D1116696

Sunward I've Climbed

SUNWARD
I'VE
CLIMBED

▲ ▲

ANNIE LAURIE MORGAN

▼ ▼

The Black Belt Press

Montgomery

Oh, I have slipped the surly bonds of earth
And danced the skies on laughter-silvered wings;
Sunward I've climbed, and joined the tumbling mirth
Of sun-split clouds . . .

John Gillespie Magee, Jr.
High Flight

The Black Belt Press
P.O. Box 551
Montgomery, AL 36101

© 1994 by Annie Laurie Morgan. All rights reserved.

Printed in the United States of America

LIBRARY OF CONGRESS CATALOGING-IN-PUBLICATION DATA

Annie Laurie Morgan, 1922-
Sunward I've Climbed / Annie Laurie Morgan
 p.   cm.
Includes bibliographical references.
SBN 1-881320-17-0 : $22.00
1. World War, 1939-1945 —France—Juvenille fiction. [1. World War, 1939-
1945—France—Fiction. 2. Physically handicapped- Fiction.] I. Title.
PZ7.M8205Su 1994   94-6583
[Fic]—dc20   CIP
                                             AC

To Phil

Yvette Hamel, 1944

PROLOGUE

Sunward I've Climbed is a true story. The narrative has been fictionalized to the extent of combining characters, inventing conversations and, in some cases, changing names.

In no other recorded instance during the Second World War did a U.S. military unit become so involved with a civilian as did the 371st Fighter Group with Yvette. *Sunward I've Climbed* is Yvette's thank-you to all her American friends who contributed so much to her recovery. The author wishes to acknowledge the following people for their help in making the book possible.

Medical Personnel: Dr. Rudolph Glocker, Dr. Samuel Yachnin, Capt. Jean Truckey, Tech./Sgt. Edward Madden, Col. Leonard Barney, Red Cross Worker Eugenia Bradford.

371st Fighter Group Pilots: C/O Col. Bingham Kleine, A. C. Wright, J. S. Green, Bernard Flory, W. R. Walling, Lloyd Hammer.

To George Deaton who got the project started, Levon Agha-Zarian, and Paul Combet who supplied information and encouragement, many thanks. Nancy Wilson and Laurie Morgan did yeomen's service in editing the text. Virginia McCullough's critique sparked the final revision. Marjorie Ballard and Virginia DuBois piloted me through the thickets of French verbs, and Philip Jutras was tireless in explaining the complexities of the Normandy invasion. To all of them, my heartfelt appreciation.

I am grateful to Alice Mauger, whose family's farm was taken over by the 371st Fighter Group about the same time as a First Army artillery unit was using the Hamel farm as a base of operations. She shared not only her firsthand knowledge of events but also the gracious hospitality of her table.

Finally, I thank my husband Phil, P-47 pilot and surgeon, who guided me through the long journey to completion of this book.

1 Sainte Mere Eglise—where Yvette
  first stayed with the 371st.
2 St. Jores—Yvette rode her bicycle
  here for sewing classes.
3 Coigny—where Yvette grew up.
4 Carentan—the largest city near
  Coigny.
5 St. Lo—Nazi headquarters in area.

1

Pierre stood at the bottom of the steps and cupped his hands around his mouth. "Yvette! Stop that damn mooning about and come help with the cows!"

His voice reverberated up the staircase of the old stone farmhouse and echoed down the second story hall. Even through the closed bedroom door, the harsh words jerked his twelve-year-old sister out of her reverie. Seated at the window, chin propped on her hand, she'd watched herself park her sky-blue Citroen in the courtyard shaded by the chestnut tree. From the seat beside her, she'd gathered her presents, and in her elegant patent leather sandals had stepped to the ground. Her red silk skirt swirled around her knees when she closed the door. The famous Paris clothes designer, Mademoiselle Yvette, had come to pay a visit to her family.

As a needle pricks a balloon, Pierre's bellow punctured her daydream. The Citroen disappeared and she was once again dressed in wooden shoes, a shapeless skirt, and a no-color blouse that hung on her like a sack. She examined her hands. They were not yet red and calloused, but it didn't take long for farm chores and Normandy weather to turn soft skin to leather. She pushed herself to her feet. Today was September the first. Only one more week of milking, and then she would go off to school. She could hardly wait!

"Hurry up, spoiled brat, or I'll come and get you!" the voice goaded her.

She crossed the room and flung open the door. "I'll be there in a minute!" she yelled. Pierre was as odious as the cows, always telling her what to do and when to do it. But as she started down the hall, she had to agree with him. She was spoiled. Of the twelve children in the family, she was her father's favorite. He, too, had an eye for style and loved the feel of good fabric. The Hamel farm had prospered in recent years, and because she'd made such high marks on her examination for the *Certificat d'Etudes* in June, he'd promised she could begin her studies in clothing design. Just one week from today she'd be on her way to Picauville. What a lucky girl she was!

From the top of the stairs she looked down at her brother's angry face. Her smile was sugary. "You called?"

Head high, arms out to the side, she paced herself down the steps as if balancing a long train behind her. Pierre watched her slow progress with mounting rage. He'd been up through the night delivering a cow of her stillborn calf. All day he'd helped with the haying. Now his sister's taunting drove his anger to the boiling point. When Yvette saw his blue eyes narrow and his jaw lock in that special way, she knew she'd overdone it. She dropped her little charade.

"I'm coming, Pierre!"

Too late. He lunged up the remaining steps and grabbed her arm. Dragging her behind him, he opened the front door and heaved her into the gravel driveway. Waving her arms wildly, she just managed to keep her balance.

"Off to the barn, Your Highness," he shouted after her. "For that little trick, milk two extra ones—Blanchette and Tulipe."

She turned around and glared at him. The prospect of the added labor made her want to scream at him and pummel his chest. A look at the angry line of his mouth made her change her tack. "Pierre," her voice quavered, "you know I'm not as strong as the others." She blinked, trying not to cry. "It always takes me longer."

Tears were wasted on Edouard—he was too much her own age—but they were often effective with the older brothers.

"Then milk faster," Pierre retorted. He sighed and rubbed his hand over his face. "I'm too tired to argue, Yvette. Get going." He shut the door before she could reply.

"Tyrant!" she yelled at him. Scuffing her shoes, she dragged her way across the courtyard that separated the house from the barn. By the time she reached its shadowy confines she was somewhat mollified. Since Michel was in bed with the flu and her father and Henri at the market in Carentan, Pierre, too, would have to do double duty.

She took two pails and a burlap sack from the store of utensils against the wall. She was quick about it. The barn was always dark, even in bright sunshine, and she peopled its murky corners with ogres ready to pounce upon her. Outside, she followed the path skirting the house and paused a moment to gaze at the lush fields, bordered by hedgerows and drainage ditches, that stretched like green bandannas all around her. A beautiful sight but, oh, the work it demanded of its caretakers! Horses, colts, sheep and lambs, pigs, rabbits, ducks and chickens needed tending to. Eleven hectares were planted in grain, four more in beets, and every day, twice a day, seventy cows had to be milked. Even in this advanced year of 1939, all work was done by hand. To be the owner, living in Paris, was a fine thing. It was quite another to be a tenant like her father. Knowledgeable as he was in the science of agriculture, he hoped that with continuing prosperity he could buy the farm, and each month money was set aside for that eventuality. Meanwhile, La Hougue's 110 hectares of fertile Normandy farmland could be made to pay only if every member of the family labored from sunup to sundown, with no vacation and never a holiday.

Yvette trudged toward three cows grazing beneath the gnarled branches of an apple tree. The one they called Tulipe was skittish and did not like to be startled. As Yvette drew near she cooed the animal's name. Tulipe acknowledged Yvette's presence with a baleful look over her shoulder and then went back to cropping grass. Yvette kneeled beside her on the burlap bag, placed the pail beneath the bulging udder, and leaned her head against the cow's ample rump. With one motion, she pulled, turned, and squeezed the soft, rough-textured teats. Jet streams of milk hit the sides of the pail with the pinging sound of bullets striking metal. Her hands were soon coated with cream. She should feel affection for the beasts, she told herself. It was their largess, demanding such good prices at La Gloria dairy in Carentan, which would bring about her own release. But all too soon, her sweaty blouse was glued to her back and a gnawing ache settled between her shoulder blades. A storm must be brewing—the flies were more vicious than usual today. They tormented the cow, and with unerring precision found the narrow band of bare skin between Yvette's hair and the collar of her blouse. Their bite was as painful as a bee sting. Tears of frustration filled Yvette's eyes as Tulipe's tail flicked again across her cheek, leaving a trail of dust. Finally, the udder was emptied, and Yvette moved on to Anemone.

Blanchette, Violette, and Noirette came and went in a blur. Her wrists and forearms felt like they were on fire. The handles of the brimming pails dug trenches in her hands as, with short, jerky steps, she made endless trips to the horse-drawn wagon to empty her pails into the big milk cans. One more week, she kept repeating. Only one more week.

By the time she finished the sun was setting. She plodded toward the barn, her thin, elongated shadow at her heels. She rinsed her pails and stacked them with the others. At the pump beside the back door of the house, she splashed cool water on her face. When she was rich and famous she would buy a tub. She would fill it with warm water and she'd bathe, not once a week as they did now, but every day! The extravagance of the thought made her smile.

Eight-year-old Claire opened the door and stepped into the yard. From a sack, she scattered feed for the chickens that were pecking in the dirt. "Finally, Yvette, you're finished!" she said.

"You're lucky to still be too young to milk," Yvette retorted, drying her face on the rough towel hung beside the pump.

Claire nodded. "I plan to stay eleven for several years."

Yvette tousled her sister's barley-colored hair, cropped straight as a thatched roof across her forehead. "I can't wait to be twenty-one. Nobody to tell me what to do."

"You've always wanted to be grown up." Claire regarded the older girl with puzzled eyes, dark brown like their father's. "Me, I shall never want to leave Maman and Papa."

Yvette shrugged a worldly shrug. "Paris is not so far away. I'll come often for visits."

The sound of a car on the gravel drive interrupted their chatter. Since their father owned one of the three cars in the village of Coigny, the children had no difficulty identifying his Renault. "Do you think Papa has brought something for dinner from the bakery?" Claire asked eagerly.

"I'll soon find out!" Yvette answered.

She jumped up the steps and darted into the pantry. As she hurried past the dining room windows, she glimpsed her father and Henri unloading supplies. She paused. Her father's luxuriant mustache, which added distinction to his face, seemed to weigh down the corners of his mouth. His lively eyes were brooding. She searched her brother's sunburned face. Gone were the jokes and the perpetual talk. Henri was silent and abstracted, his movements awkward. What had happened to make them look so grim, Yvette wondered. Even her father's walk was different. Usually he carried a sack of flour with ease; now, it burdened him. Yet in his other hand, he held the tall, white cardboard box tied with its special ribbon. Could anything be very wrong if he'd remembered that? She ran to open the door.

"*Ca va,* Papa?" she greeted him.

He didn't answer. Preoccupied, he shouldered the sack of flour into the entrance hall. Then, as if remembering, he handed her the box.

She took it in both hands. It was heavy, and as she inhaled the smell of sugar and spice that seeped out through the top her stomach growled with hunger. "Ummm," she breathed. "May I be the one to open it?"

He blinked, focusing his thoughts. "Yes, yes, Yvette. You may open it," he answered roughly.

"Papa, what's wrong?"

Although their eyes met, Yvette had the feeling that he didn't see her; that he was looking through her to something beyond. Then with a flick of his hand he motioned her toward the kitchen.

Stiff with anxiety, she paced ahead of him, gingerly holding the cake. She heard the noises her brothers made as they gathered for dinner: a door slam, quick steps in the hall, a whistle, a snatch of song. In the kitchen, Gilberte and Marguerite looked up from setting the table; Claire let out a happy squeal. "Papa remembered!"

At the fireplace, Alice Hamel left off stirring the stew pot hanging from its hook. Red-faced from the heat, she opened her mouth to protest the profligacy of the cake. Then over Yvette's shoulder, she noted her husband's somber expression. Her fine eyebrows drew together. "What's the matter, Antoine?"

As his sons crowded into the room behind him, he lowered the sack of flour to the floor, and then looked up and met her anxious gaze. "Hitler has invaded Poland."

"No!"

Yvette winced as the spoon her mother held clattered to the hearth.

"Henri and I heard the news just now in Carentan."

As her uneasy glance darted from her speechless brothers to her ashen-faced parents, Yvette wondered why they were so upset. For a long time newspapers had headlined and radios had broadcasted Hitler's demands for more "living space." When he threatened, then occupied different countries, he was denounced by politicians and commentators. Yet nothing was done to punish him. Why was this invasion so much worse than the others? "What does it mean, Papa?" she asked.

"We and the English promised Poland that if Germany attacked, we would go to war." He shook his head despondently.

Yvette regarded him with puzzled eyes. She'd seen the country on a map. It was so far away. Why would they have to fight for Poland?

Grimly, the family gathered around the dinner table. While they discussed the latest event over beef stew, bread, cheese and fruit, a sense of foreboding hovered like fog. They had lived with uncertainty for months but always there had been hope. Now peace, which had hung in such precarious balance, might end.

As always, after-dinner chores awaited. Dishes needed to be washed; work clothes required mending. Henri and Georges left for the barn to tend a mare gone lame. "Anemone is off her feed," Antoine cautioned Georges. "We'd better start her on an infusion to head off a cold."

When the tasks were done, the evening radio broadcast drew the family like a magnet. Appalled they listened to the account of Polish defenses crumbling; of planes destroyed on Polish airfields before they had a chance to fly; of refugees fleeing their burning cities. The Polish cavalry had taken a gallant stand, but heroic as they looked in military parades, they were no match for German tanks. "England and France have issued an ultimatum to the German High Command," the announcer finished in a solemn voice. "Withdraw, or we are at war."

What would Germany do? Accede to the Allied demand? Or plunge the world into a bloody conflict?

The answer came after two days of fearful waiting. At three o'clock, the bells of the Coigny church began to ring—a wild, discordant clanging, as if the village bell ringer had gone berserk. Church bells from nearby Baupte, St. Jores, La-Haye-du-Puits and Picauville joined the insistent clamor. Back and forth across the countryside they tolled their awesome message: Hitler had rejected the ultimatum. France and England were at war with Nazi Germany.

2

H er father's dreaded wake-up call seeped into Yvette's befogged mind. "*Levez-vous.*" She tried to ignore it, but the words were followed by a tapping on the door. She dragged herself from the bed she shared with Claire, envying the younger girl's blissful sleep. She didn't remember putting on her clothes, yet when she stumbled down the stairs she was dressed. As she huddled by the fire, a circle of blurred faces swam into view. Her father handed her a cup of coffee mixed with warm milk.

"Getting up the first time for the morning milking isn't easy," he sympathized. "But with your brothers gone, we all have to do our share."

Drinking the comforting brew, she recalled the events of yesterday—the last breakfast together and the family walking silently up the drive. That five of the seven brothers had been recalled to active duty was devastating beyond words. Tears mingled with good-bye hugs and kisses as the partings, brutal by their suddenness, wrenched the family apart. Now they were gone—Michel to the Maginot Line, Henri and Georges to the Belgian front, Pierre and David, the oldest, the married son, to the port of Cherbourg.

And with their leaving, Yvette's dream of becoming a *couturiere* had collapsed. She, along with the others left behind, must take up the slack. Instead of the excitement and the challenge of designing clothes, unending drudgery would be her lot. As she'd walked beside her father back to the house she'd wanted to weep for the lost chance. Fate had locked the gate and there was no escape. Noting her crestfallen look, her father had rested his hand a moment on her head. "I wish it were possible for you to go to school, but it isn't. I'm sorry about that." He'd sighed. "You aren't the only one who will suffer in this war."

She looked now from her father's harried face to her fellow milkers and wondered how he could run a farm with such a motley crew: sixteen-year-old Edouard, sturdy, but still a boy; the always sweet-natured Gilberte, whose willingness to help surpassed her strength; Etienne, dear Etienne, who cringed to see sheep led to the slaughter, whose flowers won prizes at provincial fairs; and she herself, not yet thirteen, and hating every moment of the grinding toil. Dear God, how would he manage?

Somehow they did—chained together in a lockstep of endless tasks. Yvette lived on a treadmill of exhaustion. She could sleep anytime, anywhere—sitting upright in a chair or with her eyes open at the table. She never tried, but never doubted that she could sleep standing on her head.

Daily, the war news grew more ominous. Stalin joined Hitler as an ally and together they dismembered Poland. Tales of mass killings and of uprisings suppressed seeped out. Although mobilization of the French armed forces was complete by September 20th, it came too late to help the Poles.

France and England braced for an attack. But the golden days of autumn came and went, and still the blitzkrieg did not strike. Farmers picked their apple crop, butchered hogs, and cut wood for winter fires. Jokes made the rounds about the phony war which had been declared but went unfought. Spring arrived in all its glory. Spirits lifted and hopes blossomed that, with the conquest of Poland, Hitler's appetite for more living space was finally satisfied.

But on May 8th peace was shattered when German tanks swept across neutral Belgium and their bombers reduced the Dutch city of Rotterdam to rubble. Swiftly, the Nazis advanced, trapping the French and English forces at the seaside town of Dunquerque. Every night before going to bed, Alice led her family in prayer that Henri and Georges would be among the lucky ones evacuated.

Although Yvette dreaded the arrival of the daily newspaper, she hated radio broadcasts even more. The headlines of Le

Journal de la Manche were one day old, and there was always hope that in the interim the war had taken a turn for the better. The radio brought an immediacy that was impossible to ignore. The disastrous events reported were taking place right then and there. Her parents looked so grave that she wondered if they would ever smile again. There was little to smile about.

The Maginot Line was taken from the rear—God knows what had happened to Michel—and on June 5th the French front between Paris and the sea crumbled. "Nothing would be gained by turning Paris into a ruin," the acting President, Marechal Petain, declared. And so Parisians fled the city, leaving their boulevards deserted. The Hamels sat transfixed by the radio, listening to the unbelievable—the roll of drums, the thud of German boots marching in a victory parade around the Arc de Triomphe. Yvette watched tears spill down her father's cheeks.

"C'est un desastre pour nous et pour la France," her mother moaned.

The Abbe Giard stopped by the farm that evening. Family friend as well as curate of the churches of Coigny and nearby Baupte, he came to commiserate with the Hamels over the French surrender. Yvette set another place at the table, and over soup, bread, cheese and fruit, the solemn group discussed and tried to understand the swiftness and completeness of the French debacle.

"Communist unrest, strikes in our factories, corrupt leaders, Generals living in the past!" Antoine threw up his hands in a hopeless gesture. "We were defeated before the fighting began."

"That was part of it," Father Giard conceded, "but there was something more." His dark brows drew together over sorrowing eyes. "We wanted at all costs to avoid conflict."

"France never recovered from the last war," Alice objected. "Not a family escaped losing a father, son, or brother. So many young men—gone!"

Father Giard nodded. "But Germany lost more than we did. In defeat, however, they found a purpose—an evil one to be sure. We were unwilling to commit ourselves to anything but our own selfish interests. And now we've learned a bitter lesson. Freedom belongs only to those willing to sacrifice everything to keep it. We were not willing." He stared into the fire. "For us the war is over, but our real travail may only have begun."

Two days later the newspaper printed the surrender terms which Antoine read aloud at the breakfast table. The eastern provinces of Alsace-Lorraine would be annexed to Germany. Two million French prisoners-of-war would be detained. France would be divided into two zones stretching from Switzerland to Spain. The northern zone would be occupied by German troops; the southern zone would be governed by the Petain regime, head-quartered in the town of Vichy. The French navy would be disarmed and France would be forced to pay the costs of the occupying army.

"When will they arrive?" Yvette broke a stunned silence.

"Any time they choose," Edouard retorted. "A conquering army doesn't have to ask permission."

The Boches in Coigny! Their quiet little town. It had always seemed so safe and out-of-the-way. A cow fallen in a ditch or a drunken farmer brandishing his scythe at a stranger passing through his field was the kind of excitement the village was used to. How could they adjust to an army of invaders? Yvette shivered. And these invaders were monsters, as everyone knew.

"I guess we've heard the 'Marseillaise' for the last time," Gilberte said.

"German spoken everywhere!" Edouard grunted.

"The swastika raised over the school, town hall, the post office!" Marguerite grimaced.

Antoine shook his head. "In more ways than we can imagine, 'France defeated' will be ground into our consciousness."

On that depressing note, the meal ended and the family dispersed to their various tasks. In happier times Yvette had enjoyed gathering dandelions to feed the rabbits. The field bordered the road, and in good weather neighbors passing by always stopped to talk. Today, however, neither she nor they were in a mood for chatting, and the clear sky, warm sun and gentle breeze seemed a mockery. On such a lovely day as this, men were putting other men in prison camps and France resounded to the tramp of enemy boots.

As her basket filled she became aware of a noise, faint but growing louder, that she didn't recognize. It wasn't sheep led to the market or cows crossing the road to another field. Her curiosity piqued, she made her way to the fence. Peering down the road, she puzzled over a barked command and the revving of an engine. Just then a row of soldiers came around the bend.

"Mon Dieu, les Boches!" she said aloud.

Terrified, she stood riveted at the fence staring at the ranks of men approaching. But as she stared she wondered why their marching seemed so lackadaisical—so unlike the goosesteppers pictured in the papers. These soldiers had a hangdog look, and how dirty and unkempt their uniforms were. Yvette gasped. The uniforms were blue with twin rows of buttons down the jacket. Some of the men even wore berets. Her heart leaped to her throat at this first sight of French prisoners-of-war.

At intervals, motorcyclists rode beside the prisoners. In the sidecar next to the driver sat a German guard with his gun trained on the men. If a soldier lagged behind, the guard shouted an order and pointed his gun at the guilty one to emphasize his point.

From where were they coming, Yvette puzzled. Cherbourg! That was it. The port had held out until a week ago. To keep highways open to their military traffic, the Boches must be marching prisoners along these back country roads. Where were they going? Were David and Pierre among this group?

With frantic eyes, she searched the rows as they passed. Mother-of-God, how much alike they looked—mudcaked shoes, disheveled dress, and weariness stamped on their bearded faces. What a contrast the Germans made with their gray-green uniforms so spic and span; their knee-high boots were polished to a T. And they had the air of victors—haughty caution mingled with disdain.

On and on they came until they blurred together and Yvette despaired that she would not recognize her brothers even if they were among this group. Then from the next to the last row a hand lifted in a brief salute. David! His head was high and on his rugged features she caught a fleeting smile. "St. Lo!" he called.

"Silence! Eyes front!" snarled the guard, waving his gun in

David's direction. The motorcyclist gave Yvette an angry look, and frightened, she stumbled backwards away from the fence. After the last row of soldiers had disappeared she raced for the laundry where Gilberte and her mother were doing the wash. Fleet-footed and without pause, she crossed the intervening fields. By the time she reached the creek and rushed into the cool, damp room, her heart was pounding and she could scarcely breathe.

"What's the matter?" Gilberte asked. "You look like you've seen a ghost."

"I've just seen David!" Yvette gasped.

"*Mon Dieu!* Where?" her mother demanded.

Yvette described the scene she'd witnessed.

"St. Lo?" her mother puzzled. "Ah," her face cleared, "that's where he'll be demobilized. Then he'll come home!"

Seeing her mother smile—for the first time in weeks—Yvette did not have the heart to remind her of surrender terms: the two million French prisoners-of-war who would be detained.

More excitement followed. That evening as the family prepared for bed, Pierre and another soldier appeared at the door. Exhausted and unkempt, Pierre was barely recognizable. After he was smothered with hugs and kisses, he introduced his friend, Jean-Louis, who wanted to stay the night before going on to Paris.

Over bowls of reheated stew, they told of escaping from a holding camp after the fall of Cherbourg and their three-day trek to get to the farm. Had their luck not held, they would have been among David's group heading for St. Lo.

"Must you leave tomorrow?" Antoine asked their guest.

Jean-Louis nodded. "I'll have a better chance of evading capture while the Germans are still disorganized."

"You can wear some of the clothes we give to the gypsy family who come by here every fall," Alice said. "We'll dress you like a Norman farmer."

"His hands would never pass the test," Pierre grunted, giving his friend a good-natured jab. "He was a teacher," he explained to the others.

With a chagrined smile, Jean-Louis examined his smooth,

callous-free hands. "They would never fool the Germans," he agreed. Then his expression sobered. "I doubt the gypsies will come this year. They and other 'undesirables' are being put into concentration camps."

"The gypsies mean no harm," Alice protested.

"Everyone must be productive—the Nazi idea of productive— in the New European Order," Jean-Louis answered grimly. "Otherwise, one is eliminated."

Yvette shuddered. Would the gypsies be shot? They were so grateful for the food and clothes, the field where her father let them spend the night. Kind people—wanderers.

Pierre pushed himself to his feet. "You must get to bed, my friend," he said. "dawn comes early here."

The next morning, Jean-Louis joined the milkers for coffee. He wore the baggy pants and too-big shirt that Alice had given him. Although the clothes did not make his boyish figure look like a farmer, he would be less conspicuous than if he wore a uniform. Yvette fixed food for him to take; Pierre explained the shortcut to Carentan that would keep him off the road. He thanked the family for their kindness. They pressed his hand, wished him well, and watched with trepidation as he disappeared among the apple trees.

They never heard whether he survived the perilous journey, and feared that he'd been recaptured or, worse still, shot as a spy.

3

Events of the following week kept the family in an uproar. Demobilized, David returned from St. Lo to his wife who lived on her family's farm on the outskirts of Coigny. Two days later, during a thunderstorm, Henri and Georges appeared at the back door of La Hougue. Soaked to the skin, haggard, rail-thin, they were welcomed with cries of joy, supplied with warm clothes, and seated at the dinner table where they kept their listeners on the edge of their seats with their harrowing tales of retreat from the Belgian front. "The Boches rolled over our defenses like a tidal wave. Don't let anyone tell you the French soldier is not brave," Georges's voice was angry, "but an army needs weapons. Ours were a joke." Trapped at Dunquerque, they managed to find places on a boat crammed to the sinking point with desperate men. "I looked back at that flaming beach and decided that's as close to hell as I ever want to get," Henri said.

After living for three days on tea and biscuits in the English port of Southhampton, they boarded a French ship headed for Cherbourg hoping they could fight again. "None of us knew that Rommel's tanks had entered the city," Georges continued. "We jumped on the last train out of town. It was headed for Evreux." He grimaced. "From the frying pan into the fire!"

"We had to get rid of our uniforms" Henri picked up the tale, "so we took clothes off dead refugees lying in a ditch. Poor devils, they were machinegunned while trying to escape their burning cities. We played leapfrog with the Nazis for two hundred kilometers. They were always just ahead of us or right behind. We traveled at night and hid during the day." His eyes were glazed. "How often did we get lost?"

Georges shook his head.

"When did we eat our last meal?" he countered.

"I can't believe we're home." Tears seeped unheeded from Henri's sunken eyes.

"Rouen is in flames," Georges's somber voice broke the silence that had fallen, "the Gestapo is shooting members of the Resistance, foreigners are trying to get out any way they can. And now that France is disintegrating, that jackal Mussolini has sided with the Boches."

Yvette looked around at the circle of anguished faces. Everything had happened too quickly. There should have been a respite after defeat—a time to assess damage, lick wounds, and prepare for reparations. But the victor had already occupied the country, and now the French would learn firsthand the horrors that had happened to the Poles, the Belgians, the Dutch, and Czechs that, up to now, they had only read about.

Two hundred of them arrived in Coigny. Along with their horses, trucks, wagons and weapons, they took over the Chateau du Franquetot. The elegant and gracious *Comtesse,* proprietress of the vast domain of a *Marechal* of France, was ousted by the invaders and reduced to living in a rooming house in Baupte.

Another shock followed the next day. As the family gathered for the noon meal a knock sounded on the door. It was the *Garde Champetre,* the village policeman whose grave expression warned of unpleasant news. After declining a cup of coffee, he produced from his leather pouch summonses for the newly returned Hamel sons to go to St. Lo for "processing."

"'Processing?' What does that mean?" Pierre demanded.

Monsieur Malraux gave him a baleful look. "What indeed? Even the Mayor doesn't know."

"But David has already been to St. Lo," Alice persisted.

Other than a nod and a lift of the shoulders, Monsieur Malraux could offer no further explanation.

Georges's eyes narrowed. "Henri, Pierre and I arrived at night. No one saw us. We haven't spoken to anyone. How did the Boches know we were here?"

"Someone reported you," the policeman said in sepulchral tones.

All eyes were riveted on the bearer of bad news. "Who?" Pierre demanded.

Again the policeman could shed no light. He placed three summonses on the table and held up the fourth. "I must deliver this to David." He headed for the door. "We live in worrisome times," he intoned. "And it will only get worse."

When the door closed behind him speculation on the identity of the snitch erupted. The family had no real enemies in their town, they'd thought. Competitors, yes; people who envied their relative affluence. But to tattletale to the enemy the arrival of returning sons showed real malice. "I wouldn't put it past Francois Dumont," Georges suggested to his father. "Your fellow council-man has always been bitter that our milk brings higher prices than his."

"We're just lucky, of course," his father replied dryly.

Henri grunted. "If he drank less and worked more, his farm would out-produce anyone's."

"I once told him that," Antoine said with a rueful smile. "He's never forgiven me, nor stopped reminding me that I'm a tenant, while he's a *proprietaire*."

"Due to his wife's inheritance," Alice retorted. "He's also jealous that you have seven healthy sons, and he has only two, one of whom is sickly."

"But how would he know we were home?" Georges asked.

Suddenly Antoine clapped a hand to his forehead. "I'm the guilty one," he exclaimed.

The others regarded him in startled silence. "At the town council meeting last night I took the Mayor aside to tell him that you three and David were home," Antoine began. "He promised to keep the information under his hat as long as he could. I didn't realize that our neighbor and *good friend,* Monsieur Dumont, had sidled up behind us. He must have overheard." Antoine shook his head in self-reproach.

"Let this be a lesson." Alice's voice was hard. She looked around the table. "There may be others who will use the Boches to avenge old grudges. From now on we keep our business to ourselves."

The next morning the four sons set off for St. Lo. Through the long day and the interminable night the family waited and worried. At dawn Henri and Georges returned without the other two.

"Getting us to St. Lo for 'processing' was a dirty Nazi trick," Georges fumed. "David and Pierre are on their way to Germany, 'to work for the greater glory of the Third Reich,'" he quoted bitterly. He rubbed a grubby hand over his too-thin face. "If their group had not filled the quota for the day, Henri and I would also have been seized."

As the awful truth sank in, tears rolled down Alice's cheeks. "What will become of them?" she moaned. "And Michel? Is he alive?"

Reluctantly, the Hamels set about complying with regulations posted by the German *Kommandant* at the *Mairie,* post office and bulletin board in the town square. Antoine assigned Yvette the chore of listing on a placard the names of each member of the household, their status, and current whereabouts. That this roster must be permanently displayed on the back of the front door stripped the family of privacy and gave the Nazis one more tool to ease their task of surveillance.

Gilberte, Marguerite, Etienne and Edouard accompanied their parents to the town hall to obtain their newly mandated civilian *carte d'identite.* Not yet sixteen, Yvette and Claire were not required to have an I.D. card, but, like every member of the community, they had to apply for a book of ration stamps.

The rest of the regulations were discussed over lunch. "Neither blackout curtains nor the curfew will cause us any hardship," Antoine said, "but I'm not giving up my rifle or the shortwave radio."

"And what do we do if they find them!" Alice demanded in a stricken voice.

"Calm yourself," Antoine replied. "The Boches know that every farmer has a gun. I'll turn in the one with the faulty safety catch. None of you need to know where I'll hide the good one. As for the radio, I've got the perfect place—in the closet under the stairs. They'd have to plough through ten years of accumulated debris to locate it." His mouth hardened. "We'll learn the real news of what's happening in the world, not the swill they'll be dishing out!"

"We don't need you in a prison camp on top of our other problems," Alice objected angrily. "The risk is too great!"

"Now, Maman," Etienne intervened, "there are only two hundred Boches in Coigny. They have more important things to do than search house-to-house for radios."

"They need us," Antoine added as a simple statement of fact, "and until England is conquered, they won't keep too tight a rein on Normandy. They don't want partisans nipping at their backsides while the invasion is underway."

Yvette was well aware that the obstinate look in her father's eyes would preclude further argument on her mother's part. Her father was right. Food was of immense importance to the Nazi. Sending a Norman farmer to prison camp would be biting the hand that fed them.

Three weeks later the Postmistress delivered a letter from Michel. The envelope was dirty and crumpled; the message inside was brief. He was a prisoner, on a train heading for Germany. He would drop the letter out of a window before they reached the border hoping that whoever found it would put it in the mail. "France defeated so quickly—what a terrible blow. I don't know what the future holds. Will try to communicate again. All my love, Michel."

Alice clasped the letter to her breast. "He is alive!" she exulted.

Messages in the form of preprinted post cards arrived from Pierre and David. "I am well. I work (a) in a factory, (b) on a farm helping the Fuehrer bring about a better world. Do not worry about me. Your son." Pierre had underlined "factory," David, "farm."

The cards were passed around the breakfast table for scrutiny and all agreed that the signatures were genuine.

"The Boches aren't so stupid as to deprive us of all contact with our sons," Antoine growled. "They want us cowed, not rebellious!"

Antoine's assessment of the German desire to maintain a

tractable Normandy while they prepared for the invasion of England was borne out by their actions. The Colonel heading the force at the Chateau du Franquetot made a formal call on Father Giard to request the use of the Coigny church for services for his troops. His manners were exemplary, his French excellent. Though his men frequented the cafe for beer and wine, none ever drank to excess. They treated women politely, and a group was seen stopping on the road one day to help Monsieur Lebrun extricate his cow that had fallen in a ditch. Military bands gave frequent concerts for the public at the park in Carentan.

But July faded into August and the invasion of England did not materialize. Every night, while Yvette kept watch at the kitchen window her father disappeared into the closet under the stairs. From underneath a pile of old work clothes, shoes, odds and ends, he took a box of toy soldiers. The false bottom of the box concealed the shortwave radio. He kept it tuned to the British Broadcasting station and learned of fierce air battles between the Royal Air Force and the Luftwaffe for control of the Channel. Both sides suffered grievously, but by the end of August the attrition rate for the Germans was two to one. On September 15th, in addition to the losses inflicted on the German Air Force, much of the invasion shipping was destroyed by English bombers.

Yvette knew by the look on her father's face when he emerged from the closet that the news was good. "The invasion of Great Britain is indefinitely postponed. The English didn't fold as everyone expected. They came out fighting." He pretended to parry with his fists as if in a boxing match. "Bloody but unbowed," he gloated. "Hitler may have bitten off more than he can chew!"

4

Christmas was bleak. The absence of the brothers cast a pall on any joy the season brought, and the curfew cancelled the holiday's most important celebration: midnight mass at the church in Baupte. As Yvette climbed the steps to bed on Christmas Eve she recalled the excitement of other years. Dressed in Sunday finery, the family gathered with neighbors at the church square in Coigny. There the Choir Master, wearing his top hat and greatcoat with the black fur collar, jostled the townspeople into orderly rows. Lanterns were lit and voices tuned. Then, with baton raised he set a jaunty pace while the road to Baupte glimmered with lights, and carols rose on the clear, cold air.

Yvette loved the pageantry of the midnight mass—Father Giard in his flowing robes, the chants, the organ music, the incense, the candles. In the solemnity of the occasion she hardly recognized some of her friends. How could Robert, who yesterday had called her names and yanked her hair, look so angelic as an altar boy?

The trek back to La Hougue was tiring, but hot chocolate and sweet biscuits awaited them. Then, impatient for the morning, Yvette and Claire were sent to bed. At dawn they raced each other down the stairs to find what Pere Noel had left in their wooden shoes.

Their childhood was over. They would never be that carefree again.

Winter's bitter weather affected members of the family in various ways. Alice went about her duties with dogged forbearance. Though life was difficult, none of her sons had been killed. Compared to that reality, everything else faded into insignificance. Claire and the cafe owner's daughter had become best friends.

31

Busy confiding secrets and plans for the future to each other, they had little concern left for cold and rain. Marguerite was taking care of a sickly lamb which, now that it was better, followed her everywhere. The shy girl had a talent for healing, and seeing the improvement in her constant companion offset any malaise the weather brought.

Gilberte's tolerance for discomfort seemed limitless. She volunteered for extra work and, unlike Yvette, never objected to any task. One frigid afternoon as they milked together in the barn where the cows had been moved for the winter, Gilberte began whistling a Maurice Chevalier hit she'd heard on the radio. It was a bouncy tune that grated on Yvette's nerves. She listened, clenching her teeth. Finally, she'd had enough. "How can you be cheerful when I'm so damn miserable!" she exploded.

"Pardonnez-moi, Mademoiselle," Gilberte said with a show of mock humility.

Yvette rolled her eyes.

"Now Yvette, what is so terrible about work on a farm? Caring for the animals benefits us. Most harvests are golden, and even after the bitterest winter, spring always comes. Remember what Maman says: 'God tempers the wind to the shorn lamb.' You're never called on to endure beyond your limits."

"I hate it when you talk like a Mother Superior!" Yvette groaned.

"We are so different," Gilberte laughed. "Maybe that's why we get along so well. You're the mule that balks at the load assigned to it. I'm a sheep that accepts things as they are."

Yvette shook her head. It was impossible to stay angry at Gilberte. Her wide-spaced eyes and regular features gave her face a classic beauty, but it was her smile, enfolding one like a comforter on a chilly evening, that people remembered. "Why can't I be more like you?" Yvette lamented.

Gilberte's expression sobered. "You've got something I don't have—a toughness inside, like steel. So, go on being a mule. You may need that stubbornness some day."

It was the brothers whom the frigid weather disaffected the most. They found fault with everything: each other, their parents, their sisters. Each knew he had the hardest tasks; none felt he was appreciated. Georges was particularly morose, Yvette reflected one frosty morning as, pausing to look out the dining room window, she saw him in the field where the horses grazed. She watched him clearing the drainage ditch of brambles—a winter task that everyone hated. Today, however, eradicating the bushes seemed to give him perverse pleasure. A grim smile tightened his lips. He seemed almost beside himself as, with savage blows, he drove the pick again and again into the roots. Yvette was startled by his vehemence and wondered if, in his mind's eye, he saw the brambles as Nazis and was ridding France's soil of the invaders? She knew the depth of his hatred for them. His brush in St. Lo with being sent as a slave to Germany had shaken him to the core. Finally, the task completed, he stood a moment, breathing deeply. Then, wiping a hand across his sweating brow, he shouldered the pick and headed for the barn.

Yvette thought the exertion had dissipated his anger, but, as he passed the stable Henri was cleaning, he paused to inspect his younger brother's handwork. Yvette saw the two glare at each other, Georges shake his head in disgust and mouth a criticism that brought a flush to Henri's face. He retaliated by lifting some horse manure on the tip of his pitchfork and tossing it in Georges's direction. It landed on the toe of Georges's shoe. Yvette's eyes widened as the furious Georges drew back his fist and hit Henri with a blow to the jaw that knocked him to the ground. Henri's initial reaction was one of surprise. Then, fuming, he staggered to his feet and flailing his arms, screaming obscenities, rushed to attack his older brother. Astounded and mesmerized, Yvette watched them grappling with each other. She'd seen them scuffle good-naturedly, but never had she seen them fight.

She was about to call her mother when she saw her father rush from the barn. Shouting commands, he managed to separate the two combatants. They stood apart, angry and unrepentant. Yvette could imagine her father's irate remark. "If you've got energy for this kind of behavior, I can find more work for you to do!"

They went their separate, discontented ways, and Yvette felt for her father as, shaking his head in frustration, he watched them leave. She thought of his gloomy remark on her November birthday. "I wish I could tell you that life gets better with the passing years, but in a war, everything gets worse."

The coming of spring brought relief in the weather. Winter clothes were put away, and spirits lifted with the sun's return. But June's arrival brought an astonishing development: Germany invaded its former ally, Russia. From a town council meeting following this event, Antoine brought home disturbing news. Yvette had stayed up with her mother for his arrival, and listened to her father's account of how this latest event would impinge on their lives.

"The Mayor detained me after the meeting broke up," he related. "'The Boches have been lenient with us until now,' Monsieur *le Maire* said to me. When I reminded him testily that I'd supplied them with grain, cattle, and three of my sons, he answered, 'We haven't seen anything yet.'"

Yvette listened with mounting dread as her father repeated the Mayor's rhetorical questions: who will feed those German soldiers marching toward Moscow? Who's going to furnish the leather for their boots? The Russian campaign will go on forever. When it's over, France will be denuded.

"'Of particular concern are some of our own people,' the Mayor went on. I mouthed the word 'Dumont,' and he nodded. 'Fix your car tonight so it will no longer run,' he advised me. That ended our conversation, for we noticed Dumont watching us."

"Mon Dieu!" Alice sighed. "Which should we fear the most—the foreign enemy or the one next door?"

Antoine pushed himself to his feet. "Come, Yvette. We have work to do."

She followed him to the garage where she helped him remove the generator from the Renault. They wrapped it in old cloths, and hoisted it into the hayloft where they hid it in a corner underneath a pile of hay. They propped bricks under the chassis then let air out of the tires. In a gesture of farewell, Antoine ran a loving hand along a spotless fender.

"Keep reminding yourself, Papa, that they can't use it either," she said.

5

Yvette beckoned her mother. "Maman! Here they come!" Alice hurried to the kitchen window to watch the German staff car wheel through the gateway, bump down the drive, and pause opposite the open door of the barn. From their vantage point, hidden by the blackout curtain, she and Yvette could see Antoine inside the barn. He stood at his work bench pretending to examine the damaged breast plate of a harness.

"You are Monsieur Hamel?"

At the demand in the querulous voice, Antoine glanced over his shoulder. With slack-jawed indifference, he regarded the driver, an enlisted man, and his passenger, an officer. *"Oui,"* he grunted.

"What an actor," Yvette giggled, forgetting for the moment the seriousness of the situation. "Papa should be on the stage."

"Shhh," Alice cautioned. "They'll hear you!"

Aware of how clearly voices carried across the courtyard, Yvette quickly sobered.

At a curt motion from the officer the enlisted man cut the engine.

Because gravel for civilian use had been unavailable since the occupation, the driveway of La Hougue became a ribbon of dust in dry weather and a river of mud after a rain. Last night's downpour had turned it into a morass. With a grimace, the officer put his foot, in its shiny leather boot, to the ground and sank almost to his ankle. Yvette caught a look of sardonic amusement on the driver's face as his passenger, carrying his briefcase, tiptoed his way among the potholes filled with dirty water. When the German reached the entrance to the barn his pained expression intensified. Yvette smiled.

Unlike cow and horse dung, pig manure has a pungent odor and was usually stored away from the barn. Right after breakfast Yvette had helped her father pile on a newspaper a generous amount of the excrement, which they hid near the work bench. The morning was hot and humid, and no breeze stirred.

"I'm Captain Schmidt," she heard the visitor introduce himself. He tried not to breathe as he looked vainly around for a clean surface on which to place his briefcase. Antoine made no move to clear the harness off the workbench, and finally the Captain propped the satchel on his knee. He unfastened the straps and removed a long printed form. "You are the owner of a Renault," he announced.

Antoine acknowledged the statement with a shrug.

"Regulations require that automobile owners fill out a questionnaire—"

Antoine interrupted the Captain with a wave of his hand. "I already have the gray card issued at the beginning of the occupation."

"That's no longer sufficient," the Captain explained. "The Fuehrer's crusade against the Bolshevik has required adjustments in the method of registering motor vehicles."

The sun was now above the trees and beat unimpeded on the slate roof of the barn. The wilted collar of the Captain's shirt had turned dark with sweat. He seemed to have trouble swallowing. Yvette marveled at her father's seeming indifference to the fetid air.

"Even though gas rationing has reduced the number of cars in circulation, the problems facing the automobile industry are more complex than ever."

Antoine gave the matter thought. He pursed his lips and scratched his armpit. "Doesn't make much sense to me," he frowned. "Fewer cars, fewer problems."

The effort to abide by the official policy of not antagonizing the Norman farmer, plus the heat and the stench, gave the Captain's face an apoplectic look.

"In order to maintain an adequate inventory of spare parts, the government needs a census of automobiles that are in good running condition," he said in a strangled voice.

Antoine's brow cleared. *"Ah, mon Capitaine,* 'in good running condition,' you say?" He shook his head. "You've made the trip to La Hougue for nothing. My car is—how do you call it? Oh yes— *Kaput!"* He beamed, pleased with himself for producing the foreign term so readily.

"What!" demanded the Captain, forgetting for the moment his misery.

"Oui," Antoine nodded. *"Kaput.* The generator went bad so I sent it to Paris demanding a replacement. I've heard nothing from them," he went on, aggrieved. Then a crafty expression narrowed his eyes. "You have influence? Perhaps you could—"

"But the Paris assembly plant makes only trucks and wagons now!" the Captain bellowed.

Antoine's eyebrows peaked in dismay. *"Vraiment?"*

"Their output of cars was curtailed when the new regime began!"

Antoine threw up his hands in disgust. "New—old. What's the difference? Nothing ever changes. Here in the provinces we're still the last to know what goes on in the capital" His face took on a petulant expression. "When can I get my car in working order again?"

The shock of realizing the Renault had slipped from his grasp in addition to the nauseating odor overcame the Captain. He backed hurriedly out of the barn, the open briefcase flopping in one hand, the printed form fluttering in the other. Propped against the outside wall, he began to retch. Antoine watched him a moment, then shook his head. There was no explaining the peculiar behavior of foreigners. He turned back to his workbench.

The surly driver came to the Captain's aid and they plodded back to the car. After he'd deposited the officer on the seat, the enlisted man eyed his own mudcaked shoes and slammed the door. He slid under the steering wheel and, with tires churning, backed the vehicle toward the gate. As it disappeared down the road, Alice smiled at her daughter. "It appears that you and Papa have saved the Renault."

Though the episode momentarily brightened the Hamels'

existence, it became overshadowed by the Russian campaign. The Mayor's dire predictions proved to be true. Despite initial victories, success eluded the German legions. As the Russians retreated, they put to the torch vast regions of their country so the invaders could not live off the land. The further the Germans penetrated into Soviet territory, the further their horse-drawn vehicles had to transport supplies. Horses, like men, were vulnerable to disease, suffered from the cold, and died in battle. In Normandy, the requisitioning of horses, as well as cows, multiplied, and the demand for grain and other foodstuffs was unrelenting. Leather shoes, purses and gloves disappeared from French store shelves. Bread made from white flour had become a rarity. Coffee, tea, sugar, oil, soap, fish—each week another product vanished.

On December 7th, as Antoine listened to his shortwave radio, he was astounded to hear a confused report of Japanese dive-bombers roaring out of the Hawaiian dawn and sinking much of the American fleet at Pearl Harbor. The next day's newspapers were full of the story of thousands of sailors entombed with their ships, and gloated over the disarray of the vaunted American presence in the Pacific. When, three days later, Hitler and Mussolini joined their ally, Japan, and declared war on the United States, there was rejoicing in the Hamel household.

"They're in it!" Antoine exulted. "Now the tide will turn."

But as the months of 1942 came and went, the rejoicing turned to gloom. American and English forces were losing everywhere. The Philippines, Malay peninsula, Dutch East Indies, and Hong Kong fell to the enemy. Japan controlled the Pacific. In the Atlantic, German submarines roamed unmolested. Tons of war materiel desperately needed by the English lay at the bottom of the ocean. Had American help arrived too little, too late?

At La Hougue, the difficulties of daily living were exacerbated by Georges's increasing restiveness. His surly attitude toward German soldiers when he met them in town or on the road; his resolve to somehow, some day, make *them* pay for what they had done to France; his diatribes about Nazi manipulation of French banks, "—don't you understand? They're paying us for our animals with our own money!" was a mounting source of worry. The latest episode, the mysterious appearance on the town bulletin board of a poster condemning prominent officials in the French government at Vichy of being hand in glove with the Nazi had brought the turmoil to a head. That night at dinner his mother chastised him for his recalcitrant behavior. His response was an angry, "It's my own neck!"

"Oh, is it!" his father demanded. "You know as well as we do that when someone in the village attracts attention, the rest of the family also is put under special surveillance."

For a moment the chastened Georges stared at his plate. Then, lifting his head, he looked at his father. "Papa, I want to join the *Maquis,*" he blurted.

Yvette saw her father's face turn pale, and imagined the thoughts racing through his mind. The chances of Georges surviving in the Maquisard were small. Accounts appeared frequently in the newspaper of German agents infiltrating the resistance networks. The casualties in Normandy were alarming. Three of the Hamel sons were prisoners and might never return home. If something happened to Georges also, the loss would be insupportable. She watched her father struggle with an answer other than "No!" that would reach this most conscientious of his sons.

Finally, he nodded. "Yes, I guess that would be easier," he answered in a reasonable tone.

Georges's spine jerked ramrod straight. "Easier!" His voice was incredulous. "They're fighting—all over France!"

"Sure they are," Antoine agreed. "They strike here, there, then disappear. They live the life of gypsies." He smiled. "I'd like that, too."

Yvette saw a red flush spread over Georges's face. "You think I'd be running away," he said, bristling.

Antoine shrugged. "Life with the Maquis would be a hell of lot more exciting than farming these days. Here it's nonstop work, shortages of everything, putting up with the Boches!" He jerked a thumb toward the placard nailed to the front door. "And what do we tell the inspector when he comes to check the roll-call? 'Our son, Georges? Hmmmm. We don't know where he went. One day he just—disappeared.' How long would it take them to ship another of your brothers off to Germany?"

As the argument struck home, Georges's shoulders slumped in defeat.

Another horse was requisitioned in August. Antoine and Etienne returned from delivering the animal to the marketplace in La-Haye-du-Puits with the startling news of an English-Canadian raid on the French coastal town of Dieppe. It had been a disaster. Of five thousand troops put ashore, fifteen hundred had been killed and two thousand were taken prisoner and paraded through the streets of the city. Another Dunquerque, for once again the remnant of an army had to be evacuated. Again the Nazi exulted in a victory.

How this raid impacted the Hamel household was revealed three days later when Antoine, fresh from a meeting with the Mayor, took his place at the lunch table. His face was grave. "Although the Dieppe raid was a failure, the Nazis know the Allies will come again," he reported the gist of his conversation with the town's chief official. "Next time they come, they won't attack a fortified city. They'll choose another site—an open beach, perhaps. Therefore, plans for the Atlantic Wall have been reactivated."

"Mon Dieu!" Alice groaned.

Murmurs of consternation circled the table. Still vivid in their minds was the flurry of activity that followed American entry in the war. Europe must be made impregnable. Calais, Le Havre and other major ports along the Channel had been fortified. Then the Russian and North African campaigns had diverted Hitler's attention and talk about Fortress Europe had subsided. Now the Dieppe raid had re-alerted the Fuehrer to the danger of an Allied invasion. Twenty-four-hundred miles of coast line stretching from the Bay of Biscay to Norway were to be made secure.

"How in the hell can they fight the Russians, the English, the Americans, and build that kind of wall?" Henri demanded.

"It's impossible!" Georges agreed. "Where will they find the manpower to do the—"

His voice trailed off. He stared at his father.

"From all the countries that border the Channel," Antoine answered. He rubbed a hand over his haggard face. "Every day, twenty men from the environs of Coigny must gather at the church square to be transported to their destinations."

An appalled silence fell over the group. No one wanted to ask the question: who among us will have to go?

Georges sat back in his chair. "Tell us, Papa."

Antoine looked at his son with anguished eyes. "Etienne," he answered, "and you."

If Yvette lived to be a hundred, she would never forget the look on Georges's face. In yielding to his father's wishes he'd given up the freedom of the *Maquis* for the chains of his implacable foe.

6

L eave-takings even for the day had become important, so the family gathered in the courtyard to see the conscript laborers on their way. Dressed in their oldest clothes, carrying a bundle of food, they looked like vagabonds. "Life was so simple before the war," Alice said dispiritedly. "When someone went on a trip, it was assumed they would return. Now, one never knows."

The departure of Georges and Etienne each morning meant that their work must be divided among the rest of the family. Except for mass on Sundays, Yvette's chores left her no time for other activities. Her contacts with people her own age were limited to occasional visits from an erstwhile schoolmate who bicycled out to the farm to see her. Daughter of the Postmistress, Michiline, helped part-time in the Post Office and kept house for her mother and younger brother. Through the years she and Yvette had remained fast friends. Michiline was a lively, enjoyable companion. She brought the town gossip and news of the enemy's activities, which she shared with Yvette over cups of ersatz coffee made from roasted grain. Yvette treasured these visits. They acted on her circumscribed existence like a tonic whose benefits lasted long after the dose had been administered.

Weary and hungry, the conscripts returned home at night after the rest of the family had eaten. Wolfing down the meal kept warm for them, they talked of their day's activities. Etienne had been posted to a crew working on the sand dunes near the town of Madeleine. There, an enormous bunker was under construction, housing for one of the huge guns that would dominate approach from the sea. "Hitler himself is supposed to have designed the emplacement," he related. "Incredible! A bomb would have to make a direct hit to do it any damage."

The bitter Georges was assigned to a plant in Montebourg making cement for the bunkers. "My supervisor must have been warned about me. He spends a lot of time at my shoulder. If any sabotage occurred, I'd be the first one up against the wall!"

All too soon the harvest season was upon them. Through the long hot days of August, Antoine, Henri, Edouard, the girls and Alice went into the fields. From sunup to sundown, the mowing, drying in swaths, gathering and threshing continued. Every bale of the fifty tons of hay stored in the barn had to be carried on someone's shoulders up the ladder to the hayloft. Finally it was done, but the backbreaking work took its toll.

On the first of September, Antoine got out of bed at his usual hour to call the milkers. He made it to the bedroom door where he collapsed. A frightened Alice called the others, then dispatched Henri on his bicycle to summon the family physician. After his examination, Dr. Bouclier reported his diagnosis—pneumonia complicated by a heart condition—to the anxious family gathered in the kitchen. "Monsieur Hamel is very sick, and must have complete bed rest as well as medication. I'll petition the office of the Kommandant to let Michel come home," Dr. Bouclier continued. "In hardship cases like this, they sometimes allow the oldest son to assume his father's duties."

"How benevolent!" Edouard grunted.

The doctor nodded. "When their food supply is endangered, they suddenly show a disposition to be kind."

A week later as Yvette completed her afternoon milking, she saw a gaunt Michel opening the gate. She rushed across the field calling his name. He caught her in his arms and held her close. When they drew apart to inspect each other she could not hide her dismay. The whites of his eyes were yellowed; sores crusted at the corners of his mouth. His splotched complexion, the crepey skin of his neck, made him look as if he'd suddenly become old.

"You were a little girl when I left three years ago," he smiled. "Now you're almost grown—and so pretty."

"What did they do to you, Michel?" she asked, her blue-gray eyes dark with anger.

"You'd find it hard to believe," he answered. "Besides, I don't want to talk about it now."

As they made their way down the rutted drive, Yvette explained why the house looked so neglected. "We can't get paint and nails have disappeared. We had to take the bricks from Etienne's flower garden to prop up the—"

He silenced her with his hand on her arm. "To me, it is the most beautiful sight in the world."

At the door, the others welcomed him with cries of joy. As they led him into the hall, an unsteady Antoine, dressed in his night clothes, came slowly down the stairs. "So that's why they let me go!" Michel cried.

"It's worth a few days in bed to have you back." Antoine held out his arms and the two clung to each other.

Bathed and dressed in clothes that used to fit him, Michel sat at dinner, staggered by the amount of food. "When you're hungry for so long, all you can think about is something to eat." After he'd had his fill he gave his account of what had happened to him since he'd dropped his letter from the train. It was a tale of despair and shattered pride, of forced marches and long train rides. Of weeks of idleness in holding camps, and months of unending labor in factories. The shunting from one place to another finally ended when he was sent to a camp in Germany. "I soon found out why the stalag was called 'the camp of the dead.' We ate soup made from potato skins, and slept under one thin blanket and a leaking roof. Infractions of the rules resulted in a beating. The work making barbed wire never stopped—shifts were twelve hours long. If you got sick, too bad. There were no medicines. If you died, someone else just took your place."

In anguished silence his listeners stared at the emaciated figure with the haunted eyes. "I've dreamed so often of this room, this table and all of you around it, that I wonder if you're real or have I made you up."

"The nightmare is over, my son," Antoine said in a broken voice. "You're home."

Slowly, father and son recuperated, and gradually worked their way into the daily schedule. They helped pick the apple crop in October, and in November shared in the sowing of the winter wheat.

The Allied invasion of North Africa and capture of Casablanca, plus the sinking of the French fleet by their own sailors in the harbor of Toulon, had dire consequences for the French. German troops, who had hastened to the Mediterranean port in the vain hope of capturing the fleet, stayed on as 'protectors.' The line separating occupied and unoccupied zones disappeared, and whatever power Marshal Petain had wielded at Vichy was no more. By the end of 1942, French borders were sealed and ports were closed; foreign newspapers were banned, and listening to foreign radio broadcasts was a prison offense. France was an island on which all Frenchmen were marooned. Anyone caught trying to escape was shot.

New Year's Day brought further calamity to the Hamels when Georges returned home as the family gathered for dinner. Since any deviation from the norm always portended trouble, his early arrival from Montebourg was viewed with misgivings. "What brings you home at this hour?" Antoine tried not to let his worry show.

"Bad news," Georges answered.

Her brother's abrupt answer sent a chill down Yvette's spine.

"The big-hearted foreman let me off before the others because tomorrow I leave for Germany."

Shocked into silence, no one spoke.

"When I asked him 'why me?' he said I was replacing one of my brothers who had come home."

"The swine!" Michel fumed. "That's one of their favorite tricks. Hoping we'll blame each other instead of them." His anger changed to concern. "Where are they sending you?"

"Does it matter?" Georges's voice was flat, drained of emotion. His face was a mask of despair. "It's all the same to me."

Yvette saw tears fill her father's eyes and knew what he was thinking: in protecting his son from a swift death in the Maquis, had he condemned him to a slow death in a German labor camp? The next morning, another good-bye was added to all the others that had gone before.

In March, the *Proprietaire* of La Hougue began coming every week from Paris to the farm to pick up food. Before the war he and Antoine had kept in touch from time to time to discuss crop rotation, the latest in animal husbandry, and other business matters. Now, necessity mandated his frequent visits, for hunger in the city had become acute. Among the sick and elderly, starvation was often the cause of death.

In contrast to the drabness of their lives, April arrived in a riot of color. Wild flowers blanketed roadside ditches, pink and white hawthorn bloomed with abandon, and cows were turned out to pastures that were emerald green again. Spring also brought Yvette an unexpected pleasure. It came via her friend, Michiline, who told her of a sewing class taught by her mother's friend, Madame Dubois, in the neighboring town of St. Jores. Two of the pupils in the class had had to drop out and the teacher had offered to let Michiline and Yvette take their places.

Although a sewing class taught by Madame Dubois could not compare with the Ecole de Couture at Picauville, Yvette was thrilled at this unexpected bonanza. The class met three times a week and began at eight o'clock in the morning. That meant getting up earlier than the others to milk her cows, an eight-kilometer round-trip bicycle ride, and her share of the day's chores awaiting when she got home.

Early on, the teacher recognized that Yvette had a flair for design and the determination to succeed. She gave her special attention and helped her to the limits of her ability. The hours spent at the home of Madame Dubois seemed to fly, and with every session Yvette gained more skill. "All wars end—this one will, too," her teacher encouraged her. "Don't lose sight of your dream. It has only been postponed."

Two months into the course, however, Michiline began making excuses and missing classes. When they'd begun the undertaking Yvette had wondered if her friend would stay the course. She was good at starting things, but often if they proved difficult, her interest flagged. Through the years, Yvette had accepted Michiline for what she was—warm, generous, impulsive—but undependable on the long haul. Now, Michiline had tired of the bicycle trip made in all kinds of weather and the dullness of redoing something that had been incorrectly done before. "I'm not motivated like you are," she told Yvette on the day she withdrew from the class. "You've got talent, but I'm all thumbs. Besides," she grimaced, "it's such a bore."

Yvette looked at the disgruntled expression on Michiline's face and for the first time was grateful for the discipline the farm had taught her. Compared to her daily chores, other activities seemed effortless. "I'll miss you," Yvette said.

"When you're rich and famous, I'll say I knew you when," Michiline smiled. "Watch out, Coco Chanel!"

"There's room for both of us at the top," Yvette joked.

With promises that they would keep in touch, the friends parted and Yvette continued the thrice-weekly classes alone. One afternoon in late July, after leaving her bicycle in the garage, Yvette headed down the driveway toward the house. When she stepped into the entryway, she expected to hear the rattle of crockery and smell dinner cooking on the hearth. Instead, the kitchen was silent except for a worried murmur of conversation. She hurried through the door and found her mother, pale and shaken, sitting in a chair. In front of the fireplace stood her brother, Georges.

Weary and gaunt, he was stripped of the elegance that had set him apart. His lively, chestnut-colored eyes had turned watchful, and dark whiskers bristled on his chin. Dressed in drab pants and jacket, and with a greasy looking cap pulled low on his forehead, he seemed to Yvette to have shrunk. She welcomed him with a hug and kisses.

"Are you—all right?" She backed away to examine his face.

He shrugged assent. "Considering six months of rotten food, miserable housing and twelve-hour work days."

"What are you doing here?" she asked anxiously.

"I was in the process of being transferred from one factory to another. For some reason—they never tell you why—I was issued a week's pass to come home. Transportation is so messed up, I've wasted three days getting here."

His eyes narrowed, his mouth hardened. "I'm not going back.

The whole god-damned Wehrmacht could not drag me back!"

The venomous intensity in his voice made the hair prickle on the back of her neck.

A stir at the door interrupted their talk. "Georges!" Antoine rushed to the fireplace and embraced his son. "You're home! For how long?"

Georges stepped away to look his father in the eyes. "Not long, Papa. I'm going to join the *Maquis*."

Antoine nodded slowly. "This time I won't hinder you. How can I help?"

Georges began to pace the room. "I left the train at Carentan and used the short cut. No one saw me arrive at La Hougue. *Voila,* I never came home."

"D'accord," his father answered.

"I'll need false I.D. papers."

"The Mayor has ways."

"How long will it take?"

Antoine frowned. "Last week, a counterfeiting network in La-Haye-du-Puits was smashed. Now, it's necessary to go further afield. Monday, perhaps."

Georges shook his head. "That's not good. For me to stay here past Sunday is dangerous—for you."

"To breathe these days is dangerous," his father brushed the risk aside. He hurried toward the hall. "The sooner I get word to the Mayor, the better."

As if remembering that it was the dinner hour, Alice rose from her chair and crossed to the cupboard. "You must not leave the house," she instructed Georges, "and stay away from the windows."

He nodded. "None of you should change your routines." He glanced at Yvette. "Where have you come from just now?"

She told him about the sewing class in St. Jores.

He stared at her as if he hadn't heard correctly. Then he began to laugh. He laughed until tears rolled down his cheeks. Yvette and her mother exchanged a worried look. Finally, he knuckled the tears from his eyes with grubby fingers. "Germany is being bombed around the clock. The Americans come by day and the

English at night. You never know whether the factory you leave in the evening will be there in the morning. The bridge you crossed might disappear behind you. People are dying by the thousands, and in St. Jores, girls sit around a table learning how to sew."

"Life goes on, Georges," his mother said.

"Yes, thank God." He smiled at Yvette. "Keep on with your sewing class. How about the others?" he asked his mother.

She told him of Edouard being pressed into a road and bridge repair detail; that Etienne was still building beach defenses. "Michel, Henri, and Papa take care of the farm chores as best they can. All of us do the milking."

The others straggled in. Astonished to see Georges at home, they readily agreed with his escape plans. When Antoine returned from the Mayor's house, he had good news. The process had been set in motion. Now the hardest part began—the waiting.

Georges slept the clock around. When he came downstairs the next evening, he looked more like his former self. He was eager for news of events since he'd left, but loath to spend time talking about his work. It was mind-numbingly boring, he related, doing the same thing over and over. "We never knew what we were making parts for. There were Poles, Czechs, Dutch, Belgians. We couldn't speak each other's language, but we shared a common hate: the Boches."

A plan was devised to hide Georges in the attic if wheels or boots sounded in the drive. The next day he helped his mother in the house, stayed away from windows and slipped upstairs if someone came to the door. At dinner, they planned the next day's program. After lunch, Yvette would accompany her father to town. She would make purchases at the store, buy stamps, while he called at the Town Hall to collect the monthly ration books. In short—a routine visit. As they plotted, they suddenly fell silent—listening to a tapping on the door. Georges left the table to sprint up the stairs. Etienne moved his empty chair from the table to the wall; Gilberte washed his plate and glass.

"Keep talking," Antoine whispered, heading for the entryway. He took a deep breath and opened the door. The Abbe Giard stepped into the hall. Antoine's shoulders sagged with relief. He ushered the Abbe into the kitchen where Alice invited him to join them at dinner.

"I can't stay," the Cure answered. "I've come to tell you there's been a glitch. Georges's papers won't be ready tomorrow."

"Mon Dieu!" Antoine groaned. "When?"

"Tuesday, the Mayor hopes. Give him until three o'clock." Father Giard bid the family a hasty good-bye. "I'm sorry," he told Antoine at the door. "Pray, my friend," he added, and disappeared into the darkness.

"I heard," Georges said when he returned to the kitchen. "I'm endangering all of you. Maybe I could risk not having papers."

"Don't even think about it," Etienne shook his head. "They're getting more antsy all the time. Everyone is being checked."

"I'm due back tomorrow." Georges grimaced. "When I left, one of the guards warned me not to try anything funny! Almost as if he suspected something."

"Don't worry, Georges," Antoine told his son. "We'll get your papers!"

Although her father's voice was firm, Yvette wondered if he were as positive as he sounded.

7

Even though the hours on Tuesday morning were filled with tasks, time seemed to stand still. Yvette helped Georges pack his knapsack, fixed food for him to take. She watched him pace from room to room, torn between reluctance to bid his old life *Adieu*, yet longing to be on his way. At last it was time to go. Yvette and her father hitched the horse to the cabriolet then settled beside each other on the seat. They knew that observers, hidden by the blackout curtain, watched anxiously from the window. *"Deo volente,* let our mission be successful," Antoine murmured. He flicked the reins and they started up the drive.

Never had the ride to town seemed so long. Yvette remembered when it used to be enjoyable—checking the number of milk cans at their neighbors' gates; stopping for a bit of gossip if they met someone. Today they had eyes only for the church bell tower. The first sight of it above the hedgerows meant that only one more bend in the road remained before they arrived in the village square.

"There!" Yvette exclaimed. "We made it."

"Don't count your chickens before—" The words had scarcely left his lips when they heard the hateful whine of tires, the grind of gears. "No!" Yvette groaned.

"Get ready," Antoine muttered. He pulled his cap down over his forehead while his chin sagged toward his chest. Yvette slumped beside him, letting her hands fall limp at her sides. With vacant eyes she watched the gray-green patrol car, like some malevolent, mechanical animal nose around the bend.

"Halte!"

Although Yvette knew the command jarred her father from his ears down to his toes, she marveled that he blinked as if awaking from a snooze. He straightened, pulled back on the reins, and inspected the two occupants of the approaching vehicle.

Stocky, with a high-cheek-boned Slavic face, the driver, leaving the engine idling, stopped the staff car beside the cabriolet. "We need directions," he said.

Antoine frowned; cupped a hand behind his ear. *"Comment?"*

"Here we go with our little charade," the driver growled to his companion. "We....need....directions," he repeated, enunciating as if speaking to a retarded child.

Further pretense that the foreigner's excellent French was incomprehensible would stretch credulity. Antoine replaced his befuddled look with a benign smile. *"A votre service, Messieurs."*

"Where is the Hamel farm?"

The query froze Yvette's blood. As if from a great distance, she heard her father reply, "I am Antoine Hamel."

The driver held out his hand. "Your papers."

The search through all his pockets seemed to take forever. Was that another of his charades; a further ruse to gain the upper hand, Yvette wondered. She watched the driver grow increasingly impatient. Then she noted that since the cabriolet was higher than the patrol car, her father looked down his nose at its two occupants while they had to look up to him. The detail pleased her and she was sure it had not escaped her father's notice.

"Ah, voila!" The card was finally produced.

After examining the card the driver handed it back with a curt nod. "Your son, Georges, was due back at his job yesterday. He hasn't shown up."

Antoine's eyebrows lifted. "Due back? From where?"

"Don't play games! You know he was issued a pass to come home. Where is he?"

Yvette held her breath.

"Pass? To come home?" Antoine rose from his seat. "He never arrived," he shouted. Under Antoine's accusing stare, the driver shifted in his seat. He glanced from the papers beside him on the seat to his companion.

"Two of my sons are prisoners-of-war. Now a third has disappeared in Germany!"

Her father's voice was not only angry, but, Yvette noted, it carried easily to his friend, Andre, working with his nephew in a field adjoining the road. As the two of them hastened toward the fence, their tools glinting in the sun, two burly farmers in a wagon filled with hay approached from the rear. Curious about the disturbance, they drew alongside the cabriolet, thus blocking the road. Yvette glanced at the newcomers as if she'd never seen her mother's cousins from Vierville before. "It isn't fair," Antoine wailed. "Three sons—just gone! How can I tell their mother?" he appealed to the farmers in the wagon. "She won't recover from this latest blow."

"Three sons gone?" one of the wagoners asked. "Did you say three?"

Antoine nodded in despair. "Two have been in Germany since the war began," he moaned. "Now they inform me the third has— vanished."

"Good God!" the driver of the wagon sympathized. He jerked a thumb toward the load his wagon carried. "I'm on my way to the chateau to deliver this hay for *their* horses. Meanwhile I don't have enough for my own. They take our sons away yet expect us to grow more wheat."

"It's getting worse all the time," the farmer at the fence agreed. "My two sons are prisoners. I'm trying to run a farm with a sixteen-year-old boy!"

"The injustice of it!" Antoine lamented. Yvette buried her face in her hands.

The mutters grew louder and mean. With mounting apprehension, the occupants of the patrol car eyed the workers gesticulating with razor-sharp tools and the wagoner jiggling a long, snakelike whip. "Somebody in St. Lo screwed up and left us holding the bag," Yvette heard the driver grunt.

"Let's get the hell out of here," his companion agreed.

"Quiet, old man," the driver called to Antoine. "We'll look into this and get back to you." He shifted into reverse, and with a screech of tires, sped back the way he had come.

"Thank God," Yvette breathed.

"We're not out of the woods yet," her father cautioned. "*Merci,*

Andre," he called to his friend at the fence, "and to you, Marcel,"
he tipped his hat to Alice's cousin. "That was close."

Marcel winked and gave a final snap to his whip; Andre
brandished his hoe. They bid each other *adieu,* Antoine clicked
the reins, and he and Yvette resumed their way to town.

They parted in the church square. She headed for the general
store, he for the City Hall. It was 3:15. She dawdled over her
purchases, chatted at length with the owner. In the Post Office,
she gave up her place in line to a neighbor in a hurry. Despite her
delaying tactics, her father was nowhere in sight when she
returned to the cabriolet. Had another glitch developed?

To wait in the carriage would be conspicuous. She glanced
around, wondering how to occupy her time. The school adjoining
the town hall was deserted—the *rentree* would not begin for
another month. At the Delacroix house next the school, Madame
was working in her garden, but she was a busybody and loved to
poke around in other people's affairs. Across the street, Yvette
saw the glow of the forge through the open door of the
blacksmith's shop—no possibilities there—and further on the
cafe. Since girls her age did not frequent the cafe unaccompanied,
that too was no help. As a last resort she crossed the square to the
town bulletin board. Scrutinizing the public notices would keep
her busy for a little while. As she feigned interest in the accumu-
lated, dog-eared announcements, she heard footsteps behind her.
"Ah, Mademoiselle Hamel. How are you?"

Yvette dreaded turning around. Even before the war, she'd
disliked Monsieur Dumont. His oily, too-friendly manner had
grated on her nerves. Ever since Georges's and Henri's close call
in St. Lo, and the dismantling of her father's Renault, she had
despised him. That he was a Nazi sympathizer was well known
now. His fortunes had improved. His milk drew the highest prices
in the region, and seldom was his livestock requisitioned.

She greeted him with as much cordiality as she could muster.
As she turned back to her inspection of the public notices she felt
his eyes appraising her. "It seems only yesterday that you were
just a child," he said. "Now, you're a young woman and," he
moved a step closer, "quite an attractive one."

The sound of his breathing through parted lips, the smell of his cloying cologne repelled her. Yet at this crucial time, she mustn't offend him. "Well, everyone grows up, don't they, Monsieur Dumont," she smiled.

"Indeed they do—some more pleasing to the eye than others." He patted her lingeringly on the arm. "And how is your family?"

She shrugged. "As well as can be expected."

"These are trying times," he agreed. "Do you hear from your brothers, David and Pierre?"

A little wriggle of alarm angled down her spine. "Not as often as we'd like."

"And the handsome Georges. He was just home, wasn't he?"

Panic gripped her. How did he find out! "Home?" She gave him a puzzled look. "Was Georges coming home?"

Monsieur Dumont looked momentarily flustered. "I suppose it was just a rumor, my dear."

"Who told you?" She had to know!

She watched him stiffen at her persistence, and berated herself for her clumsiness. She looked at him wide-eyed. "I mean, I wondered if you'd heard anything from the Mayor—something that, perhaps, he hadn't had time to tell us."

Her implication that Monsieur Dumont, rather than her father, was privy to the Mayor's confidence was not lost on him. Amused, and disgusted, she watched him preen. "We discuss matters that are not generally known. But," he leaned closer so that their shoulders touched, "this rumor came through a contact at head-quarters in St. Lo." He smiled slyly. "It doesn't hurt to keep a finger in all the pies, *n'est-ce pas?*"

"How clever you are," she breathed, trying to stem her rising alarm. Where was her father! "Perhaps George's homecoming was delayed."

"That must be it," he agreed.

Out of the corner of her eye she saw a bicyclist pedaling hard toward the town hall. He glided the last few meters, propped his bicycle against a tree, and disappeared through the door. Was that the courier, she wondered desperately. She must keep Monsieur Dumont occupied.

"How lucky for the Mayor to have someone like you to act as a liaison between him and the St. Lo authorities," she burbled.

"I don't say this to everyone," he took her hand to emphasize his point, "but the *Kommandantur* does not entrust everything to the Mayor's office. Our Mayor is a good man—do not get me wrong—but these days there are matters which are delicate, and require a certain finesse." He gave her hand a squeeze.

She longed to snatch her hand away. Instead, she gritted her teeth and nodded solemnly. "And you're the one they contact?"

His oily face broke into a smile.

"Yvette!"

Her father's call flooded her with relief. It had the opposite effect on Monsieur Dumont who dropped her hand as if it were on fire. "I didn't know your father was here," he blurted.

"He was getting our ration books," she explained.

Monsieur Dumont's eyes narrowed. "I was in the Town Hall just now. I didn't see him."

Yvette shrugged. "Papa doesn't get away from the farm very often. You know how he likes to talk. He was probably visiting with someone and forgot the time." She gave him a warm smile. "I do appreciate your information about Georges. Maman and Papa will be so thrilled to see him when he arrives." She edged away. *"Au revoir,* and again, thanks."

"What was that all about?" her father demanded when they were seated in the carriage.

"I'll explain later," she answered. "Did you get it!"

"Just!" Antoine sighed with relief.

As they headed back to La Hougue, he described the circuitous route now needed to obtain false I.D. papers. They originated on an underground printing press in Bayeux. A functionary in the city government, a member of the Resistance, made a weekly trip to Valognes to visit his dying mother. He sometimes carried documents back and forth and agreed to drop Georges's papers off at the midway point—Carentan—where a railroad clerk would deliver them to the Mayor's office in Coigny.

But this week, the official's visit to his mother had been postponed a day and, on the way to Carentan, the train was delayed by a bridge which was being repaired.

"The Mayor and I sat looking at each other, growing more nervous every minute," Antoine said. The bicyclist whose arrival Yvette had shielded from Monsieur Dumont's prying eyes was indeed the courier. Antoine patted the pocket of his coat. "I've got the papers here."

His long tale had brought them to the gate of La Hougue, and in the excitement of getting Georges ready for his trip, her father forgot her encounter with Monsieur Dumont. She hoped that, given time, she also could erase the repugnant episode from her mind.

Georges became Lucien Travert from Lessay—an expert in dealing with draft horses. Since so many dray teams had been requisitioned by the Wehrmacht, he no longer had a job in the city where the famous horse fairs used to be held. He was traveling to Brittany to work on his uncle's farm. Food was secreted in every pocket; grease and dirt aged his I.D. card. As the family watched his blue jacket disappear behind a hedgerow they hoped that his dream of fighting with the Maquis would finally be realized.

8

Her father cupped Yvette's chin in his hand and examined her face. "Happy Birthday, *ma petite*. You're getting too grown up to be called 'my little one' any longer."

"Being sixteen used to sound so exciting." She grimaced. "Now it only means I have to get an I. D. card."

He let his arm drop to his side. "How much longer can this war last!"

The bleak November light coming through the kitchen window emphasized the grooves bracketing his mouth and showed up the gray streaks in his hair. Today he little resembled the young man that Yvette loved to look at in the family album. His black hair had curled around a forehead free of wrinkles; his lips had curved in a rakish smile. From his Spanish grandmother, he'd inherited his flashing eyes and taste for fine clothes. What a *gallant* he was in those days, her mother would remind him, with just the right show of jealousy. He would twirl his mustache and they would smile at each other in a knowing way.

Her parents didn't banter like that any more. Gaiety was one of the many things the war had robbed them of. Yvette couldn't remember the last time she'd heard her father's deep-throated laugh or her mother singing at her work. Any frivolity at the dinner table brought disapproving looks. "How can you joke when David and Pierre are prisoners and Georges is in constant danger?"

The surrender of Italy, the capture of Corsica, and the retreat of German soldiers from Russian soil brightened the waning weeks of 1943. But as pressure on Germany mounted, so did the suffering of the countries under Nazi domination. Requisition of livestock, grain, and workers increased, and reprisals against members of the Resistance were more frequent and brutal. Surveillance of the population living along the Channel coast expanded alarmingly.

At the beginning of the occupation the inspection of the poster listing the members of the household and their whereabouts had been sporadic and cursory. Yvette remembered a Captain who, on his way down the drive, had paused in the field where the horses grazed and picked a handful of mushrooms. He'd asked her father to cook him a mushroom omelet, gave the poster a passing glance, then sat at the kitchen table to eat the delicacy while carrying on an amiable conversation with the family. After thanking them for their hospitality, he'd bid them a cordial *adieu*.

But that casual appraisal was long past. The inspector came often now and verified the occupation and location of every member of the household. Yvette lived in dread that her father's story about Georges would be challenged and she would return some evening from St. Jores to find that he'd been apprehended to fill Georges's place.

Fear of seizure dominated their lives. The bitter cold of January and February in 1944 brought disease and death to malnourished workers on the coastal fortifications, and there was a continual search for replacements. The demand for woodsmen to fell trees for stakes planted in open fields to prevent glider landings, for quarrymen to dig limestone to supply cement for gun emplacements, and artisans to repair bomb damage was unremitting. Sweeps through the countryside gathered those who might, for whatever reason, have been exempt before.

"Charles Devries was taken this morning," Antoine told the family at lunch one day."

"No!" Alice answered.

"When I left the broken scythe at the blacksmith's shop, he was being led away. His father stood in the road with tears streaming down his face. 'But I have a doctor's certificate and the Mayor's permit,' he pleaded. The Boches shrugged. 'Those excuses don't count any more,' they said."

"Of what use to them is a feebleminded boy who limps?" Alice exclaimed.

"He can push a wheelbarrow," Edouard answered. "That's all they care about—live bodies."

Antoine looked from Michel to Henri. "From now on, it would be safer for you to stay off the roads and away from town."

"Not get off the farm!" Henri protested.

"Here you're fairly safe," his father answered. "But if you give the impression of not having enough to do," he made a grabbing motion, "you could be hooked like Charles Devries."

"Prisoners! On our own land!" Henri exploded.

"Better our land than Bocheland," his father answered.

Their confinement told on already jangled nerves. "Yvette flits about free as a bird, while we're chained like dogs to a stake," she overheard Henri grumbling to Michel.

In truth, she was the most mobile member of the family and tried to compensate for the others' isolation by bringing bits of information back from her thrice-weekly trips to her sewing class. More and more German troops were being stationed in St. Jores, she related. Telephone lines between St. Jores and Carentan had been cut for the third time in three weeks; the Boches had flooded the marshes southeast of the city to prevent gliders and parachutists from landing.

One cold, gray morning in late February she set out at her usual time. Soon after she'd left the country road and joined the highway to St. Jores, she heard behind her the dreaded thrum of a heavy duty motorcycle. The *feldgendarmerie!* Go on by, she prayed. Don't stop! But as if her plea had attracted its attention, the vehicle drew abreast and the driver motioned her to pull off the road.

The sight of a special agent of the Nazi police, even at a distance, made the hair prickle on the back of her neck. Her worst nightmare was to be accosted by one. She'd often told herself how stupid it was to let a uniform frighten her. Yet the dark green overcoat, black boots and belt, gun in its holster, helmet and goggles, and the gold medallion on a heavy chain around the neck conjured up scenes of midnight seizure, interrogation and torture.

"Your papers!"

Her heart pounded as with clumsy fingers she groped in her string bag for her I. D. card. She handed it to the driver who in turn passed it to the *feldgendarmerie* riding in the sidecar. Yvette braced herself.

"Look this way."

She flinched involuntarily, when instead of meeting the policeman's eyes she saw her own frightened expression reflected in his mirrored goggles. Stony-faced, he compared her features to those pictured on her *carte*.

"How tall are you?" he asked.

"A meter, um—seventy-two," she blurted.

He measured her visually from head to toe, then took a pencil and small notebook from his pocket. "Write your name."

As the driver passed her the writing tools, panic gripped her. How had she signed the card? Sometimes she began her names with flowery capital letters; other times she merely printed them. She hated the card and had scarcely looked at it since her sixteenth birthday. As she fretted, she became aware of the policeman's attention riveted on her. "You seem to have trouble remembering your name," he snapped. "Perhaps this is not your card."

"Oh yes, that's my card!" she answered. Had she replied too quickly? Under their suspicious stares, she gripped the pencil like a vise, and scratched out the letters of her name. It seemed to take forever. She handed back the notebook and pencil and held her breath. The policeman examined it without a change of expression.

"Hand over your bag."

She passed it over and with mounting alarm waited while he examined the contents. He even poked through the ingredients of her lunch. What had happened to trigger this kind of scrutiny? Was this something to do with Georges?

"Where did you come from just now?"

"I live on a farm near Coigny."

"Where are you going?"

At the mention of St. Jores, both men stiffened. What was the name of the teacher? How many girls were in the class? Where was the house located? Did she return this way last night? One query followed another like bullets from a machine gun. Her mind in turmoil, she tried to give coherent answers. As abruptly as it had begun, the interrogation ceased. Frozen-faced, the inquisitor stared through the windshield then, without turning his head, spoke in German to the driver.

"Return home," the driver told her. "If you go to St. Jores, you will be stopped again. Those inspectors will not be as restrained as we were."

He thrust the bag and card at her and the motorcycle sped on its way. Yvette pedaled to the farm as if pursued by demons. As she and her mother worried over the severity of the questioning, Madame Houtecourt brought the mail, as well as an explanation.

"Two Boches, throats cut and minus their uniforms, were found this morning in a drainage ditch between Pretot and St. Jores."

"Mon Dieu," Yvette murmured.

"More reprisals," her mother lamented.

And so it was. Twenty members of the Resistance—the ratio was now ten to one—caught in the region of La Manche, were herded into the church square in the village of Beaucoudray and shot. Yet oil tanks persisted in burning mysteriously, telephone lines were cut with regularity, and German corpses continued to float facedown in drainage ditches. The Hamels lived in fear that one day Georges's body would be among those slumped against a wall.

Throughout March, American and English bombers came in ever-increasing numbers. Like distant thunder their rumble could be heard in Coigny as they headed for railroad marshalling yards, communication centers, oil depots and munitions dumps to the east and south. As the milkers gathered one morning after a particularly violent nocturnal attack, they expressed relief that Coigy had nothing to attract them.

That very night, however, the rumble grew louder until the family was deafened by the roar of planes. One ear-splitting explosion followed another, and fire lit up the sky as if the sun were rising. Clouds of dust and ashes billowed into the air. When the reverberations had died away, the shaken family gathered in the hall.

"It was too close to have been Carentan," Antoine conjectured.

"Could it have been Baupte?" Alice asked fearfully. The farm of the Hamel's oldest daughter, Denise, and her husband, Paul, lay on the outskirts of the town.

Antoine put a protective arm around his wife. "As soon as the curfew's lifted, we'll find out."

They arose at dawn, prepared to dispatch Etienne to Baupte when the sound of a wagon in the drive brought everyone to the door. White-faced, Denise, Paul, and their four-year-old son, Bernard, told of the night's disaster.

"Baupte is—gone!" Denise said. "Nothing is left but the church and *presbytere*," She shuddered. "It was awful. There was no place to hide."

"Everybody is homeless," Paul continued. "The town is being evacuated."

"What were the bombers aiming at?" Antoine asked.

"The railroad bridge," Paul replied. "The Boches are fortifying the islands of Guernsey and Jersey. Trains carrying ammunition from Carentan to the port at Barneville-Carteret run twenty-four hours a day. Baupte is about the midway point. By destroying the bridge, the Allies could disrupt the pipeline." He grimaced. "They missed the bridge, but demolished the tracks on either side and blew up a munitions train."

"Some of our cows were killed," Denise continued, "but by some miracle, the house wasn't hit and none of us was hurt."

"Everyone is sure that the bombers will be back to get the bridge," Paul said grimly.

"If the Allies are intent on cutting off supplies to the Channel Islands, that could mean an invasion right here in our neck of the woods." Etienne's voice held suppressed excitement.

The possibility that the long-awaited Allied invasion might take place in this spit of Normandy, called the Cotentin, set off a spate of arguments pro and con. The thirty-mile-wide peninsula with its drainage ditches and small hedgerow-bordered fields would be totally unsuitable terrain for an invasion of such

magnitude, Antoine reasoned. But they'd need a port, Henri
countered. Cherbourg would be perfect. "It's too heavily de-
fended," Michel objected. And on and on, until like all invasion
plans about which they could only speculate, this one, too, was
left in limbo.

The Hamels set about accommodating the refugees. Paul and
Bernard took beds left vacant by Pierre and Georges, and Denise
joined her sisters in the big room that overlooked the courtyard.
The Abbe Giard declined the Hamels' offer of sanctuary. "I must
watch over the church," he explained. And so he continued to live
in the *presbytere,* traveling around the region to take care of his
scattered flock.

In the following days more refugees arrived. An elderly ex-
tailor, Monsieur Olivier, and his tiny wife, a former seamstress,
were installed in the guest room. For a merchant couple and their
nephew, Jacques, cots were set up in the dining room. The
merchant couple tarried only a few days, then traveled south to
stay with relatives. Jacques asked if he could remain with the
Hamels in order to keep an eye on his *bureau de tabac* which had
been damaged in the bombing, and also to deliver to his
customers in the region the cigarettes, stamps and other items that
he'd managed to salvage. Antoine readily agreed, and Jacques
became a fixture in the Hamel household. He helped with farm
chores, and in the evening listened with Antoine to the shortwave
radio. He was knowledgeable about messages that frequently
were transmitted by code to Resistance fighters, and sometimes
disappeared for days at a time, returning without explanation.
Though he never told them, the family assumed that Jacques was
a courier between Resistance groups.

Every morning and evening Paul returned to his and Denise's
farm to care for their animals. On one of these trips he brought his
wife's harmonium back to La Hougue. He set it up in the dining
room and there, on Sunday evenings, the family gathered for a
songfest as they used to do. Henri played his accordion, Etienne
his trumpet, and the five-year-old war that had dominated their
lives was forgotten for a little while.

9

The capriciousness of the death of Suzanne, one of her friends in the sewing class, was a numbing experience for Yvette. She arrived one day in late April at the home of Madame Dubois to find the class, as well as the teacher, in tears. Madame Dubois related the bizarre event which had occurred the night before. To prevent birds from eating the berries on their currant bushes, Suzanne had helped her mother cover the bushes with old curtains, which formerly had hung in their dining room. Soldiers arrived during the night, claimed the white curtains were a landmark for planes bombing the railroad bridge, then shot and killed the entire family. When Madame ended her account with "The worst part of it is—" Yvette covered her ears. The worst part was always the same—a jealous relative, an erstwhile friend, or a neighbor, getting even for some real or imagined slight, had denounced the family to the Nazis.

"When the Boches start shooting people like Suzanne, no one is safe," the teacher concluded. "Everything we do could be interpreted as a signal—what a nightmare!"

As if to compensate for the gloom which permeated their lives, May ushered in glorious weather. Winter clothes were put away and the sun shone from cloudless skies. But those clear skies brought increasing destruction. Baupte and Carentan were frequent targets for the bombers, which came by day and by night. Adding to the apprehension were the more and more frequent attacks by Resistance groups on railroads and communication networks. In retaliation, the Germans shot more hostages. After a train ferrying Nazi troops to Cherbourg blew up, French civilians equal to the number of soldiers being transported were forced to occupy each railroad car. At any moment, a member of the family might be snatched to ride the trains. As the grip tightened on the oppressed, tension mounted on the oppressor. The Allied invasion was coming. Everybody knew it. But when—and where?

"The uncertainty must be driving them crazy," Yvette said as she watched a group of soldiers jog along the road. Formerly, the thud of hobnail boots, the singsong chant, HI-LI, HI-LO; HI-LI, HI-LO as they marched double-time from the Chateau to Baupte and back again had reminded her of little boys with toys playing at war games. Now, the sudden breaks for the hedgerows and the mounting of machine guns on the banks of the ditches looked grimly real.

Jacques joined her at the kitchen window as the last of the soldiers jogged out of sight. "Wouldn't they love to know," he smiled maliciously.

Yvette gave him a sidelong glance. "Wouldn't we!"

Their eyes met. "Soon," he answered noncommittally.

A massive buildup of German forces in the region added to the anxiety. "St. Jores is running over with soldiers," Yvette reported. Sainte Mere Eglise bristles with armored cars, field artillery and tanks, the Hamel's harness maker disclosed. "The 91st Airborne Division has been moved to Carentan," the Mayor related. "They're everywhere, the bastards."

Etienne kept the family informed about beach defenses that General Rommel had devised: hundreds of thousands of mines planted in the sand; stakes topped with explosives hidden by high tide; tetrahedra strengthened with concrete, barbed wire strung by the mile and, looming over all, the big guns protected by their concrete bunkers. "If, by some miracle, Allied soldiers get beyond the beaches, they could be drowned in the flooded marshes." He shook his head. "I pity the poor devils who will be the first to land!"

As May drew to a close, the Hamel's shortwave radio vibrated with messages for the Resistance—garbled phrases, numbers in sequence, lines of poetry—but hopes for an imminent Allied invasion evaporated when June began. The weather took a turn for the worse. It deteriorated further on the 2nd and 3rd. By the night of the 5th, rain beat against the slate roof of La Hougue and wind moaned around its eaves.

"I guess the Boches are celebrating tonight," Edouard said as thunder rumbled overhead. "No invasion in this kind of weather."

Yvette nodded, and closed the book she was reading. "They must feel very safe."

Henri left off banking the fire. "When you think about it, this would be a good night for the Allies to attack. They would take the Boches completely by surprise."

Edouard gave his older brother a sarcastic look. "General Eisenhower could really use you on his staff."

"They have this little problem, Henri," Etienne explained in a voice he used with his four-year-old nephew, Bernard. "From England, an invasion has to come by sea. And storms make the sea very rough."

"By now, the Boches are in the sack," Henri ignored the logic of the other two. "Probably half of them are drunk." He nodded. "It's a good idea."

"Then you wait up for them," Etienne suggested. "I'm going to bed."

"Me, too." Yvette pushed herself from her chair. "Maybe by July the weather will clear and we can start hoping again."

At midnight an all-too-familiar rumble roused her from a deep sleep. She opened her eyes and groaned. Moonlight streamed through the bedroom window. The storm had passed—and the bombers were back. She shook Claire by the shoulder. "Get up!" she called to her other sisters, and swung her feet to the floor.

As they stirred the rumble grew louder. How low they sounded. "Hurry!" Yvette urged. "They're headed this way. We must get downstairs." She stumbled across the room and flung open the door. Too late! The planes were already overhead. She cringed, waiting for the explosion. The thunder of engines beat against her ears, rattled windows and shook the floor, but as quickly as they had come the planes were gone.

"Thank God," she murmured, letting her taut shoulders droop with relief. "Tonight we're not the target."

As she crawled back into bed, she felt momentary guilt. Their own deliverance meant someone else would suffer. Too tired to wonder for whom the bombs were meant, she fell asleep.

Thirty minutes later the reverberation of another wave of planes broke into her slumber. This time Gilberte sounded the alarm. Again the stirring, the effort to arise. Again the planes were upon them, low-flying like the others, and then they, too, were gone. An ear-splitting yell from the hall brought them upright in their beds. Yvette was the first one to reach the door. She found Etienne staring into the night from one of the three large windows that stretched the length of the hall. "Look!" he cried.

The rest of the household quickly gathered. Awed, they gazed at what seemed a multitude of parachutes, scattered like confetti in the sky. In the bright moonlight they were clearly visible, scarcely two hundred meters above the ground. From some of them, bundles of different sizes and shapes dangled; others carried soldiers. Silently, they drifted toward the trees. Moments later, they were lost to sight. The distant sound of gunfire rumbled across the countryside, and from the direction of Sainte Mere Eglise, the horizon glowed as if on fire.

"What can it mean?" Yvette asked.

"We'll soon find out," her mother answered. "Papa and Jacques are listening to the radio."

"Do they think that this is the—"

"Shhhh," Etienne broke in. "Listen." From a clump of apple trees near the fishing pond, a mechanical "click-click" was clearly audible. An answering "click-clack" came from a stand of oaks near the wash house. The pattern was repeated again and again.

"They're signaling to each other," Henri said.

Finally, the clicking noises were stilled and all was peaceful as before. The moon disappeared behind a cloud, and in the darkened fields below, not a trace remained of the airborne visitors.

Footsteps on the stairs announced Antoine's return. He hurried toward the group at the window. "Jacques is convinced," he cried. "This is it!" He raised his fists above his head. "The day we've waited for so long!"

Shouts of "Bravo!" "Hooray," and ear-splitting whistles echoed up and down the hall.

Amid the tumultuous rejoicing, Yvette felt a tug on her arm. "We have something important to do," Madame Olivier reminded her.

They hurried to the guest room, and took from the big armoire the red, white and blue flag that they had pieced together from strips of cloth. They tacked it to the pole hidden under the bed, and after they'd sung a few bars of the "Marseillaise," they hung the flag from the windowsill.

"Ours will be the first French flag to welcome our liberators!" Madame Olivier boasted.

"Maman and Papa will be so proud! I can't wait for them to see it." Yvette kissed Madame Olivier goodnight and hurried from the room.

There was no settling down in her own bed, however, for bursts of gunfire and sporadic explosions kept the family on edge until morning. Although the parachutists had gone, evidence remained that they had landed on the farm. "The underbrush around the lambing shed was trampled," Henri reported to the milkers gathered in the barn, "and look what I found inside the shed." He held up the wrapper from a candy bar. "Chocolate!"

They passed around the crumpled paper and sniffed an aroma they'd almost forgotten. "That's something to tell our grandchildren about," Gilberte said. "Ours was the first soil the parachutists touched."

"They tangled with the Boches in the Chasse," Etienne reported. "I found the remains of Tulipe in the field. She must have wandered alongside the Boches's camp last night. They butchered her, and cooked her hind quarters for supper. I guess they were saving the rest for today but the parachutists surprised them— burned their camp. Trucks, tanks, everything. Three of the Boches are dead."

"Mon Dieu." Gilberte murmured.

"During the fight part of the fence was torn down," Etienne continued. "I found Blanchette and Anemone in the road."

Subdued, his listeners contemplated what this first skirmish of the invasion portended: that while the battle for Normandy raged, they would be caught defenseless in the crossfire.

Finished with her milking, Yvette left the barn for the house. She noted at once that the flag on the windowsill was missing. Who had taken it down, she wondered uneasily. As she stepped into the hall, she heard her mother's angry voice. "God in heaven, what were you thinking of! We're surrounded by Germans and you hang out a French flag to taunt them!"

Filled with apprehension, Yvette hurried into the kitchen where a furious Alice, clutching the flag, stood over a cowed Madame Olivier crouched by the fire. "Maman," she cried, "I'm as much to blame as she is."

Alice whirled on her daughter. "And what if our liberators are driven out?" she demanded. "The Boches would kill us all." She sighed, turning again toward Madame Olivier. "Yvette is too young to remember the last war but you lived through it. You should know better."

The chastened lady nodded. "I'm sorry. My joy got the better of my good sense."

Clasping the flag as if she thought it might escape, Alice swept from the room. The culprits eyed each other. "Next time don't pay attention to the whim of a dotty old lady," Madame Olivier said.

Yvette crossed the room and gave her a hug. "We did the wrong thing for the right reason," she answered.

"I did so want our liberators to know we were good French." Madame Olivier sighed. "I feel terrible about endangering the family. *Mon Dieu,* let's hope the Boches were too occupied with the parachutists to notice the flag."

"I'm sure they were," Yvette said with more conviction than she felt. She headed for the door. "I'd better change for breakfast."

As she climbed the stairs to her bedroom, her mother's cry, "the boches would kill us all!" rang in her ears. Had they seen the flag and even now were on the way to the farm? She thought of Suzanne's family, executed for covering currant bushes with white curtains. Compared to that trivial act, what she and Madame Olivier had done was a monstrous affront.

Claire stood at the washstand when Yvette came into the

room. Over her shoulder, she watched Yvette step out of her shoes. "Maman is furious! You're really going to catch it for hanging out that flag!" She reached for a towel to dry her face.

"I've already caught it!" Yvette retorted, pulling off her blouse. "I don't need any more from you."

"That was a stupid thing to do. What if the Boches had spotted it?" Claire cocked her thumb and forefinger to imitate a gun. "Rat-a-tat-tat," she pretended to mow down a group of people. "We'd all be dead just like Suzanne's—"

The thud of running boots in the driveway silenced her. Frozen, the girls listened to a pounding on the door. "They saw it!" Claire whimpered.

From below, they heard shouted commands, the sounds of splintering furniture and breaking crockery. Yvette longed to hide—in the armoire, under the bed, anywhere—but Claire's nightmare imitation of the family's execution goaded her into action. Snatching a dress from the armoire, she yanked it over her head, and dashed to the door.

"Where are you going?" Claire cried.

"To tell them it was my idea," Yvette answered.

"Wait for me."

Her sister's plea went unanswered as Yvette raced barefoot down the hall. She looked over the banister and stopped, rooted to the spot. Hands upraised, face ashen, her father was slowly mounting the stairs. A German soldier prodded him upward with a gun held to his back. On the steps below, a second soldier crouched, while two others stood guard at the door. None of them had heard her approach, but at the clatter of Claire's sabots, the soldiers spun in Yvette's direction. Paralyzed, she stared into the muzzles of four guns.

At the release of pressure on his back, Antoine glanced over his shoulder. "Don't shoot!" he screamed. "It's my daughters, not the parachutists."

Weak with relief, Yvette uttered a silent thanks. It wasn't the flag! She felt Claire's hand slip into hers as their shaken father continued up the stairs. At the top, he turned left toward his bedroom. "Go right!" the guard jabbed him savagely.

Antoine winced with pain. "There are no parachutists here," he insisted.

"We know some of them landed on your farm," one of the guards snarled. "Stop wasting our time."

"Tell us where they are," another cajoled, "and we'll let you go. Most of them drowned in the marshes. It won't take long to round up the stragglers. Why risk your neck?"

Antoine could only shake his head. With an impatient gesture of his gun, one of the soldiers motioned the girls down the stairs. "Go to the kitchen," he said.

Yvette and Claire found the rest of the household seated at the table guarded by two soldiers standing at the fireplace. As the girls scurried to their places, one of the soldiers drew a dagger from its scabbard. It was covered with dried blood. "I got one of them in Baupte," he grinned. "We'll get the rest of them before too long."

The family waited in rigid silence. Finally, footsteps sounded on the stairs, and Antoine was shoved into the room. A sharp command released the guards at the fireplace and, slamming the door behind them, the soldiers fanned out from the courtyard. Some searched the stables, others the barns. Watching at the window, the Hamels relished the enemy's mounting frustration when no airborne troops were found.

Antoine described what happened upstairs. "They examined every armoire, and under each bed. They even climbed into the attic. They're so obsessed with these parachutists, they didn't mention the extra grain that we've hidden there." He smiled with satisfaction. "They are scared."

The approaching clatter of horse-drawn wagons, rumble of trucks, and rhythmic cadence of marching men attracted the squad leader's attention. At his command, the search party abandoned their unsuccessful efforts and hurried up the drive to join their comrades. It was a far different unit making its withdrawal than that which had arrived in Coigny four years ago. Dust covered the faded trucks, wagons squeaked, horses plodded. Even the sidecar-motorcycles which had terrified Yvette now had a bedraggled look.

"I guess they're headed for St. Jores to beef up the troops

already there," Henri said. He shook his head in frustration. "I wish we knew what's happening!"

The day that had begun in such an extraordinary fashion continued with an air of unreality. From the beaches east of Sainte Mere Eglise came sounds of unimaginable strife: the boom of shells lobbed by battleships, the whoosh-whoosh-whoosh of antiaircraft fire, the rending crash of exploding bombs, the chatter of machine guns. Buffeted by the unrelieved commotion, the Hamels went about their daily chores. Snatching moments whenever they could, they listened to the radio. Vichy acknowledged that enemy paratroopers had landed, but those who had not drowned in the marshes were being rounded up and shot. Everything was under control.

"Even discounting the lies, it's hard to imagine that an invasion could succeed," Antoine said uneasily at lunch. "The odds against it are so enormous."

An evening broadcast from Berlin reiterated that the "feeble attempt to breach the Atlantic Wall" was an utter failure. This boast was followed by a special bulletin from the Military Governor of Paris. "German soldiers have been given orders to shoot Frenchmen found cooperating with invasion forces." And last, from Vichy, Pierre Laval exhorted his countrymen to live up to the armistice terms the French government had signed in 1940 and cooperate with German authorities.

Antoine glanced at the clock, and nodded to Jacques. "Now it's time to get the real news from the BBC."

As they unearthed the radio from its camouflage, Antoine was glad they had hidden it so well. In the Germans' zeal to find the parachutists, they had made only a halfhearted inspection of the closet, then hurried to search more obvious places. Astounded, Antoine and Jacques listened to the events of D-Day or, in French, *le Jour J*, as the invasion had now been labeled. The news seemed too good to be true. They rushed to tell the others what they'd learned.

The parachutists were American, not English, as the Hamels had assumed. "The Yanks are pouring onto the beaches at La Madeleine, and Sainte Mere Eglise has been captured," he related.

"Another American foothold has been made at Vierville, and the English and Canadians are moving inland from the beaches of the Calvados!"

"The Boches are finished!" Edouard whooped.

"Surprised, not finished," his father cautioned. "They've been preparing for this invasion for a very long time."

10

Yvette let the tailgate of the milk cart fall with a bang. "I wish Maman would stop reminding us to be careful every time we leave the house. You'd think we were two-year-olds," she grumbled.

"That's because you and Claire act like two-year-olds." Etienne lifted a milk can into the back of the cart. "You have this stupid idea that just because the Americans have landed danger is past. There's fighting all around us. The war's not over by a long shot."

"I bet it is for us," Claire firmly announced as she adjusted the horse's bridle. "Once the Americans capture Carentan, that's it for the Germans."

Etienne rolled his eyes at the futility of discussing anything intelligent with a twelve-year-old sister. He stowed the last of the milk cans on the cart and closed the tailgate. "Let's go," he snapped.

Claire took the seat beside him while Gilberte and Yvette climbed in the back. With the heavy cart in tow, the horse shuffled from the barn and set out on the long trek to the field where the girls' cows were grazing. *Le grand labour* was the field most distant from the house and their mother had insisted that, during these perilous times, Etienne go with them.

Yvette settled herself against the side of the cart, leaned her head back and closed her eyes. The steady plop, plop, plop of the horse's gait was soothing, and halfway between sleep and wakefulness, she reflected on the events of the past few days. The departure of the Oliviers had left a vacuum. During their three weeks' sojourn at La Hougue they'd become like members of the family. Though urged to stay by everyone, they'd insisted that in the uncertain days ahead, they would be no help to the Hamels, they would only be in the way. And so, with their meager belongings stowed in the little horse-drawn cart, they'd set out for Periers to stay with a cousin. Jacques, too, was gone. He didn't come down for breakfast one morning, and Henri discovered that his few possessions were missing. Perhaps after the war, he would tell them about the secret missions, the reason for his sudden disappearances.

The most exciting event, of course, had been Papa's experience the night of *le Jour J*. After everyone else had gone to bed, he'd sat by the fire to read awhile. Suddenly he became aware of a tapping on the kitchen window. More curious than afraid, he reasoned that the Boches would have smashed the window, therefore the tapper must be someone needing help. He hurried to the front entrance and opened the door. Out of the darkness stepped three American parachutists. *"Mon Dieu,* they were formidable!" he told the milkers over coffee the next morning. "Tall, with blackened faces, each of them was a walking arsenal. I gaped, then invited them in. Wary as cats, they eased into the hall. I closed the door behind them and when I turned around, I looked down the barrels of three drawn guns. 'Boches?' their leader demanded. Before I could assure them there were no Germans here, they spread out to search the kitchen, dining room, the pantry. Finished with the ground floor, they started up the stairs. *'Non, s'il vous plaît!'* In garbled English, I explained there were no Germans. Only family—wife, children. *'Boche? Aucun!'* Thank God, they finally believed me. They apologized; said they'd been warned that some of us would be harboring Germans. The leader explained that they were lost—dropped by their plane into the wrong zone. All day they'd fought skirmishes with the Germans while trying to find their way to Sainte Mere Eglise. I regretted having to tell them they were still ten kilometers away, but my news that the Americans had captured the town cheered them. They asked if they could sleep a few hours before going on. I readily agreed, built up the fire, and they lay down to rest. Before I left the room they were asleep."

By the time the milkers arose the next morning, the parachutists were gone. The only evidence of their passage was a slip of paper on the kitchen table bearing the word "Merci."

"Such fine young men," her father had murmured. "Go with God," he'd added.

Yvette recalled how disappointed she'd been to have missed them. Probably they were the only Americans that would come their way.

The cart came to a halt, and Yvette roused from her reverie. "Everybody out," Etienne said.

He helped unload the milk cans, then, leaving the girls with admonitions to be watchful of the dangers that were all around them, he set off for his own duties in the adjoining field.

Time passed slowly for Yvette. The milking bored her beyond words, and even this early in the morning, the weather was hot. Finally, it was done. Etienne returned, and they set out on the journey home. It always seemed longer going back. Yvette wished the horse would bestir himself, but knew that Etienne would not force him to a faster pace merely because she was tired and hungry.

As they made their way across *la grande vallee,* Etienne suddenly pulled back on the reins. "Look at that!" He pointed to a ditch at the far side of the field.

Echoing his astonishment, the girls stared at the row of gun barrels protruding from the hedge. Contrasted with the bright green foliage, their dull gray finish had a menacing look. "Are they real? How did they get there?" Yvette asked.

"We'd better take a look," Etienne said.

"No!" Claire whimpered. "Let's go home! Remember what Maman said."

"You've certainly changed your tune!" Etienne retorted.

"She's right," Gilberte reasoned. "We'd better go home."

Just then, a figure dressed in khaki dashed from the hedge, waving his arms. *"Allez, allez,"* he shouted at them. *"Avion!"*

Now they, too, heard the drone of the plane. "Go, Etienne!" Gilberte urged.

As Etienne prodded the horse into a trot, the others searched the sky. "There!" Claire pointed above the trees of *le grand labour.* *"Oh, mon Dieu, Boche!"*

Suddenly, the plane with the all-too-familiar swastika painted on its tail went into a dive. The scream of its engine sent the horse into a frenzy and it bolted, dragging the milk cart in its wake. Etienne clung to the reins; Claire dropped to the floorboard and hid under the seat. As Yvette and Gilberte clutched the sides of the heaving vehicle, the guns of the plane exploded and bullets marched toward them with the roar of an onrushing train. The cart took an abrupt swerve to the left and, paralyzed with fear, the girls watched bullets seam the earth where moments before they had been riding. The ditch across the field erupted with gunfire and a hail of missiles streaked for the plane. It veered, then as if shot from a cannon zoomed upward and disappeared into the clouds. Though the episode was over in a minute it seemed to have lasted a lifetime.

Etienne managed to rein in the horse and kept him at a fast pace while the shaken group mulled over who the soldiers were and what they were doing in the hedge. As they passed the chicken coop they saw their father standing halfway up the drive. "Papa!" Claire yelled, "there are soldiers in the hedges of *la grande vallee!*"

He merely nodded, waving them on. As they cleared the corner of the house, they couldn't believe their eyes. The courtyard was alive with American soldiers. Some unloaded supplies from trucks; others carried boxes into the house. At the front door, two guards were posted.

"They arrived soon after you left," their father explained. "We were as flabbergasted as you are."

Yvette regarded the scene with anxious eyes. "Where will we go, Papa?"

"We're staying here," he answered. "The Commanding Officer said he needs only one room to set up his headquarters. He wanted to be upstairs, so I offered him your bedroom since it's larger than the others. You girls can move to the guest room."

The suddenness of the change in their lives left them speechless. In a daze, they unloaded the cart. Antoine explained to the guards at the door that they were members of the family. How bizarre to have to be identified before entering one's own house.

Conversation at breakfast was taken up with modifying their daily schedules, which the new arrangement mandated. For safety's sake the cows must be brought to pastures nearest the house. Of more concern was the fact that the men would have to forego work in the fields.

"No beets this year, Papa?" Michel asked.

"It looks that way," his father answered.

Murmurs of dismay arose. Planted in June, harvested in November, beets provided the diet staple for the cows during the winter. Without them, hay was insufficient to sustain the animals, leaving them vulnerable to ailments that often led to death.

"What else can we do? To be in the fields would be dangerous—for us as well as the Americans. Since you'll have no field work," he went on addressing his sons, "you can do your share of the morning milking and take over entirely in the afternoon. That will free the girls to do more of the housework for their mother."

As the discussion continued, there was a knock on the door. It was a clerk from the Colonel's staff who said that headquarters would be vacated long enough for the girls to move their belongings to another room.

After Denise's cot and one of the four-posters had been transferred to the new location the girls emptied the big armoire and the bureau of their possessions. The five occupants filled the small guest room to the bursting point. Yvette grimaced as she looked around at the mounds of rumpled clothes, the knick-knacks stacked against a wall. "This is going to take a lot of getting used to!"

"We're lucky," Gilberte countered. "Think of all the refugees with no place to stay."

Yvette groaned. "I bet you could find something nice to say about hell."

"Well, it would keep you nice and warm," Gilberte smiled.

Yvette shook her head and crossed the room to look out of the window. She saw Etienne standing at the door of the barn holding the bridle of the now-unharnessed horse. Ostensibly, he was inspecting the reins for damage; in reality he was trying to take in the activity that swirled around him. "I know just how you feel,"

Yvette murmured. "Everything is so strange." As she turned to leave the window, she noticed a figure sidle through the gate.

"Uh oh," she grunted. "What is *le Minable* doing here?"

The others joined her to inspect the seedy-looking figure standing at the gate. His shifty eyes explored the courtyard; an astonished whistle puckered his lips. With his cap pulled low on his forehead, it was easy to see why he'd been nicknamed "the Worm."

"He knows Jacques has gone—that nobody here has cigarettes," Denise muttered.

"He didn't come for cigarettes," Marguerite answered. "Look at him. He's taking count."

Indeed, he seemed to be doing just that as, muttering to himself, his head swiveled from side to side. "Why doesn't Etienne turn around!" Claire exclaimed.

As if he'd heard her, Etienne glanced over his shoulder. He scowled when he saw the Nazi collaborator from St. Jores. He walked purposefully toward le Minable, said something, then shook his head. The interloper pretended disappointment but continued to linger and to look. Etienne edged him firmly out the gate, bid him a curt "Adieu," and waited until he walked reluctantly away. Then he hurried toward the house. Moments later, two guards were posted at the gate.

"Locking the barn door after the horse has bolted," Denise said. "*Le Minable* will be busy soon telling his Nazi bosses how many Americans are posted here."

By late afternoon deployment was complete and twenty-seven pieces of artillery dominated the fields of La Hougue. "They've got everything from 155mm down to machine guns," Henri reported. The Colonel, his staff, members of the gun crews and support personnel, some two hundred men in all, were bunkered in barns and granges. A mess tent had sprouted in a grove of apple trees, and a first aid station had taken over a stable. For the first time since its invention, a telephone was installed on a Coigny farm.

As the Hamels' dinner ended, Colonel Norton came to the kitchen with his interpreter, Captain Howell. The Commanding Officer's upright figure, short-cropped hair and observant eyes looked very military but his smile was ingratiating. Through the Captain, he apologized for the inconveniences that the artillery unit of the First Army was causing the family and hoped that their stay at La Hougue would be brief. In return, Antoine welcomed the unit and offered any services which the Colonel and his staff might lack.

Actually, they were badly in need of a scout, the Captain said. "Someone who can slip into St. Jores tonight, estimate the number of troops, identify their units, locate their artillery. Is there someone in the family familiar with the town who would volunteer?"

Henri was on his feet as soon as the Captain finished speaking. Antoine nodded. "This is my son, Henri. He knows the area well."

"Good," the Captain answered. "Come with us and I'll explain the procedure."

The Americans bid the family a cordial *adieu* and, followed by Henri, withdrew to the hall.

"The Americans have posted guards at the entrance to the marsh," Henri reported when he returned. "They'll give me the password when I go through their *barriere* so there'll be no trouble when I come back." He looked at his mother's troubled face. "I'll be all right, Maman. I survived Dunquerque, remember?"

"You had an army with you then," she answered. "This time you'll be alone."

"An army couldn't slip in and out of St. Jores undetected as I hope to do," he smiled.

He waited until dusk, then dressed in dark clothes and with the password, "Tumbleweeds," fixed in his mind, he set out on his journey. At midnight, the family was jarred awake by a high-pitched, unnerving whistle, followed by an explosion. The house seemed to shudder on its foundations. Yvette and her sisters jumped from their beds, unsure of what to do. "That didn't sound like a bomb. What could it be?" Yvette asked in a shaky voice.

"I don't know, but it was close." Claire cried.

"We can't just stand here," Denise snapped. "Let's go—"

Another explosion silenced her. The door burst open. "Hide!" their father yelled. "Guns from St. Jores are shelling us."

As the sisters huddled underneath the beds, the guns of La Hougue retaliated. The earth heaved and windows rattled. The crash of tree limbs and the lowing of cattle added to the din. After what seemed an age, the firing ended. The shaken family gathered in the hall to assess the damage. All agreed that, by some miracle, none of the shells had hit the house.

At dawn the distraught family worried over Henri's continued absence. That he'd gotten lost was inconceivable. Blindfolded, he could find his way around the region. The other possibilities were too grim to think about. As breakfast ended, a knock sounded on the kitchen door. Yvette opened it to find the Colonel and the Captain waiting. She noted that they, too, were edgy and red-eyed from lack of sleep. "Henri? He is back?" the Captain asked.

"Not yet," she answered in a worried tone.

Her father joined her at the door and the question was repeated. Again, the Captain got a negative response. "No word—at all!" he demanded.

"We have heard nothing," Antoine replied. "We are very concerned."

Yvette saw mistrust flicker in the look the officers exchanged. Her mind recoiled. Henri was now a suspect in last night's shelling. As she listened to her father tell of the visit of *le Minable,* he seemed to be grasping at straws to place the blame. Yvette could see that from the Americans' point of view, Henri was the more likely culprit. He was eager to make the trip; his parents agreed willingly to let him go. Her heart sank as with curt nods, the officers proceeded up the stairs.

The morning hours dragged. Traffic in and out of the house, the unexpected jangle of the telephone rasped on nerves that were already overwrought. After one such call, a flurry of footsteps on the stairs was followed by the Colonel's precipitous departure. Thirty minutes later he was back, accompanied by a very relieved Henri. After the family's welcome had abated, Captain Howell apologized. "We're sorry that we doubted you. It's hard to know whom to trust."

"There are collaborators," Antoine acknowledged. "They make it difficult for the rest of us."

When the officers left, Henri told of his venture which was successful until his return to the Americans' barriere. Not only had the sentries changed during his absence, but "Tumbleweeds" was no longer the password. The guards seized him as a spy and hustled him to the Chateau for interrogation. Through a succession of misunderstandings, he was thrown into a cell.

Henri wiped a grimy hand over his face. "I could see myself up against a wall—a target for their firing squad. Thank God the provisions officer overheard the jailer complaining that a prisoner insisted on getting in touch with the C/O at La Hougue. The provisions officer had talked to the Mayor about a source for milk and eggs, and the Mayor recommended our farm. Eventually the pieces of the puzzle fell into place."

"Did you get the information the Americans wanted?" Michel asked.

"More," Henri answered grimly. "The town is being evacuated. Even refugees are leaving. Besides taking over the Quinette place, the Boches have established a lookout post in a tall pine tree beside the police station. From there, they can see all of Coigny."

"And the guns on the Quinette farm can zero in on La Hougue," Michel grunted.

"What can we do?" Yvette asked. "Hide under the beds all day?"

"They aren't aiming at our house," Henri answered. "They want to knock out the guns."

"That's not much comfort when the walls shake and the windows fall out," she retorted.

"No one promised that deliverance would come cheap," Alice reminded them. "It's already cost our liberators dearly. We, too, must be prepared to pay the price."

11

The shelling of the Hamel farm by the guns of St. Jores was sporadic at first, but soon the bombardment fell into a pattern. Beginning at five in the afternoon, it coincided with the evening milking as if to punish the family for harboring the enemy. After the firing had lasted an hour, the guns fell silent until dark. Then the terror began again.

As the days passed, the two hundred members of the artillery unit became more and more an extension of the family. At dawn they filled their helmets at the back door pump, then propping their pocket mirrors against the fence posts, they washed and shaved. Coffee was left warming on the hearth for the guards at the door. Many of the soldiers joined the family in the kitchen after supper. They brought little gifts, their French-English dictionaries, harmonicas and accordions. They taught the girls American songs, showed snapshots of their families, played chess, checkers and dominoes, and talked about "after the war." The morning milking always drew a crowd. *"Permettez-moi,"* became a frequent request as, one after another, "city slickers" tried their hand at what looked like such an easy task.

The soldiers drank milk by the gallon. Antoine was glad to give it to them, for the battle for Carentan prevented La Gloria Dairy from picking up the cans at La Hougue, and the milk would have gone to waste. He also supplied fresh eggs to supplement their army rations, and sometimes Alice fixed extra food at noon which Gilberte and Yvette carried on trays to the upstairs headquarters. Captain Howell expressed the appreciation of the Colonel and his staff. He'd inhale the aroma of thick vegetable soup, an omelet seasoned with *ciboulette*, or chicken rotisserie and heave a blissful sigh. "The smell alone makes us ravenous. Please give our thanks and compliments to your mother."

Among the group of novice milkers was a young man named Jeff. Because he spoke French fluently, he and Yvette struck up an acquaintance. He was from Mobile in the state called Alabama, he told her. The city was founded by the French even before New Orleans, and enjoyed a reputation as a center of French culture. He'd learned French from his grandmother and planned to study at the Sorbonne after college. "I didn't know the Army would give me a free trip to France," he joked, "but this tour isn't exactly what I had in mind." She called him Mon Professeur, for, born teacher that he was, he insisted she learn not only the slang she picked up from the other soldiers, but English as it should be spoken. He loaned her his dictionary, and on mornings when he was off-duty, he explained grammar to her while she milked.

The artillery unit had been with the Hamels for two weeks when an extremely high tide, coupled with a four-day gale, destroyed the artificial port which supplied the American forces. Replacement of personnel and supplies slowed to a trickle. Yvette overheard a group of artillerymen talk in anxious tones of thinning ranks and dwindling stores of ammunition.

"It seems that Hitler can control even the weather," she reported at lunch one day. "What will they do?"

"What will *we* do if Hitler's threat to 'throw them back into the sea' comes true?" Claire wondered apprehensively.

The others, too, expressed anxiety at the precarious foothold the Allies had established in Fortress Europe. Would another Dunquerque develop? Or a stalemate?

Captain Howell eased their fears. He came to the kitchen one evening as the Colonel's spokesman to apologize for the artillery unit's lengthening stay. "We had expected to be out of here by now, but the destruction of the port threw our timetable out of kilter." He went on to explain that repairs on the artificial port were completed and supplies are already moving. "We hope to make up for lost time." He shook his head. "The Germans don't give up easy. They're fighting for every foot of ground."

Enemy fire took a mounting toll of the Americans. Minor injuries were treated at the first aid station in the stable. The seriously wounded had to be transported to La Fiere, an evacuation hospital near Sainte Mere Eglise. After a particularly intense shelling one afternoon Michel sought out Yvette in the kitchen. She saw by his expression that something was wrong. "I've got bad news," he said.

"What is it?" she asked, dreading to hear.

"Your Professor was hit by a shell fragment."

"He's not dead, Michel!" she pleaded.

"No, a head wound," he answered. "They think he'll never see again."

She cried out as if in pain.

"The medics are working on him now. They're getting ready to take him to La Fiere."

An engine sputtered in the courtyard. Yvette hurried to the window in time to see two corpsmen fasten a stretcher to a waiting jeep. She stared in disbelief at the blanket-covered, motionless figure whose head was swathed in bandages. Only this morning he'd joined her while she milked.

"Today's drill is on the verbs 'to have' and 'to be,'" he'd said briskly, parking himself beside her on a three-legged stool.

She'd groaned. "Not again!"

"Practice makes perfect," he'd admonished, wagging his finger at her. Then laughing, he'd dodged the jet of milk that she had squirted at him.

Now tears filled her eyes as she watched the jeep drive out the gate. At the collecting station in Houtteville, the Professor would be transferred to an ambulance, and the tortuous trip to La Fiere would begin. She'd heard the medics describe it as a nightmare of narrow, pot-holed roads lined by burned-out trucks and tanks. Detours were frequent and, in the blackout, driving into a ditch was an ever-present danger. Enemy stragglers and unexploded mines posed added hazards. Not many of the severely wounded lived through the ordeal of the journey. Would her Professor be one of the few who did? Given his wound, would he rather not?

The constantly changing battle lines brought an ebb and flow of soldiers to the farm. One day it was an advance infantry platoon cut off by enemy action from the main body of their unit. Their radio had been destroyed and, running low on ammunition, they'd wandered in circles until spotted by an artillery post in one of the fields of La Hougue. Another day, two German deserters were found hiding in the hay loft. The sixteen-year-olds had been sent to Normandy after six weeks of basic training to throw the enemy back into the sea. Terrified at the magnitude of the Allied invasion forces, they were grateful to surrender to one of the artillerymen.

Sometimes at dusk troop carriers from the infantry unit that occupied the Chateau would file into the courtyard of La Hougue. With their faces blackened and dressed in camouflage, the soldiers would mill about the barns while officers hurried to the upstairs headquarters to consult with their artillery counterparts. A short time later the infantry Major and his adjutant would return, and at their muffled commands, the trucks, like panthers on the prowl, crept up to the road and disappeared into the dark.

Though isolated from their neighbors and ignorant of happenings outside the farm, the Hamels were kept informed of major events by Captain Howell. From time to time he came to the kitchen after supper for a chat. He described the capture of Carentan, the drive on Cherbourg, told of the establishment of an Army Air Force Fighter Group on a farm near Sainte Mere Eglise.

"We've seen the planes flying over the farm." Etienne whistled. "Formidable!"

"What are they called?" Yvette asked.

"Thunderbolts!" the Captain answered. "The Germans dread to hear them coming. They're superb in air-to-air combat, but also make mincemeat of their tanks and trains."

"What farm is it?" Antoine asked.

"It's near the evacuation hospital at La Fiere," the Captain answered. "It's called Le Londe."

"I've heard of it," Antoine nodded. "Not many farms in this region have fields big enough for an airstrip."

On June 26th Cherbourg surrendered to the Americans, but German demolition experts left the port facilities in a shambles. "The city held out longer than we'd hoped," the Captain related, "and with their panzers arriving from the east, they hope to keep us bottled up in the peninsula. We can't let that happen. It's time to break out."

By the first of July, the rumble of truck convoys on highways to the east and west of La Hougue went on day and night, and overhead there seemed no letup in the thunder of planes headed for targets in the south. The very routineness of sweeping the kitchen that morning emphasized for Yvette the changes that had occurred in their lives. She paused at the window to reflect. No mail, no morning newspaper was delivered; she couldn't remember the last visitor they'd had. Trips to the market had been suspended as well as Sunday attendance at church. She frowned, watching Etienne and Edouard joke with some of the soldiers outside the barn. Despite her father's efforts to keep them busy, without field work they had too much idle time on their hands. "It's all so strange," she murmured.

Her mother looked up from fixing a pot of coffee. "Funny," she said. "I was thinking exactly the same thing. We don't hear bird calls any more, and the cows don't low except in fear."

A nerve-jarring whistle put an abrupt end to their musings. Cringing, they stared at each other. The explosion sounded distant, but a second quickly followed, much closer than the first. Footsteps clattered on the stairs and Claire dashed into the room. "Why are they shelling at ten in the morning!" she cried.

Before her mother could answer, a third shell struck the chimney then rattled along the slate roof until it fell harmlessly into a pond. The three older girls burst into the kitchen as a fourth shell exploded, splintering glass in the dining room.

"Under the table!" Alice commanded.

Frantically, they moved the heavy piece of furniture to the middle of the room. Huddling under its dubious protection, they clung to one another. What did the change in schedule mean? Was this a counterattack, or just another Boche reminder: you've given aid to the enemy, therefore you must pay. Finally the torment ended and the shaken group crawled from their shelter.

With his sons at his heels, Antoine rushed through the door. "You're safe, thank God!" he exclaimed.

Still dazed by the unexpected attack, Alice nodded. "And you?"

"We were in the barn. Nothing there was hit," he answered.

"The pump doesn't work, the roof over the *cremerie* collapsed, and the windows in the dining room are gone," Michel said. "God knows what would have happened if the shell that hit the chimney hadn't been a dud!"

There were swift footsteps on the stairs, and a sergeant passed the kitchen door on the run. His shoes beat a hurried tattoo across the courtyard, and when he reached the barn he started calling names. A group gathered quickly and listened intently to his instructions. When the men dispersed and the sergeant returned, the Hamels expected an explanation, a word of caution, anything to help them prepare for future eventualities, but he hurried past the kitchen and took the stairs to headquarters two at a time.

"None of them seem to care about us," Claire complained.

"They have to follow orders," Henri answered.

"That doesn't help us protect ourselves," she insisted. "What can we do?"

Yvette glanced around the kitchen. "Why don't we make this room as safe as possible. When the shelling starts, we can all come here."

Her father nodded. "That's a good idea."

Everything from propping mattresses against the windows to removing flammable material was suggested. Alice assigned each one a part in the endeavor. "We must get it done before the evening milking begins," she said. "Meanwhile, the pump must be repaired, and the windows in the dining room boarded up."

Lunch was a haphazard meal. Uncertainty permeated the air. How dreadful not to know what was going on upstairs—what plans were being laid; what damage would result. As soon as they had eaten, Gilberte and Yvette ironed the shirts that they had promised to deliver to the officers that afternoon. By spelling each other at the ironing board and heating the irons over the fire, they managed to get the dozen garments finished by two o'clock.

They folded the khaki shirts and carried them upstairs. The atmosphere in the room had an urgency they'd never sensed before. Though Captain Howell thanked them graciously, and managed to joke, "We'll be the best-groomed officers in the

American Army," it was obvious that his mind was elsewhere and his effort to be pleasant was forced.

"I have a terrible feeling," Gilberte said when she and Yvette returned to the hall. "Something awful is going to happen."

It was so unlike Gilberte to be morose; Yvette became even more uneasy. She tried to dampen her own anxiety by admonishing the older girl. "Don't say that. Shake off those gloomy thoughts." She took her sister's arm and led her down the stairs. "We're lucky, remember?" she went on, hoping to divert Gilberte by imitating her perpetual optimism. "Think of all the refugees with no place to stay. At least here at La Hougue we're safer than they are."

Yvette waited for Gilberte's smile of recognition, but she continued her silence as if she hadn't heard.

"Tell me," Yvette pleaded. "What is it?"

"I don't know," Gilberte answered in a faraway voice. "Something—" She shook her head.

12

There was no more time for talk. Their mother was already supervising the project of making the kitchen as safe as possible. Gilberte and Yvette joined the others in removing anything that would splinter, shatter or catch on fire. The beautiful Limoges china which had been a wedding present to Alice from her family was carefully wrapped, packed in boxes and stowed in the closet under the stairs. When all was secure, linens were stripped from some of the beds, and their mattresses carried down the stairs. Two were placed on top of the kitchen table, hopefully providing a safe hiding place; others were stuffed into the window frames to lessen the danger of flying glass. When Etienne snuffed out the last chink of light, Yvette looked around the room and shivered. "It'll be like living in a cave."

"In this kind of war, a cave is the safest place to be," Michel replied.

The week's mending awaited Yvette, and she left the gloomy kitchen and climbed the stairs to her bedroom. She longed for a little while just to be alone. The day's events had been unnerving: the shelling at the unaccustomed hour, the kitchen turned into a cave, and Gilberte's uncharacteristic behavior. The look of dismay on her sister's face had been chilling. Had she had a premonition of disaster? And if so, what could it be? If only they knew what to prepare for! The Americans' need for secrecy was obvious, but surely Captain Howell trusted her father enough to tell him something!

She closed the bedroom door, shutting out the jangle of the telephone, the clatter of footsteps on the stairs. How blessed was the silence after so much turmoil. From the armoire she took her sewing basket and the shirts with collars that were frayed. Thank

God it was the mending she had to do and not the afternoon
milking. She sat at the window and began to turn the collar of a
shirt. Soon, however, like a magnet, the activity in the courtyard
attracted her attention. Soldiers loaded equipment and guns on
trucks that lined the driveway. The Colonel seemed to be
everywhere, conferring with this group and that. A jeep carrying
Captain Howell made a hurried exit out the gate. Later he
returned, accompanied by the infantry officer from the Chateau
who had been to La Hougue many times before. They looked so
grim, so focused on the coming conflict, Yvette gave an involun-
tary shudder. What lay in store for the Hamels as a result of their
endeavor?

"Yvette!"

She heard the voice above the hubbub. Oh bother! Henri was
such a pain in the *derriere*. The fewer chores he had, the lazier he
got. She was already working harder than he was, but he seemed
to spend his time thinking up things for her to do.

"Yvette!"

Gritting her teeth, she crossed the room, and flung open the
door. Henri waited at the foot of the stairs. She glared at his
upturned face. "Whatever it is you want, the answer is 'NO!'"

He cupped a hand behind his ear. "Come on down. I can't hear
you. There's too much noise."

She was about to yell another taunt when the front door
opened and two of the Colonel's aides hurried into the entryway.
They paused beside Henri, gave brother and sister a tentative
smile then stood a little aside, waiting for one or the other to go
up the steps or down. Realizing the impasse must be broken,
Yvette made her reluctant descent. The aides raced past her to the
upstairs headquarters.

With hand on hip and a disgruntled expression, she con-
fronted Henri. "Well?"

"You realize, Yvette, that something unusual is going on," he
began.

"I'm not deaf or blind," she retorted, "just tired." She held out
the garment she still carried. "This happens to be your shirt I'm
mending."

"With the Americans here, you have had a lot to do," he conceded, "but since today is out of the ordinary, we thought that by starting now instead of waiting until five, we'd miss the evening shelling. If all of us help, we should be through in an hour."

She gazed at him wide-eyed. "Through with what, Henri?"

He gave her a tight little smile.

"I milked this morning," she explained as if to someone with a limited attention span. "Remember what Papa said? That you and the rest of the brothers would take over in the after—"

"Look around you," he interrupted, waving toward the court-yard. "Something is going on. We've got to finish the milking before—"

"We?" she demanded. "Where are you when we're cooking and cleaning, washing and ironing and all the rest of it? You're out at the barn with the soldiers cracking jokes!" How long had it been, she demanded, since he'd done a full days work? He'd become so lazy, he was getting fat around the middle.

Listening to her bluster, he hung his head as if acknowledging the truth of her accusations. She knew his contriteness was a put-on. Still, it felt good to vent her outrage. "And in the time you're taking to talk me into doing your job, you could be half through," she finished.

He looked up and met her eyes. "It's just this once, Yvette. I promise."

She'd run out of steam. Henri was as tenacious as a bulldog. He wouldn't let go until he wore you down.

She sighed. Her shoulders drooped.

"You'll do it?" he wheedled.

She groaned. "Yes, but just this once!"

"Good girl!" He patted her shoulder. "Put on your sabots and we're ready to go."

She dragged her way to the pantry. From its hook behind the door, she snatched her apron and tied it around her waist. Sliding her feet into the wooden shoes, she recalled the day the war began. She was sitting at her bedroom window, lost in a reverie. Only one more week of milking and she would be off to school. She could hardly wait. Five years later, here she was.

Glumly, she joined Gilberte in the barn. Engrossed in her own malaise, she'd forgotten her sister's distress. She grabbed two pails and her burlap sack from the stack of utensils against the wall. Scuffing her feet, she headed for the door.

"To milk ten cows is not the end of the world," Gilberte said as she followed Yvette outside the barn.

"Henri can outdo a cat in thinking of ways to get out of work," Yvette grumbled.

"Doesn't the extra effort make sense if we can avoid the shelling?" Gilberte asked.

"How do we know it will?" Yvette nodded toward the soldiers loading the trucks. "If the lookout post in St. Jores is watching, a few shells now would wipe out half the unit."

Gilberte winced at the thought. She watched the activity in the courtyard. "You can tell by their gestures, the number of cigarettes they smoke that they are scared. How many of them will be killed today? Think about that, Yvette, instead of getting upset with Henri."

A pang of guilt assailed Yvette. How selfish to be so absorbed in her own fatigue that she forgot what the Americans faced. "You're right, as usual," she said, chagrined. "I wouldn't want to be in their shoes."

Heading for the field next the house, the girls began calling their cows. The change in schedule made the animals uneasy, and they were reluctant to obey. The hot sun, her weariness, the cow's ponderous movements irritated Yvette beyond endurance. Her guilt was forgotten. "Come on you stupid beasts!" she bellowed.

Gilberte gave her a sidelong look. "Does that really help?"

"It helps me," Yvette retorted. "Finally!" she grunted when the first two of their herd approached.

Gilberte placed her stool next to Paquerette, and Yvette knelt beside Narcisse. She rested her head against the animal's rump and began the pull, turn and squeeze motion that, by now, she must have done a thousand times. Listening to the mutter of engines, the barked commands that wafted from the courtyard, she thought back to the day the Americans had arrived. Only three weeks ago. *Mon Dieu,* so much had happened since then, it seemed a lifetime. She recalled the last morning that she had milked with the Professor. She saw him sitting on the stool beside her, a book open in his hand. He wagged his finger at her, then smiling, dodged the jet of milk she squirted at him. Tears blurred her eyes as she watched the jeep carrying him to La Fiere bump up the drive. Had he survived that awful trip?

"This isn't so bad, is it?"

Yvette lifted her head. Dear Gilberte. Always making the best of things. "Of course not," Yvette answered in a saccharine tone. "Milking is my favorite way to spend an afternoon."

To soften the sarcasm of her retort, she turned her head and grinned at her sister. The grin froze as she watched Paquerette explode and Gilberte, with a splotch of red staining her blouse, hurled backward to the ground. Yvette tried to scream, but no sound came. An excruciating pain shot through her. She felt herself falling, falling, falling into a mist. Suddenly, the world went black.

13

Yvette tried to locate the voice—faint and far away—but she was too tired. "Yvette! Speak to me!" Footsteps pounding, another voice, and out of the blackness, light. It took all her strength to open her eyes. Henri loomed over her.

"She's alive! Thank God!" A sob.

"Take her to the house." The other voice was Michel's. "I'll bring Gilberte."

She felt Henri's arms lifting her. The world spun, and blackness closed around her. She awoke atop the mattresses on the kitchen table. Her parents stood at her side. Why were their eyes red and their mouths so twisted?

"The medic will be here in a minute," her father said.

The pain returned—so all-encompassing it clouded her perception of its origin. She felt her energy ebbing away. A mist dimmed her father's distraught face, and suddenly she felt very cold. "Papa," she whispered, "am I going to die?"

She heard a shuffle of feet at the door, and the Abbe Giard's black-robed figure wavered toward her. He leaned over and kissed her cheek. "I've come to pray with you," he said.

Her fingers closed on the rosary that someone slipped into her hand. She tried to listen to the sacrament for the dying, but lethargy overwhelmed her. The words asking for her salvation came from a great distance. Unencumbered by her body, she floated on a cloud. How peaceful it was, away from the weeping. Now she could rest.

But as she drifted toward that cool and quiet space, voices and the scrape of hurrying feet intruded on the stillness. The spell was broken. Why hadn't they let her go?

"She's coming around!"

Her eyelids fluttered. The medic held an inverted bottle above his head. A tube curved down to her arm. The fingers of his other hand were pressed against her wrist. "There you are!" he smiled.

The kitchen was crowded with soldiers. Captain Howell stood next to her father, the Colonel behind her mother. Where was Gilberte?

Another bustle at the door. Two corpsmen entered carrying a stretcher. As they crossed the room toward the table, her mind recoiled. "No," she moaned.

"Yvette, you need a doctor," her father said gently. "The Americans have arranged it."

"Not La Fiere," she pleaded.

"Don't be afraid," the Abbe said. "I'm going with you."

"Maman! Don't let them take me away!"

Tears streamed down her mother's face. "It's for your own good, my sweet."

Yvette shook her head. If they took her to La Fiere, she would never see home again.

The corpsmen eased her from the mattress to the stretcher. The effort exhausted her. As she was carried to the door, the weeping faces blurred together.

The medic followed the stretcher to the jeep, covered Yvette with a blanket, then held her hand a moment. "Go with God," he said.

"She's really in bad shape," Yvette heard him murmur to the driver. "If she makes it to the hospital, it'll be a miracle."

The mutter of the engine as the jeep started up the drive sounded to Yvette like a death knell. She sank into oblivion. When she regained her senses, a dim light shone above her, and another face was looking down at her. A bottle dripped more fluid into her arm, and the jeep had been replaced by an ambulance. As it lurched to avoid a pothole, she moaned. Father Giard came to crouch beside her. "I'm here, Yvette. This is Major Barney. He's going with us to La Fiere."

The Major took her hand. "Hang on, sweetheart," he said.

His big hand was warm and solid. Yvette clutched it as if she was indeed hanging on. He spoke to her in a soothing voice, and though she understood little of what he said, listening to him eased her fears. She drifted in and out of perception.

Cold air brought her back to awareness. The ambulance had stopped. In the darkness she could barely see the Abbe's face. Outside the open door, she heard voices. Her pain was sharp and throbbing, and the jerking motion as they lifted her was agonizing. In a haze, she saw other ambulances drawn up before a sprawling tent. The corpsmen carrying her stretcher joined the grim procession trudging with their blanket-covered burdens toward the entrance.

Inside, the tent was crowded with wounded. Room was made for Yvette on the dirt floor against a wall. The stench of urine, blood and vomit was pervasive and from all sides came tortured cries.

"Severe shock. Let's get her into the operating tent. Alert Dr. Yachnin."

The orders seemed to come from the bottom of a well. Yvette looked up to see a khaki-clad figure swim above her. "Our first civilian casualty," she heard him say.

"Nobody warned us it would be like this!" a woman answered.

Wearily, the man rubbed a hand over his face. "How could they?" he asked. "We wouldn't have believed them." He turned to the next stretcher.

A needle pricked Yvette's arm and gradually the noises and the smells receded. More jolting as her stretcher was lifted—would they never let her rest?—and she moaned as they settled her on a surface that was hard and flat. Bright lights beat upon her eyelids.

"God, what a shame! How young and pretty she is!"

Slowly Yvette opened her eyes and looked up at a circle of white-masked faces. Where was she? What were they doing to her? She tried to speak, but a gauze mask dripping an icy liquid was pressed over her mouth and nose. The smell was sickeningly sweet. Gradually, her agitation slackened and she began to drift.

"She's not going to last much longer. We've got to get going! Is she out?" The words echoed hollowly.

"Almost," came the faraway answer.

Yvette let go of her last hold on consciousness. She had no

more strength to fight. She didn't hear the final, "Now."

• • •

"Yvette! Yvette! Wake up. Look at me!"

The woman's voice rasped like sandpaper across her nerves. Leave me alone, she wanted to say. But her tormentor would not go away. She tapped Yvette on the cheek, continued to call her name. The harassment was finally beyond ignoring, and Yvette reluctantly opened her eyes.

"Bon jour!" The face was strong and kind; her dark hair drawn back into a snood. *"Moi,"* she pointed to herself, "Captain Truckey." She made motions of spooning food into her mouth. *"Manger?"*

The thought of eating made Yvette gag, and she drifted back into the stupor from which she had been so rudely summoned.

"No, no," the nurse insisted. "Look at me."

Why were they pestering her? Yvette pried open her eyelids. Another woman, dressed in a gray uniform with a Red Cross emblem on her cap, stood beside the nurse. "This is Miss Bradford," Captain Truckey introduced the Red Cross worker. "She'll help you eat a little soup." The nurse's eyes were moist as, with gentle fingers, she smoothed Yvette's hair back from her face. "I'll see you later, my dear," she said, then disappeared.

"I speak a little French," Miss Bradford said, pulling up a stool. "How are you feeling?"

"Ca va," Yvette answered. Actually, she felt awful—weak as a kitten, and her legs did ache so. She lay flat with her range of vision restricted to a patch of tent above her face. A heavy weight anchored her to the cot. Liquid dripped from a bottle into her left arm. There was something odd about her right one. She must determine what it was. Later. Right now, she was too tired. Her eyes began to close, but Miss Bradford was as annoying as the nurse.

"It's time to eat," she insisted. She held a glass straw to Yvette's lips and imitated a sucking noise. "Now you," she smiled.

While the warm liquid dribbled down her throat, vague recollections and distorted images flickered across Yvette's mind. Miss Bradford's murmurs, "good girl," "that's fine," stirred memories of the farm and a hen clucking to her chicks. Yvette was washing her face at the pump. The evening milking was done, and she was hot and sweaty. The door opened and Gilberte appeared on the stoop. Her eyes were enormous and fixed on Yvette as if asking for help.

"I'm coming, Gilberte!"

Her sister shook her head.

"Wait!" Yvette cried. But when she rushed to the stoop, Gilberte was gone.

The straw fell from Yvette's lips.

"More," Miss Bradford urged.

But Yvette didn't hear.

14

As she hovered between sleep and wakefulness, Yvette felt someone stroke her hair. The years fell away, and she was five years old, recovering from a bout of measles. It was her birthday and her father had brought her a cake. He'd sat by her bed and smoothed her hair back from her feverish face. How could his big, calloused hand be so gentle?

"Yvette."

She stirred, reluctant to let the good dream escape. She'd had so many bad ones lately—

"Yvette."

Slowly she opened her eyes. "Papa!" she breathed. "You're real!"

Smiling, he nodded.

"You've come to take me home."

"No, dear heart." His smile faded. "You need medicine and care that we can't give you. The Americans have agreed that you can stay with them until they leave."

"It's so awful," she moaned. She saw his involuntary shudder, and knew his walk down the aisle between the rows of cots in the recovery tent had shaken him to the core. "How long have I been here?" she asked.

"A week. I came as soon as I could. So much fighting all around Coigny the roads have been impassable. I rode Michel's bicycle, and prayed for its good health all the way!"

She managed a smile. "Maman? She is all right? How is Gilberte? And the others?"

"They send their love," he answered.

"What's happening at home?"

Her tongue felt heavy and her words sounded slurred, but she did not want to let him go. She rested her hand on his arm.

"The Americans left La Hougue yesterday," he said. "A new battle is shaping around Periers. The Colonel, the Captain, and many others asked to be remembered to you."

"How strange it must be without them," she murmured.

"No more sentinels at the door," he answered. "The courtyard looks so empty. I miss Captain Howell."

She nodded.

"Is there anything that I can bring you?" he asked.

She shook her head. "Everyone is so kind. I haven't gotten used to this monster." The plaster cast extended from her waist up to her neck. It held her right arm at an oblique angle above her chest and immobilized her left arm down to the elbow. There, needles inserted into her veins connected her to bottles of fluid hanging from a stand beside the cot. The entire contraption allowed her to move her head only from side to side.

"The doctor said it will be six more weeks," her father sympathized. "You'll have to be patient as well as stubborn, my little mule," he smiled.

"Patience," Yvette sighed. "Gilberte has it and to spare." Her eyes closed. "Too bad she can't loan me some—" Her hand slid from her father's arm.

He leaned over and kissed her good-bye. He smoothed her pillow, then rose from his chair. As he gazed at her pallid face, the dark smudges under her eyes, he managed to stifle a sob, but could not hold back the tears that streamed down his cheeks.

Time had little meaning for Yvette. She slept a lot, sulfa drugs controlled infection, morphine reduced her pain, and intravenous infusions kept her fluids in balance. At the end of ten days, she felt more alert. Perhaps it was the new privacy that gave her spirits a lift. She'd awakened one morning to find her bed surrounded by sheets hung from a metal rod. Thus she was shielded from the sight of the ghastly injuries of the other wounded in the recovery tent. In order that she not feel isolated, a portion of one of the sheets facing the entrance to the tent had been folded back, and she could watch who came and went.

When Yvette thanked Captain Truckey for the seclusion the

new arrangement afforded, the nurse apologized. "We should have done it sooner since you're our only female patient. You must let us know if you need anything."

Yvette considered asking for medication to relieve the tingling in her legs and feet, but a look at the Head Nurse's exhausted face reminded her of the endless complaints that she must listen to. "Three hundred wounded are admitted almost every day," Miss Bradford had told Yvette. "Sometimes Dr. Yachnin operates for eighteen hours at a stretch." No, Yvette decided, the tingling would eventually go away. She wouldn't bother the Captain with her little aches and pains.

Word about the wounded French girl spread around the hospital complex, and corpsmen, members of the operating room crews, ambulance drivers and other medical personnel stopped by to say hello. They brought gifts of daisies stuck in a can, an apple, or a treasured piece of chocolate. The nurses fixed her hair with bows and ribbons and Miss Bradford painted her fingernails with bright red polish.

Dr. Jones, the Admitting Officer, made rounds every day, and when he finished his examination, he'd sit beside her to talk—he in French and she trying out her limited English. He met Antoine who now came daily to the hospital on his bicycle, and the two of them became friends.

One morning at the end of the second week, there was a rustle at Yvette's "door." Her invitation to *"Entrez"* revealed an officer she'd never seen before. He bowed from the waist, wished her *"Bon jour,"* and from behind his back produced a small French flag. "Do you not know what day this is, Mademoiselle?" he asked.

Amused, she shook her head.

At that, he placed his hand over his heart, and keeping time by swinging the flag he sang his own enthusiastic version of the "Marseillaise." When he'd brought the national anthem to a resounding close, he stood a moment at attention. "Today is Bastille Day, the 14th of July, and soon France will once again be free."

His French was terrible, his singing off-key. It didn't matter. Yvette gave him a big smile, and thanked him as he pinned the flag to the sheet beside her cot. "I'll think of you every time I look at it," she promised. He wished her well, and bowing again, withdrew.

She was still smiling when moments later, Nurse Truckey came into her cubicle. "Happy Bastille Day to you!" the Captain said. "We heard that performance all the way to the operating room tent!" With a mock grimace, she stuck a finger in both ears.

Yvette nodded. "But wasn't it kind of him to remember."

The Head Nurse noted that, for the first time, Yvette had color in her cheeks. "You look much better today, my dear," she smiled.

"I feel better," Yvette agreed. "Soon I will be up and about and then I can go home."

The Captain's smile faded. Her face grew suddenly still.

Now, what have I said, Yvette worried. Does she think that I'm dissatisfied with the care that I've received? *Mon Dieu!* If only I could speak English better!

A cry of "Nurse! Nurse!" sent Captain Truckey hurrying away. As Yvette listened to her soothe the hysterical soldier lying in the next cot, her worries about being misunderstood were forgotten. She eyed the cast supporting her arm. It was cumbersome and uncomfortable, and she was stuck with it for another four weeks, but compared to the soldier's injury—his spinal cord had been severed by a bullet—her wounded arm was a minor inconvenience.

That afternoon, she awakened from a nap to see Dr. Jones, Miss Bradford, and a tall man with graying hair duck through the doorway to her cubicle. The stranger wore a white lab coat over a baggy scrub suit, and his eyes smiled at her from behind steel-rimmed glasses. *"Bon jour,* Yvette," he said in an accent that was gruff but not unpleasing. "I'm Dr. Yachnin," he went on, "the surgeon who operated on you. I've stopped by to see you several times, but you've been asleep." He nodded toward his two companions. "They must be doing something right. You're looking better."

"They're very good to me," she answered. "Everyone is."

He didn't check her arm, the flow of fluids dripping into her veins. Instead, he sat in the chair beside her cot She wondered why his deep set eyes probed hers so fixedly—almost as if he were assessing her emotional rather than her physical state. Prickles of apprehension angled down her spine when, with a grave expression, he leaned toward her and rested his elbows on his knees. "Though I speak French as well as English, there's something I must tell you that's very difficult to say in any language."

Alarmed, she glanced at Dr. Jones and Miss Bradford standing behind the surgeon. Their expressions, too, were somber. Something was terribly wrong. Her arm? Wasn't it healing properly?

"When you were brought to the hospital, none of us expected you to live." Dr. Yachnin shook his head as if seeing again the mangled body on the operating table. "Fragments of the shell that struck the cow shattered your legs and severely damaged your arm. The shock to your body was almost more than it could take."

Afraid to breathe, she waited, her eyes fixed on his face.

He put his hand on hers. "We managed to save your arm, Yvette, but we had to amputate your legs—the right one above the knee, the left one, below."

She stared at him in horror. What insane thing was he telling her? "That's not true!" she cried. "My legs and feet tingle—they hurt!"

The doctor nodded. "The symptom is called 'phantom limb pain.' It's normal after an amputation."

"I have no legs?" Her voice was shrill with rejection. Her face was as white as her plaster cast. Vacant-eyed, she stared at the ceiling. "Why didn't you let me die?"

He regarded her profile—the blue-gray eyes swimming in tears, the fine patrician nose, the determined chin. "Why did you live?" he countered. "You should have died when the shell fragment tore into you, on the journey in the ambulance, or while you were waiting in the admitting tent. But you didn't. Something deep inside wouldn't let go. I had nothing to do with that." He put his hand under her chin and turned her face to look at him. "The road will be long and hard, but you can walk again."

It was a lie! He was saying that to soften the blow. The chances that she, a farmer's daughter from a little town, could find the means for such an undertaking were impossibly remote.

He saw her distrust. "It would take a miracle? I agree." He tapped her forehead. "But that's where the miracle must come from. Other people can help, but whether or not you succeed, is up to your own determination."

His face was gray with fatigue as he waited for her to speak. Her response was stony silence.

He pressed her hand, then pushed himself to his feet. With a nod to his two companions, he left the tent.

"Can we do anything?" Miss Bradford asked.

Yvette shook her head. "I'd like to be alone."

Dr. Jones nodded. "We'll be back later."

She watched them leave through the parted sheets then turned her face to the wall.

15

Her body shook with sobs. She cried herself into exhaustion then fell into a troubled sleep. The mutilated Professor and her wounded tentmates wove in and out of her dreams. With heads bandaged, and missing limbs, they performed a macabre dance. An empty wheelchair pursued her. She couldn't escape it for she had no legs. She lived again the moment of her injury, felt herself falling into the blackness and cried out in terror.

A hand touched her hair. She opened her eyes and looked into her mother's distraught face. "My sweet, my sweet," Alice murmured. "Are you all right? Was it a terrible dream?"

"It's gone now that you're here," Yvette sighed.

Her father stroked her hand while her mother dried her eyes. As her mother leaned over to kiss her, Yvette smelled the fragrance of the fine lavender soap put aside before the war and used only on special occasions. What a heavenly contrast to the odor of antiseptics that permeated the recovery tent. "We're sorry we missed Dr. Yachnin's visit," Alice said. "He sent a jeep to fetch us so that we would be here when he talked to you. The driver was delayed getting to La Hougue. By the time we arrived here, it was too late."

Fresh tears stung Yvette's eyes. "I'd felt so sorry for these soldiers around me. Now I'm a cripple—just like they are. I didn't know it until Dr. Yachnin told me," she said bitterly.

Her mother sat beside her. "That should give you something to consider, dear heart. If you don't think of yourself as a cripple, then you won't be crippled."

"Please!" Yvette turned her face away. "I heard all that from Dr. Yachnin. I don't want to listen to it again!"

Alice nodded, outwardly unperturbed by the rebuke. Only a tightening of her lips, a difficulty in swallowing indicated the devastation she felt at the hopeless look on Yvette's face. She longed to cradle her child's head on her breast and tell her that everything would be all right. But that would be a lie. The road ahead was filled with all-but-insurmountable obstacles.

"How is Gilberte?" Yvette asked.

She wondered at her mother's hesitation, her concentration on smoothing a slight wrinkle from her skirt. "As well as can be expected. The others send their love," she went on, without pause. "Father Giard has quite a tale to tell of being seized by the Americans after he left you at the hospital. It seems that German spies have been dressing as priests to infiltrate the American lines."

"Mon Dieu, is he all right?" Yvette asked.

Her father nodded. "He was detained all night and released only after the American officer who rode in the ambulance with you vouched for his story."

Yvette recalled the officer's warm, strong hand that had held hers during the agonizing trip to La Fiere. So many strands had interwoven to bring her here.

"I'm sorry to have to cut short your visit," Miss Bradford said from the doorway. "Your driver has to take an ambulance to Baupte. He can drop you off in Coigny on the way."

Alice and Antoine took their reluctant leave. "Your daughter won't be alone," Yvette heard Miss Bradford tell her parents as they left the tent. "I'll stay with her."

Despair again engulfed Yvette as she listened to the ambulance drive away, She didn't want the Red Cross worker to return. She wanted to sink back into solitary grief and bemoan the ways that her handicap would blight her life. In a few moments, however, Miss Bradford appeared, carrying a book, and sat beside the cot. "I'll read to you for a little while, if you like," she said.

Yvette gave her an apathetic nod. Whether Miss Bradford read aloud or not did not interest her. Instead of listening to the story's beginning, she thought back to that afternoon that would forever change her life. She felt anger building inside her like she had never felt before: at Henri for manipulating her, at the hated Boches for shelling the farm, and at fate that had placed her in that exact spot at the precise moment. She seethed with resentment too overwhelming for tears, and almost choked on her rage. Gradually, like all powerful emotions, her rancor spent itself, and despite her efforts to ignore Miss Bradford, her attention began to focus on the tale of the girl born in the little Alabama town. Soon she was so caught up in how the girl, with the help of her teacher, overcame the triple handicaps of being blind, deaf, and mute, that she forgot her surroundings and herself.

"It's fiction, of course," Yvette said when the story ended.

"No, Yvette, it's fact. Although her teacher, Annie Sullivan, is dead, Helen Keller still lives." Miss Bradford slid the book onto the table. "I'm giving this to you—it's a translation from the English which I read when I studied French in college." She gave a little shrug. "I always take it with me when I travel. It gives me a lift when I get discouraged." She stood up. "I must be going, but I'll come back and see you soon."

After the Red Cross worker left, Yvette eyed the book, and grimaced. Another pep talk. That made three she'd had. Enough! But despite her efforts to dispense with Helen Keller, her thoughts kept returning to the girl's magnificent achievement, and the first glimmer of encouragement broke through her despair.

Claire accompanied her parents on their next visit to the evacuation hospital. She brought Yvette a souvenir from home— the doll with the beautiful china face which had decorated the top of the bureau in their room before the Americans took it over. Handing it to her sister, she was shy, ill-at-ease; while the others talked, she who usually was a chatterbox, was silent as if afraid of saying something that could be misconceived. Finally, Yvette grew impatient with her uncharacteristic behavior. "Claire, I'm your sister. Remember? Stop acting like I've got a disease you're afraid you'll catch!"

Claire's expression was so startled, Yvette laughed. That got Claire laughing, too. As her sister leaned over to kiss her, Yvette thought of her mother's admonition: if you don't think of yourself as a cripple, you won't be crippled.

Hungry for news, she listened to events that had developed since her wounding. The Boches had been driven from St. Jores. Denise, Paul and Bernard were among other refugees returning to Baupte; fighting raged at Periers, Lay Haye du Puits and St. Lo. "Today we hung out the flag that you and Madame Olivier made," her mother smiled.

The episode with the flag had happened to a different girl, Yvette reflected. The one with legs. From now on, the watershed in her life would be her injury.

"I asked the doctors if there was anything that we could do for them," her father said. "Guess what they wanted above all else? Fresh milk! Today we brought a big jug full, and *Mon Dieu,* they drank every drop of it on the spot!"

How amusing, they all agreed, that American soldiers, who were so well equipped with everything, would think that fresh milk was a treat!

The visit ended shortly thereafter when Alice noted that her daughter's energy was waning. Though she protested she wanted them to stay, Yvette fell asleep as soon as they were gone.

The next morning, a conversation outside the tent wall awoke Yvette. She recognized Captain Truckey's voice, but that of the man that she was talking to was unfamiliar.

"—and the nearest civilian hospital is the Pasteur in Cherbourg," Nurse Truckey was saying. "You can imagine the state it's in. She'll die there."

Yvette understood only bits and pieces of the man's reply. The gist of it seemed that the stranger agreed he had the facilities, "but what is it you want me to do?"

"Take care of her as long as you can," Nurse Truckey answered.

"Then what?"

"I'll have to leave that up to you."

Yvette heard the squeak of leather as weight shifted from one foot to the other. Finally, the stranger spoke again. "I'll arrange it," he said.

"Good!" Nurse Truckey answered. "Come and meet her."

"Please," the man demurred. "I've got a weak stomach when

it comes to battlefield hospitals. It's so nice and remote in the sky." It was an apology. "We don't see the carnage we cause below."

"There's enough here to last you a lifetime. Come on," Captain Truckey insisted.

The voices faded out of earshot. Briefly, Yvette wondered what the two were talking about, but since this snatch of conversation was one of many that routinely filtered through the tent wall, she paid it no particular attention. What did surprise and please her was the fact that she'd understood as much as she had. Every day, her ear had become more attuned to English and, slang aside, she could glean something from most conversations that she heard.

As she closed her eyes to go back to sleep, the scrape of footsteps in the aisle, the greetings that the Head Nurse called out to the wounded soldiers aroused her again. Moments later, Captain Truckey appeared at her cubicle door, followed by an officer whose face was white from shock.

"Yvette," Captain Truckey said, "meet Colonel Kleine."

He was tall and slim, carried a helmet under his arm, and over the left breast pocket of his khaki uniform, he wore a pair of silver wings. Though his hazel eyes were dazed from his walk between the cots, he managed to smile and say, *"Bon jour,* Mademoiselle."

Yvette recognized the voice she'd heard outside the tent. She returned his greeting in English, puzzled why an Air Force Colonel had come to see her. In sketchy French combined with English, Captain Truckey explained that the Colonel was the Commanding Officer of the Thunderbolt Fighter Group located near Sainte Mere Eglise. "Those are his planes that land practically on our roof!"

The Colonel made a show of ducking at the barb. Yvette told him that his planes had also been spotted flying over her family's farm. "Thunderbolts are formidable!" she finished.

"And loud!" the Captain got in the final dig. Her face grew serious as she turned to Yvette. "Dr. Yachnin told your father that we would care for you as long as we were here," she began. "Today we received our order to move on. We leave day after tomorrow."

Colonel Kleine

The suddenness of the change filled Yvette with apprehension. Her eyes shifted from the Captain to the Colonel and back again. What would happen to her now?

"You know that military hospitals are not allowed to treat civilians," the Captain went on. She gave the Colonel a sidelong glance. "In Yvette's case, there wasn't time to fill out the paperwork to get permission."

He nodded solemnly. "I understand."

"—and since we can't take you with us to our next bivouac, Colonel Kleine has offered to have his Group assume your care for as long as that is possible."

Yvette's comprehension had slowed during this rapid exchange, but when she grasped its significance, her eyes widened in amazement. "You're going to need a lot of treatment for a long time," the nurse continued. "Neither your parents nor a French civilian hospital can supply it. This seems a good solution."

Yvette gazed at the tall stranger who had become so all-important in her life. He smiled encouragingly. She struggled with the English words to thank him property. "My parents and I are very grateful," she managed lamely.

"We'll do everything we can to make you comfortable," Colonel Kleine replied. He turned to Captain Truckey. "That's settled then. I'll get the ball rolling."

Yvette had never heard that expression before, but it must have meant *d'accord*. "Send word to me when you're ready to leave, and I'll have an ambulance pick her up," the Colonel said.

"Right," Nurse Truckey nodded.

The rapidity with which the arrangements had been completed made Yvette's head spin.

"When will your parents be back?" the Captain asked.

"Papa will come tomorrow."

"I'll explain everything to him then."

The two Americans bid Yvette good-bye and departed.

As the sound of their footsteps faded, Yvette stared at the ceiling. What a strange turn her life had taken. How would her parents react? With a resounding "yes." The Pasteur Hospital in Cherbourg was the alternative!

The cast on her arm was covered now with names, addresses, encouraging messages, and funny sayings. She would miss all the people who had been so kind to her—especially Nurse Truckey, Miss Bradford and Dr. Jones. She glanced at the slim book on the table. "Other people can help you," Dr. Yachnin had said, "but whether or not you succeed is up to you."

16

Through the open tent flap, Yvette saw her father arrive on his bicycle, and Captain Truckey hurry to meet him. She wished she could overhear their conversation, but imagined the gist of their exchange by the swift transition in her father's expression from extreme distress to immense relief. His efforts to vocalize his gratitude were met by a shake of her head to show there was no need. They took leave of each other with smiles and warm handclasps.

Yvette was smiling when he entered her cubicle. "You know."

Antoine blinked, still dazed. "How did the Colonel hear of you?"

Yvette repeated the conversation at her bedside. "That's all I can tell you."

For a moment, they looked at each other in silence, bemused by the rapid turn of events. From the time Antoine took his seat beside the cot until his departure, a stream of visitors came to bid Yvette good-bye. Some had tears in their eyes; others tried to joke. The pile of going-away presents on her bedside table grew.

Dr. Jones stopped by to say farewell. He greeted Antoine with affection, then bent over and kissed Yvette. From his pocket, he took a small silver medal and dropped it into her hand. "When I left home, my fiancee gave this to me to assure my safe return. I know she'd like for you to have it."

Yvette regarded the familiar figure crossing the river under the twin burdens of the Christ Child and the world. "At times your load will seem as heavy as St. Christopher's," the doctor said.

She nodded. "I know."

"Remember what Dr. Yachnin told you."

"I won't forget," she promised.

"Everybody is pulling for you." He was one of those with the tears.

He put an arm around Antoine's shoulders. "Courage, my friend." With best wishes to the Hamel family, he hastened away.

A nurse came to feed Yvette her lunch, and Antoine, too, made ready to depart. "I can't wait to tell Maman about Colonel Kleine and the Fighter Group. She'll be as surprised as I am—and as relieved!"

"You'll come and see me at the airfield?" she asked anxiously.

"Of course!" He kissed her good-bye. "Maman and I will be there as soon as possible. *A bientot, ma cherie.*" He smiled, and with a wave of his hand, he was gone.

After her nap, Yvette watched stretcher bearers carry her tent-mates to ambulances for evacuation; heard the sound of hammering, and vehicles coming and going. Tents were struck, cots folded. "A place has to be found for everything from operating tables to aspirin," Miss Bradford told her. "To move a four hundred-bed hospital is not an easy task."

The next morning during the final phase of the hospital's departure, two stretcher bearers appeared at Yvette's bedside. She returned their greetings, and instructed them on how to pack her trinkets in a box. One of them spoke a little French, and he joked that moving a boutique was not in his job description.

As the soldiers carried her to the ambulance, she looked around at the remnants of equipment remaining to be packed. Soon the field would revert to a pasture, she reflected, and after awhile, people would forget that a hospital had been here. What had happened to her legs? Were they buried along with other legs, arms and hands under that group of beech trees near the road? Or burned in an incinerator? She'd never asked, and now, she would never know. Nor would she ever wear the black patent sandals of her daydreams. Her last pair of shoes had been clumsy wooden sabots.

As the ambulance bumped over the rutted road, she thought of the people at the hospital who had been so kind to her. Gradually, however, she became aware of time passing, and the journey lengthening. Why was it taking so long to travel the four kilometers between La Fiere and Saint Mere Eglise? She lifted her head from the pillow. "Are we nearly there?" she asked.

The French-speaking corpsman sitting beside the driver gave her a puzzled look "We've just begun," he answered. "It's at least twenty kilometers to Cherbourg—not counting detours."

"You've made a mistake!" Yvette exclaimed. "I'm going to Sainte Mere Eglise."

"Wait a minute," the corpsman said to the driver. As the ambulance slowed, he examined the typewritten form he took from his pocket. He showed it to his companion, then held it up for Yvette to see. "The Pasteur Hospital, Cherbourg," he said. "Plain as day."

"No!" she moaned. "Oh, no!"

Alarmed, the corpsman leaned over the seat. "Are you all right?"

Yvette closed her eyes. "—and you know what shape it's in. She'll die there!" Captain Truckey's conversation with the Colonel reverberated in her mind. Tears slid down her cheeks. Had she survived the artillery blast at La Hougue only to die in Cherbourg?

"There's no hospital in Saint Mere Eglise. Why do you want to go there?" the corpsman asked.

"The Commander of the Thunderbolt Fighter Group is going to take care of me," she answered.

The corpsman stared at her as if he feared she might be hallucinating. He translated her extraordinary statement for the driver. She heard only his last sentence. "Since when did the Air Force start playing nurse to wounded French civilians? Do you think she's O.K.?"

The driver looked around at gutted buildings, burned trucks and tanks that littered the drainage ditches. "If she isn't, what can we do for her here? Besides, that's a written order. We have to follow it or have a hell of a good reason why we didn't." He stepped on the gas and the ambulance lurched ahead.

Yvette lapsed into hopelessness. Soon the evacuation hospital would be gone and no one would knew what had become of her. Her father would think she was with Colonel Kleine; the Colonel would assume that her family had made other arrangements for her care. She would become lost among the wounded and dying at the Pasteur.

The corpsman checked her periodically, but she didn't seem to be in pain. His orders were plain and had come down through regular Army channels. There was nothing to do but go on. He turned his attention to helping the driver follow the circuitous route which, before the destruction brought by the invasion, had been a straight shot to the northern port.

Finally they reached the city, and picked their way through rubble-strewn streets past buildings whose shattered windows gaped like dead eyes. They asked directions of civilians still dazed by the fierce bombing and shelling they had endured. They found the entrance to the hospital and drove between stone pillars into the courtyard. The bronze bust of Louis Pasteur looked down benignly upon the ambulance as it wove its way to the unloading ramp.

A nun approached the driver and corpsman carrying the stretcher toward the admitting desk. They tried to explain why two American soldiers were delivering a French civilian to the hospital. The corpsman showed her the copy of his orders, and Yvette saw a worried frown crease the nun's forehead when she read the dreaded diagnosis: *doublee amputee*. "Our facilities are overcrowded, our nurses stretched to the limit. Medicines, bandages—. *Rien!*" She spread her hands in a gesture of depletion.

"What are we to do?" the driver asked. "We can't take her back. The evacuation hospital has already gone."

The rigors of the journey had exhausted Yvette, and the haggling over her disposition filled her with despair. She wanted to cover her ears and blot from her view the disputants jostling to be rid of her. She was helpless—at their mercy. Finally, the Americans won the argument. With a resigned gesture, the nun acquiesced. Yvette closed her eyes. This was to be the end.

She awoke on a pallet in a corridor. A single light bulb burned in the domed ceiling. At the end of the hall, she saw pale sunshine seeping through a dirty window. It must be late afternoon or early morning. But which afternoon? Which morning? How long had she slept?

Other pallets lined the wall, and all around her, she heard moans and cries. She'd grown accustomed to the sounds of pain. They no longer touched her. Like the clink of instruments, the shuffle of feet, they were part of the background noises of a hospital. She felt sticky with sweat, her throat was parched.

"Water!" she cried. "Can someone bring me water!"

She heard swift footsteps, and a girl knelt beside her. She slipped an arm under Yvette's neck, and held a cup to her lips. Yvette drank greedily. Never had water tasted so good. "Thank you," she said when the cup was empty. She examined the girl's young face. "Are you a nurse?" she asked.

"No, I'm a volunteer," the girl replied. She smoothed Yvette's hair back from her face. "How were you wounded?" she asked.

"A German shell," Yvette answered.

"They killed my mother," the girl said. "I will always hate the Boches." Her gentle touch contrasted sharply with the venom in her voice.

Yvette nodded. "It will take more than my lifetime to forgive."

The girl rose to her feet. "My name is Janette. I come every day to help the nurses. This is not my station—I was just passing through the hall—but I'll stop by to see you tomorrow." She smiled encouragement, then disappeared.

Tears filled Yvette's eyes. Someone knew she was alive!

She drifted in and out of sleep. Day and night merged into a continuous filament of time. She was given fluids, and fed soup by whomever was available. A bedpan was periodically placed under her, then periodically removed. A harried doctor stopped by to examine her and, looking grave, made notes on a chart. Her thoughts grew jumbled. She was back in the evacuation hospital with her friends. Helen Keller read to her from a book she'd found on the table beside the bed while Yvette ate an apple that Dr. Jones had brought. She must run and pick the flowers from the garden. She'd promised Maman she'd have them gathered by dinner time. If only she weren't so tired and hot. Perhaps she could persuade Henri to pick them. It was his turn.

A wet cloth on her forehead awoke her. The hazy image of a girl kneeling beside her swam into focus.

"I've stopped by several times," Janette said. "You were asleep."

She dipped the cloth again into the water and bathed Yvette's face. Tepid as it was, it felt deliciously cool. "You're running a fever," Janette said anxiously.

Vaguely, Yvette remembered a nurse putting a thermometer between her lips. After she'd read the gauge, she'd frowned as if Yvette had done something wrong.

"I have good news," Janette smiled. "You're moving to a room."

A room! Away from the noise, the smells, the view of the single light bulb in the ceiling. "When?"

"Soon," Janette replied. "You're next in line."

Her answer puzzled Yvette. She imagined a queue of patients waiting beside a bed. For what? Suddenly, she knew. A bed was a place to die. "I don't want to go!" Yvette cried. "Make them leave me here!"

"You'll be all right!" Janette tried to soothe her. "I'll come and see you every day."

Yvette didn't hear. She was beyond despair. How cruel to give her a bed only to let her die. She sank into a stupor from which her friend's best efforts could not rouse her. Regretfully, Janette got to her feet and hurried off to the other wounded she must care for.

During the night, Yvette's fever worsened. By morning she was delirious, calling to her mother, her father, demanding water and more water. Wavering figures stood over her, consulting worriedly together. She felt herself being lifted. The motion was agony for her arm. A needle's prick gave her blessed release.

She regained consciousness lying on a surface that was soft yet firm.. The air was cool and fresh. Her head no longer throbbed, nor was her mouth dry as dust. She listened to the patter of rain on a roof, heard the scrape of a chair, and then a voice. "She's coming around."

Another dream? She opened her eyes. Her father was leaning over her. His cheeks were wet with tears. "My sweet, my sweet," he murmured.

A man standing at the window approached the bed. He was trim, in his mid-forties, and wore a medical corps insignia on the collar of his uniform. "Hello, Yvette," he smiled. "I'm Dr. Glocker. We've come to take you to La Londe."

17

The paperwork necessary for release of patients from the Pasteur was minimal. That done, Dr. Glocker stood at the door of Yvette's room and listened to the Mother Superior's summary of the meager attention paid the girl during her eight-day stay. "We did what we could," she finished with a sigh of resignation.

"That you've maintained a program of care at all under these appalling conditions is remarkable," he said.

"At least in changing her cast, we may have saved her arm," the nun added.

"Mademoiselle Hamel will always be grateful," he assured her.

Yvette lifted her head from the pillow. "May I have my old cast back?" she asked.

The nun fixed her with a blank stare. "Why? It was filthy and smelled to high heaven."

"My American friends had written their names and addresses on it," she explained.

"It was destroyed," the nurse shrugged. "Like they all are."

"Oh no," Yvette said, disappointed.

Mon Dieu! With things as they are, do you think we have time to—"

"There, there," Dr. Glocker soothed the exhausted nun. "Yvette meant no harm. Thank you again for all that you've done. We must be going. Could we have two stretcher bearers, please."

With a curt nod, the Mother Superior turned on her heel and hurried away.

Cowed, Yvette eyed the new cast. Indeed she was grateful, but now her ties with all of those who had taken such good care of her were broken. Cities with such names as Minneapolis, Santa Fe,

Chattanooga, Hoboken would no longer be connected with familiar faces.

As two aides carried her stretcher down the hall, Yvette located the spot under the domed ceiling where she had lain. Who among the wounded here would be "next in line" for her empty bed? She hoped to catch a glimpse of Janette, but her benefactress was nowhere in sight. What a pity she couldn't thank her and tell her good-bye. Yvette's last view of the admitting desk made her cringe. With time, she hoped her memory of the struggle between the nun and the corpsmen to be rid of her would fade. In the courtyard, she was placed head-first in the ambulance, thus enabling her to look out the windows of the rear doors. As the vehicle swayed from the driveway to the road, she did not look back. That nightmare was over.

Her father sat beside her on the journey south and told her of his efforts to locate her. His tale of just-missed encounters, red-tape entanglement, and language misinterpreted sent chills down Yvette's spine. "Finally, I got word through to Colonel Kleine. He was livid. 'To hell with Army regulations!' he fumed. 'I gave my word. I want her brought back here!'" Antoine's voice broke. "He provided the ambulance, the driver and the doctor, who not only speaks French but could provide medical assistance in case you needed it. I prayed all the way that we would not be too late."

Yvette gazed at his careworn face. No need to burden him with what a close call it had been. Instead she demanded news of home. "And how is Gilberte?"

He told her that her older sister was coming along, then moved on to other topics. Yvette had wondered before at her father's avoidance of details concerning Gilberte's condition but, as always, his account of rapidly moving events which had unfolded since their last encounter pushed aside further questions. After Denise, Paul and Bernard had gone back to their farm in Baupte, a family of five whose home in St. Jores had been destroyed asked for asylum at La Hougue. "The battle for La-Haye-du-Puits and Lithaire is desperate. An evacuation hospital the size of the one at La Fiere has been set up outside of Carentan. The number of American soldiers injured every day is appalling."

Yvette shuddered as she recalled the shrieks of pain, stench of infected wounds, the sight of spurting blood that had greeted her in the admitting tent at La Fiere. Now the same scene was being repeated at Carentan. When would the carnage stop? She remembered the soldier with the severed spine in the cot next to hers. He was a German, and yet she'd borne him no malice. Was it only when facing death that different beliefs and nationalities could be put aside?

"A member of Georges's Resistance network stopped by the farm to tell us that Georges is alive and well," her father continued. "No word from David or Pierre. Since German cities are being flattened, we should be grateful that the Boches allowed David to work on a farm," he grunted sarcastically.

Time passed quickly for Yvette as her father continued his account. *Le Minable* had disappeared, but other traitors were being rounded up and punished. Except for deserters and stragglers, the Cotentin was rid of the Boches. The harvest was delayed because of unexploded shells and hand grenades. "There will be little grain to thresh this year," he reported grimly.

Yvette wished that her father could prepare her for what awaited her at La Londe, but he was as uninformed as she was. "All I can tell you is that the Colonel assured me they would take good care of you."

Another hospital tent, Yvette decided, where she would be placed alongside other wounded. She hoped that someone would be as thoughtful as Captain Truckey and surround her cot with sheets.

The sight of refugees pushing carts piled with family belongings was depressing. Yvette was touched by the sight of a little girl with scraped knees and rundown shoes, who held a headless doll in one hand, and clutched the shirttail of an older boy with the other. She was crying but he paid her no heed. He trudged along as if in a trance, hot, weary, covered with dust.

"We're almost there," Dr. Glocker announced.

The ambulance slowed, then lurched across a culvert into a lane. Twin rows of plane trees lining the lane had recently been cut. Their hastily severed stumps stuck up like giant teeth erupting from green gums. "It's a pity the trees had to go," the doctor said, "but the airplanes never would have cleared them on takeoff." He pointed out the airstrip off to the right. "The engineers suffered terrible losses. They had to repulse German attacks at one end of the strip while they laid pierced planking at the other. In one morning alone, seven soldiers successively lost their lives while driving one bulldozer. In spite of the fighting, they cleared, leveled and matted the runway in seventy-two hours."

"Remarquable!" Antoine exclaimed.

Details of the struggle for Sainte Mere Eglise were now well known. The town was the pivotal point on which had hung the success of the American landings in the Cotentin. If it had not been captured, the peninsula might still be under the Nazi heel.

"Welcome to La Londe," Dr. Glocker said.

Through the back window, Yvette saw the archway under which they'd passed. Mossy, vine-covered, the arch was set into a long wall made of the gray-white rock of Valognes. For hundreds of years, city halls, cathedrals, chateaux, and monuments had been constructed of the durable stone, giving buildings of the region their characteristic appearance.

"I'm a history buff," Dr. Glocker said, "and I've done some exploring of the place. Six hundred years ago, when this archway was built, massive gates closed off the entrance. The walls of the house are a meter thick, there are hidden passages for quick escapes, the wooden beams in the ceilings are—"

Yvette's attention was diverted from the doctor's account by the activity going on around her. She heard men's voices calling to each other, tires crunching in the dirt, footsteps hurrying to and fro. Finally, the ambulance came to a stop.

Antoine peered through the windshield at the big stone farmhouse. "What happened to the family that lived here?" he asked.

Dr. Glocker shook his head; the driver shrugged. "When we arrived, they were gone."

Antoine and Yvette looked at each other, sharing the same thought. Only city-dwellers would be as offhand as that. They imagined the turmoil that had followed the American request: we need your farm. Family heirlooms must be put away, clothes packed for a journey of uncertain duration. Animals could not be abandoned. They must be boarded with friends and relatives. What to do with fields of unreaped grain? Left unattended, they soon choked with weeds. And pens of rabbits, chicken, geese—

"I'll only be a minute," Dr. Glocker interrupted their musings. "But I'll open the back so you won't get too hot."

Yvette had begun to feel claustrophobic in the confines of the ambulance, and she welcomed the breeze that wafted through the open doors. As she looked around, she drew comfort from her view of barns, stables, the apple press, and rose trellis. Though on a larger scale than La Hougue, La Londe was much like home. A wooden sign with red painted letters on top of a cow shed intrigued her.

"What are Foxhole Follies?" she asked the driver.

He smiled. "That's the briefing room for the pilots, the theater when we're lucky enough to get a movie, a place for the Colonel to have meetings." He pointed out modifications in some of the other buildings. The stable by the gate was now a chapel, Group Material occupied the apple press, and Transportation had taken over the largest of the barns. Headquarters was located on the upper floor of the farmhouse and the officers' bar was in a pantry next the kitchen.

As Dr. Glocker's "I'll only be a minute," stretched to a quarter hour, Yvette grew uneasy. The scene at the Pasteur admitting desk replayed itself in her mind. She wished she could eavesdrop on the doctor's report to the Colonel. Did he stress her helplessness; the duration and extent of the care she would require? Might her nurses resent the burden she would add? The Colonel could even now be regretting his impulsive gesture.

By the time the quarter hour had lengthened to thirty minutes, Yvette's nerves were raw. She was sure of the reason for the delay— the doctor could not face her with the disappointing news. She listened to the aimless conversation her father and the driver pursued and wanted to scream, "Don't you care what happens to me?"

She'd turned her head to hide her tears when her father's

"There he is," riveted her attention on approaching footsteps. She strained for a glimpse of Dr. Glocker's expression as he bent to get into the ambulance, but the visor of his cap hid his face. "I'm sorry to have kept you waiting, but Colonel Kleine was very busy." The doctor slid onto the seat, turned around, and gave Yvette a big smile. "He's delighted you're here and will come and see you as soon as possible."

Relief washed over her. She had not been abandoned. But as they circled the courtyard and passed through the gate, she wondered if that feeling of helplessness was a foretaste of what she faced from now on—a seesaw between fear of rebuff and longing for acceptance, equally humiliated by both.

Her father noted her listless look. "You must be tired," he said.

"A little," she agreed.

He stroked her hair and, to distract her, told her about the girl who had stopped by to see her in the hospital room.

"Janette!" Yvette exclaimed.

He nodded. "You were asleep and she didn't want to disturb you."

Yvette told him of the tasks that Janette had performed. "Her help meant so much to me. She reminded me of Gilberte."

Yvette noticed that, as usual, the mention of Gilberte brought a fixed smile to her father's face. Gradually, his hand on her head grew still, the smile faded. With foreboding, she listened to his despairing sigh. Suspicions which she had smothered until now demanded to be faced. "Papa, tell me about Gilberte."

His despondent expression gave way to one of release. It was time the subterfuge was laid to rest. He talked, and through his eyes, she saw events of that hot July afternoon unfold. "Shells fell all around us. One shattered the kitchen window, another sliced off the top of the courtyard chestnut tree. A truck in the driveway blew up, and its flames caught a barn on fire. It was pandemonium. Suddenly, Gilberte appeared at the door." His eyes brimmed with tears. "'I'm all right,'" she said, "'but Yvette needs help.'"

Holding her breath, Yvette braced herself for the blow to fall.

"Those were the last words she spoke. She collapsed on the floor. We laid her on a mattress in the dining room. A few moments later, Henri carried you into the kitchen. You were so lifeless, we thought we had lost both of you."

"Gilberte—dead." Yvette shook her head. "Say it isn't so!"

Antoine rubbed a hand over his haggard face. "The morning that I first visited you in the evacuation hospital was the day that we buried her in the church cemetery."

"Why didn't you tell me?"

"The doctors warned us not to. The shock might have been too much."

"And all that time, you and Maman had to pretend."

Yvette recalled the last time she'd seen Gilberte—kneeling beside Paquerette. Tears ran down her cheeks. "*Le Minable* is still alive—Gilberte is dead. My God!"

The ambulance shuddered to a stop. While the Americans alighted, Antoine hastily dried her tears. The back doors opened.

"Here we are." Dr. Glocker said.

18

ntoine joined Dr. Glocker and the driver outside the ambulance. Though Yvette did not relish the prospects of a stay in another hospital, she was impatient to be freed from her cramped quarters. She was exhausted. Not only had the revelation about Gilberte drained her emotionally, but the board-flat stretcher aggravated the pain in her back, and the new plaster cast encasing her from neck to waist restricted her breathing.

"Yvette."

She lifted her head from the pillow. Framed by the doorway were Dr. Glocker and two soldiers whose helmets displayed the Red Cross emblem. "Meet Sergeant Barnes and Sergeant Davis." The doctor indicated each in turn.

She responded to their "Hi, Yvette," with an English "Hello," and noted how poorly their welcoming smiles masked their dismay. The shock of noticing that she had no legs was more than most people—even medics—could successfully hide.

"These fellows have come to take you to your quarters," Dr. Glocker went on. "Are you ready?"

"Yes, indeed," she replied.

Sergeant Barnes climbed in beside her, and a few moments later the medics had lifted her stretcher free of the ambulance. She smelled the grass, felt the sun on her face. In the distance she heard the rumble of aircraft engines. Her father gave her hand a squeeze.

In front of a row of tents sheltered by tall hedges, a group of soldiers was gathered. A hush fell on them as Dr. Glocker's little entourage approached. Then, calling greetings, they hurried toward her. Bewildered, Yvette looked up at Dr. Glocker. "They're waiting for me?"

"For you," the doctor nodded. He began the introductions: a stocky, balding man with lively eyes, was "our dentist, Dr. Cohen, and this little fellow," he clapped the shoulder of a towheaded, handsome giant, "is Dr. Roberts."

"We're glad you're here, Yvette," Doctor Roberts welcomed her.

"Dr. Lerossi," the introductions continued. "His French is nearly as good as mine, so don't talk about him. Lieutenant Harris, Corporal Mulligan—" The names began to blur together as, wide-eyed, Yvette inspected one smiling face after another. "And I've saved the best for last." Dr. Glocker singled out a tall, thin, beaknosed man wearing a white chef's hat. "When he gets mad, he throws pots and pans around," the doctor whispered loudly, "so be nice to him." The improbable hat the cook had donned bobbed and weaved as he nodded to Yvette. "Anything you want to eat, sweetheart, just let me know."

"Thank you all very much," she stammered. "You are most kind."

"It's time to get you settled," Dr. Glocker said. The men opened a path for her, and the doctor led his charges toward the tents. "My God! Poor kid," Yvette overheard one of the men murmur before she was out of earshot.

"There's the mess tent." Dr. Glocker pointed out the first and largest tent in the row. It was separated from the others by a gap in the hedge through which a dirt track ran. "That road connects the medical unit with the rest of the airfield," he explained.

As the doctor talked, Yvette looked around for the big tent marked by its red cross that would be her future home, but nothing resembling a field hospital was in sight. "This way," Dr. Glocker said, heading for a small tent across the dirt track from the mess. He ducked through an open flap, waited for the others to follow, then waved his hand around the twenty-square-foot expanse. "Your salon, Mademoiselle."

She stared at him. Was she not to be housed with the other wounded?

"In good weather," the doctor continued, "three sides of the tent can be opened. You'll be able to see what's going on, read, if you like, and have visitors." He rested his hand on the back of an unusual looking chaise longue that occupied the center of the room. "The maintenance crew constructed the aluminum frame from leftover airplane parts, and Dr. Cohen, our dentist, made the back and seat from parachute shrouds. He even included our Group's number," the doctor added, pointing out the "371st" in contrasting colors woven into the seat.

Antoine managed to exclaim, "Extraordinaire!" but Yvette was speechless. The privacy the room afforded was beyond her wildest dreams.

"And now let's have a look at your bedroom." The doctor preceded the group through an opening into an adjoining tent. *"Voila!"* he said.

Yvette gasped. Sunshine streaming through an open flap reflected off the sky-blue floor onto shimmering folds of parachute silk that lined the ceiling. The same luminous material was a bedspread for the cot and served as cases for three large pillows forming a headboard. A bedside table, painted blue to match the floor, held a mirror, comb and brush, an issue of the magazine called *Yank,* and a jar of daisies. Above the cot hung a light bulb covered by a pink flowered shade. Cartoon drawings of "Frisky," a woeful-looking pilot with a cowlick, decorated the opposite wall. Two arm chairs and a little steamer trunk completed the furnishings of the room.

Tears filled Yvette's eyes. "I don't know what to say."

Dr. Glocker patted her hand. "You don't have to say anything, my dear. We're glad you like our little surprise, and hope you'll be comfortable here." He helped the medics lift her onto the cot, and arranged the pillows behind her head. As she heaved a sigh of relief, he smiled. "That's better, eh?"

"Much better," she assured him.

The doctor turned to Antoine. "You and your family are welcome to visit any time."

"My daughter and I are overwhelmed," Antoine said. "Words cannot express—" He stopped, unable to go on.

The doctor put his hand on Antoine's shoulder. "The pleasure is ours. And now, we'll wait outside while you tell your daughter good-bye. As soon as your father leaves, Yvette, someone will be checking on you."

When the Americans had left, Antoine sank into one of the armchairs beside the cot. He and Yvette stared at each other.

"My own room," she breathed.

"Incredible!" Antoine gazed around the dazzling tent. "It looks like a fairy godmother waved her wand."

Yvette inspected the doily that covered the top of the bedside table. Each corner of the decorative mat made from parachute silk had been embroidered with flowers. She shook her head. "All the little details. So much work—for someone they'd never seen. When you describe what the Americans have done, Maman and the others won't believe it."

"I can hardly believe it myself," her father answered. "I'd better go. They're waiting." He leaned over and kissed her good-bye. "Thank God we found you!" he said. "Thank God and Colonel Kleine!"

As she listened to the mutter of the ambulance fade into the distance, she gazed at the ceiling, and thought back over the events of the past half hour. The contrast in her reception here and at the Pasteur was almost too startling to be true. The welcoming smiles, the beautiful tent—were they real, or only a dream? Mesmerized, she watched the folds of parachute silk undulate in the summer breeze. Her weary mind began to wander. She felt herself floating above the cot. Perhaps the trip from Cherbourg with Papa and Dr. Glocker was an illusion, and in truth she was still lying in the corridor at the Pasteur.

She was burning with fever. How thirsty she was. If only someone would bring her water! She called, but no one came. "She'll die there," Nurse Truckey said. Terrified, she jerked awake. "Help me!" she cried.

A slim, dark-haired man dressed in khaki appeared at the open tent flap. "Are you all right?" He hurried across the room to the cot.

She closed her eyes, then opened them quickly again. "You're still here!"

He took her hand. "I'm here. I'm Dr. Lerossi."

She recognized him now—one of those whom Dr. Glocker

had introduced. The one who spoke good French. She heaved a sigh of relief.

"Dr. Glocker told me about the Pasteur Hospital," he said. "It's behind you now. Try to put it from your mind."

"Sometimes it's hard to separate the bad dreams from—"

"I understand. Now you're safe." He smiled. "Twelve hundred men are looking after you."

She searched his eyes. "Why is all this being done for me?"

"That's a long story," he answered. "After your tiring trip, you need to rest. Some other time. O.K.?"

She shook her head. "Now. Please?"

"All right." He sat down beside the cot. "It was Colonel Kleine's idea. Quite by chance, he heard of you." Dr. Lerossi described the early days of the invasion, the struggle to get the 371st Fighter Group operational at La Londe. "About the third week of June, the Colonel learned that an evacuation hospital had just been set up at La Fiere. As the ranking officer responsible for safety in the area, he charged over there to find out what idiot had picked a spot practically at the end of our airstrip to erect a medical unit. Their Commanding Officer was away, but Colonel Kleine intercepted the Chief Surgeon, Dr. Yachnin, coming out of the operating room tent. You can imagine that, conditions being what they were, both men were somewhat testy. They exchanged some choice words; finally arrived at the same conclusion. That since their facilities were a *fait accompli,* they were stuck with each other and would have to make the best of things. They shook hands, and the Colonel turned to leave. Just then, the Head Nurse happened by on her way to her quarters. Dr. Yachnin introduced her to the Colonel, the three of them chatted a moment, and Colonel Kleine departed."

Yvette inwardly shuddered at the precarious timing of the encounter. If Colonel Kleine had left earlier or Nurse Truckey had arrived a moment later, they never would have met.

"A couple of weeks after that, our field got weathered in," Dr. Lerossi continued, "and Colonel Kleine decided to invite the nurses at the evacuation hospital to be our guests at a dance. He thought a diversion like that would boost morale for members of the 371st Fighter Group and for the hospital personnel as well. Since I'd never seen the setup at La Fiere, the Colonel invited me to go with him to issue the invitation. We drove over in a jeep to talk to the Chief Surgeon about the arrangements. We didn't see him, however, for two hundred wounded had just arrived. The admitting tent was a madhouse."

Yvette nodded. Would that scene always haunt her?

"We decided to come back another time, and were headed for the jeep when the Colonel spotted the Head Nurse coming out of the recovery tent. He greeted her and introduced me." Dr. Lerossi shook his head. "She was red-eyed from lack of sleep, and faced another two hundred wounded to care for. She asked why the Colonel was there, and he told her about the dance. 'I'm sorry, it's impossible,' she said. 'We work twelve-hour shifts—more if needed. When we're not on duty, I assure you, we're asleep. It'll be that way until we move on.'

"The Colonel was very sympathetic," Dr. Lerossi continued. "He even offered to have some of our doctors go over and fill in. She thanked him, but said they'd been trained to work as teams. To introduce newcomers into the system would be difficult."

Dr. Lerossi lifted his eyebrows. "The Colonel doesn't like being stymied. He pursed his lips, stuck his hands in his pockets. 'There must be something I can do to help,' he growled. Suddenly, the nurse grabbed him by the arm. 'There is! Come with me. I want you to meet someone!' She urged him toward the recovery tent. The Colonel resisted. 'I'm squeamish about battlefield hospitals,' he confessed.

"'This someone is special,' the Head Nurse insisted. 'Someone whose life might depend on you.'"

Dr. Lerossi laced his hands together. "That did it for the Colonel. While I stopped at the surgical tent to have a look around, he followed the Head Nurse into the recovery tent."

Yvette knew this part of the story well: how shaken the Colonel had been at seeing the rows of wounded, his anguish when he'd stood beside her cot.

"—that we'd come to France as liberators, unprepared for the destruction that we'd brought," Dr. Lerossi's story continued. "War was for soldiers. His first sight of a civilian caught in the middle was a shock. That you were wounded by a German shell because Americans had occupied your family's farm distressed him terribly. As soon as he and I returned to the field, he called a staff meeting and told them what he had in mind. 'The least we can do is take care of her,' he said, 'so let's get going.'"

Dr. Lerossi leaned toward her, resting his elbows on his knees. "Everybody helped, officers as well as enlisted men. Your tents were put up by the maintenance crew, a guy in Materiel had the idea of lining the ceiling with parachute silk." His eyes glowed remembering that idyllic interlude in the turmoil of the war. He recounted a couple of episodes that had stuck in his mind: a tough old armorer with tattoos on both arms adjusting the pink flowered shade over the hanging light bulb. "God knows where he found a lamp shade!" A grizzled crew chief's care in arranging on the bedside table the doily he'd embroidered. "We had a ball! In the midst of destruction, we had created something beautiful." He smiled. "So there you are."

She looked into the hazel eyes regarding her. Was he to be another link in the chain of those to whom she owed her life? So many links now—Edward, the medic who had given her the first transfusion; Major Barney, who'd delivered her to the evacuation hospital; Dr. Yachnin, Dr. Jones, Nurse Truckey, Janette, and Colonel Kleine. Had they not been there when she'd needed them, she would not be here.

Dr. Lerossi noted her pensive look. "You're tired. The story went on too long."

"A story that ends like this is never too long," she answered.

He stood up and took a little bell from his pocket. He swung it to and fro so she could hear its silvery peal. "Use this when you need something," he said, placing it on the table. "My tent is right next to yours."

She shook her head. "I wish there were some way I could express how grateful I am."

"There is," he smiled. "Get better."

"I plan to," she answered, settling into her pillows.

He was right. She was tired. She closed her eyes and felt

herself drifting off. No more nightmares—this was real.

He studied her sleeping face. So young, so pretty. What a crime! He felt her fingers protruding from the cast. The circulation seemed O.K. A miracle her arm was saved. A miracle, and a good surgeon. He checked her pulse, watched her shallow breathing. She wasn't out of the woods by a long shot. She would need lots of care. He would see that she got it.

19

The afternoon light had waned when Yvette awoke. Through the open flap, she saw the elongated shadow cast by her tent. She must have slept a good two hours. Now she felt an urgent need to go to the *"commodities."* In the evacuation hospital, she'd despised having to ask someone to help her. Here, she hated her dependence even more. Who among the twelve hundred soldiers had been assigned the unpleasant chore? Reluctantly, she reached for the bell.

"Hi. You're awake." Dr. Lerossi's greeting stayed her hand.

He crossed from the doorway to the cot. *"Ca va?"*

"Much better," she answered.

"That's good. You're about to have a visitor, and I'm sure you'd like to freshen up. First, you'll need a bedpan," and with those few easy words, the request she'd dreaded to make was taken care of. Your nurses will be the two medics who brought you to the tent," the doctor went on. "Their names again are Davis and Barnes. Excellent, both of them—anxious to help." He eyed her tangled hair spread on the pillow. "I thought we'd prepared for everything but," he shook his head. "we overlooked your *coiffure*. That presents a problem."

"After eight days at the Pasteur, it must look a mess," she agreed.

He reflected a moment, then nodded. "Short. That's it. One of our cooks doubles as a barber."

Mon Dieu! Yvette silently groaned.

He noted her pained expression. "He's very good. I've never heard any of the men complain."

A G.I. haircut. She would look awful!

Dr. Lerossi glanced at his watch. "He won't have time to cut it this afternoon—he's busy with chow. I'll make arrangements with him for tomorrow."

It was the only solution, she realized, but having to relinquish her hair was another blow. For as far back as she could remember, she'd worn it long—to her waist as a little girl, then shoulder length when she grew older. Her thick dark curls had always been a source of pride. That, too, was to be taken from her.

"But that doesn't help us now," the doctor went on. He rubbed a hand over his chin. "I guess I could have a go at it."

"You!"

"The 371st Fighter Group is not exactly running over with hair dressers. You have to take what you can get."

She sighed, assumed a put-upon expression, then, "Who's the visitor?" she asked.

"Colonel Kleine."

"Mon Dieu, I must look my best."

"Sergeant Barnes will show up in a minute. When he's finished, I'll be back."

The medic's knowledge of French was rudimentary. To Yvette, the language barrier seemed to make their encounter easier. The instant intimacy their roles required proved somehow less stressful without verbal communication. The tall medic with the olive complexion had a quiet, serious air. He was broad-shouldered with muscled arms, yet as he went about his tasks, his hands were gentle. When he began to clean and dress her wounds, she turned her face away. She didn't want to see the dismay on his face at what remained of her legs. As he drew the sheet up to cover her, their eyes met. He held her hand a moment, then gathered his utensils and made his way to the door. Watching him leave, she understood more clearly than before that from the moment she was injured, pity was the only emotion she would arouse in any man.

This realization had little time to fester, for Dr. Lerossi reappeared soon after the medic departed. "We've got to get going," he said briskly. "They'll be here in a few minutes." He sat down in the chair and rubbed his hands together. "O.K. How do I begin?"

"First you pick up the brush," she instructed him.

He reached toward the table. "One brush picked up," he intoned.

"Now you're on your own."

"You're a big help," he grunted. Tentatively, he began to untangle the snarls that hung about her shoulders. His first attempts were clumsy, but as the natural waves fell into place, he grew more dexterous. Gradually, she began to relax. She closed her eyes and gave herself up to the luxury of the rhythmic strokes. The doctor's touch was a gentle as Papa's.

The brush clattered on the table. "Now you're presentable."

"Ohhh, that felt so good," she answered.

He looked at her enormous eyes in her too-thin face. "I know you hate to lose your hair. It's beautiful. But cutting it seems the only answer."

She nodded. *"D'accord."*

He turned his head toward the open tent flap and listened. "I hear a jeep. They're coming."

"Will you be here?" she asked anxiously. "I'll hardly know what to say."

"I'll be here," he assured her. "You don't need to make a speech. Just be yourself."

As he spoke, they heard footsteps approach and Dr. Lerossi crossed the room to welcome the visitors. Her eyes widened as, removing their hats, Dr. Glocker and three officers dressed in olive drab uniforms, ducked through the open flap. The five tall men seemed to fill the tent. Dr. Glocker, acting as interpreter, made the introductions. "You know Colonel Kleine, of course, Yvette."

"Bien sur," she returned the Colonel's smile.

"And this is Deputy Commander, Lieutenant Colonel Daley, and Executive Officer, Lieutenant Colonel Duggan."

The two men, who looked very young for their rank, murmured *"Bon jour,* Mademoiselle," but their welcoming smiles could not conceal their shock.

The Colonel expressed his delight that she'd arrived safely, and hoped her health would markedly improve during her sojourn with the Group. Even without Dr. Glocker's help in translating, Yvette understood the Colonel's Texas drawl. His remark, "—and if these fellows don't treat you right, just let me know and heads will roll," delivered with a twinkle in his eyes, set everyone at ease.

Yvette replied that no heads need roll, for everyone had been extremely kind.

"That's good to hear," the Colonel replied. He took a letter from his pocket. "I'd like Dr. Glocker to read this to you, and then translate it—if that's necessary," he added. "They tell me your English is getting better all the time."

She shook her head. "I have the long way to go."

"It'll come," the Colonel encouraged her.

Dr. Glocker unfolded the letter and read aloud: "We, the officers and men of the 371st Fighter Group, admire the valiant spirit you have shown in the face of disaster. When you feel discouraged, remember that twelve hundred men are betting on you. We want to have a part in your future, and with this in mind, would like you to accept our gift of two thousand dollars to assist in your recovery. We wish you a long and useful life."

The doctor showed the letter to Yvette. Above the date and title of the 371st Fighter Group, Yvette's full name had been printed. Below the body of the letter, six officers had signed their names: the Colonel, the two members of his staff who accompanied him, and the C/Os of the three fighter squadrons that made up the Group. "The money is to be used for your rehabilitation, Yvette. Colonel Kleine will keep it for you until you leave us."

Yvette was dumbfounded. Twenty-four thousand francs—more money than she had seen in all her life. What an astonishing gesture. As she gazed at the three officers at the foot of her cot, tears filled her eyes. "My English is *inadequat* to say 'thank you.' My French also," she added. "I'm grateful for the kindness you have done to me already. To *comprendre* this added gift—" She stopped, unable to go on.

"They understand, Yvette," Dr. Glocker intervened.

"It's a small thing compared to your loss," the Colonel said. "If there's anything more we can do, let us know."

She looked around the shining room. "I'm already being treated like a princess."

His grave expression lightened. "That's the way we want it. Dr. Lerossi will keep me informed about your progress."

With warm wishes for her continued improvement, the two staff members joined the Colonel and Dr. Glocker in bidding her good-bye. She listened to their footsteps fade away. "Unbelievable," she murmured.

"He's a good man," Dr. Lerossi said.

"Where did the money come from?" she asked.

"He passed the hat around—everybody put in what he could."

"Mon Dieu," she murmured, shaking her head.

Through the open tent flap she watched the jeep grow smaller in the distance. If only they could make her whole again. To dance across a floor, leap a brook, skim the stairs, run with the wind. But neither the might of the United States Army nor all the money in the world could give her back her legs. She would forever remain incomplete—a fragment of what she used to be.

Dr. Lerossi read her thoughts. "If only we were magicians as well," he said.

"You've done the next best thing—given me a chance."

A shuffle of feet at the entrance interrupted their talk. The cook entered, carrying a tray. Draped over his arm was a napkin; a long white apron covered his fatigues. He paused a few paces from her cot, and clicked his heels. *"Votre dîner, Mademoiselle."* He deposited the tray on the bedside table and whipped off the cloth that covered it.

A daisy in a cartridge case stood alongside a rolled white napkin. The pork chop, potatoes, green peas and carrots were artfully arranged around a cup of applesauce.

"It's beautiful," she smiled. "My compliments to the chef."

Muttering to himself, the cook pointed to her glass.

"What's the matter?" Yvette asked Dr. Lerossi.

"He's apologizing for the powdered milk. He wonders if it ever saw a cow."

She looked at the cook. "All my life I've drunk fresh milk. This will be a new experience."

"You'll let me know if the food doesn't please you," he urged.

"I'll love it. You're too kind."

"Bon appetit," he smiled, and bowed himself out of the tent.

"It's a work of art," Yvette said after he'd left.

"It's guaranteed to put color in your cheeks," Dr. Lerossi answered. "Barnes is eating with the early shift, so Davis will help you with your meal. I've got some things to do, but I'll check back with you later. Eat well," he said as he left the tent.

Actually she had no appetite at all. She wished she could do justice to the meal the cook had taken such pains to prepare, but the constriction of the cast inhibited her breathing. She longed to draw one deep, satisfying breath. The thought of trying to swallow food made her ill.

"Yvette, *c'est moi, le* Sergeant Davis."

Not only in looks, but in manner, the stocky, blond medic was the opposite of his counterpart, Barnes. Animated, quick-moving, he tucked her napkin underneath her chin, cut up her meat, then didn't stop talking in his melange of French and English from the moment he sat down in the chair. As he fed her, he told her unabashedly about himself. His family was from the mountains of West-by-God-Virginia, and he found life in the Army Air Force so much easier than scrabbling for a living on the farm, he still couldn't believe his good fortune. He had seven brothers and sisters; aunts, uncles, and cousins by the carload, and altogether, they made quite a clan. Even as a child, he'd loved taking care of people, and being a medic fitted him to a T.

"I wouldn't be a pilot for a million francs," he went on. "I haven't got the guts to fly," he made a sweeping motion of taking flight, "much less get shot up by enemy flak and those *sale Boches* diving at you from the clouds." The 371st Fighter Group had had some rough times during the invasion, but since the Germans had been driven from the Cotentin, things had calmed down around Sainte Mere Eglise.

Although Yvette understood about half of what he said, his discourse so intrigued her, she ate more than she thought she could. Finally, a growing discomfort prompted her to say, "Enough, *merci.*"

Davis frowned at the food remaining on the plate. "Dr. Lerossi is not going to like that."

"I have the problem with the breathing." She demonstrated by trying to take a deep breath.

He ran a finger underneath the plaster at her waist. "Whew! No wonder," he exclaimed. "It's too *constricte*. You should have told us sooner." He stood up. "I'll get Doc, and we'll fix you up right away."

The relief was instantaneous. As soon as Dr. Lerossi cut a window in the cast, a look of bliss spread across her face. "This type of cast does tend to get claustrophobic," he sympathized.

"I'll be glad to get rid of this monster," she sighed. "It's hot, it itches, and I can't do anything for myself." She frowned, puzzled. "Nobody ever explained why I need such a big cast just because my arm was hurt."

She waited a moment for his answer. "Can you?" she persisted.

He slid the cast shears onto the table and sat beside her. "It wasn't just your arm, Yvette."

She inspected his sober face, and got very still. "What do you mean?" she said.

"Your right shoulder was badly injured too, and both your collar bones were broken."

"So?" She stopped breathing.

"The possibility exists that you might not have use of your right arm."

Her mind refused to accept that terrible potentiality. "No, no, no!" she shook her head.

"We won't know until we take the cast off."

Her head fell back on the pillow and she broke into sobs. He didn't comfort her. Instead, he clasped his hands tightly together and waited as, through her tears, she expressed her rage at this added insult to her body. Finally, her crying spent itself. He dried her eyes.

"Are there any more little surprises," she demanded in a sarcastic voice. "Today has been full of them. My father told me that my sister, who I thought was getting better, is dead. Now I learn that my right arm may be useless!"

"Try to understand," he answered. "No one wanted to hide anything from you. Your father was obeying doctors' orders; the doctors were following their best instincts and training. Your body and mind can absorb only so much shock. It seemed prudent not to tell you everything at once."

"'A miracle her arm was saved,'" she quoted bitterly.

"It's a miracle you're alive."

"No legs, an arm that doesn't work. Why would I want to live!"

"You've come this far against terrible odds. You've got to keep on."

"I've heard that before," she answered indifferently. "It's so easy for others to say."

"What do you want me to say!" he demanded. "That you should have died. That life isn't worth living? Well, I don't believe that."

"A burden—for the rest of my life." Her voice was flat, lifeless.

He put his hand on hers. "I don't want to raise false hopes, but the signs so far are encouraging. Be patient for two more weeks."

Her face was white from shock, but there had been no whines, no hysterics. Just cleansing anger. That was good. "We'll keep you so busy, the two weeks will fly."

She didn't answer. Her outburst had used up her meager store of energy. He took a capsule from his pocket; held a glass of water to her lips. "This will help you sleep. Call me if you need anything."

Her eyes closed. He checked her vital signs. Her cast gleamed in the twilight. "Let her arm be all right." he pleaded. "Give her that."

20

A flurry of raindrops on the roof of her tent awoke Yvette. As always when she opened her eyes, the plaster cast was the first thing she saw. This morning it recalled in sharp detail Dr. Lerossi's painful revelation of the night before. For the thirty days since her injury, she'd assumed that her arm was healing properly. That nerves might be damaged beyond repair and bones not knit as they should had not occurred to her. What would she do if her right arm proved to be useless? Without the help of both, she could never learn to walk.

When Sergeant Barnes appeared, she sensed that Dr. Lerossi had told him she knew about her arm. He seemed even more gentle than yesterday as he took care of her needs. When he finished, he sat looking at her in his quiet, intense way. He told her in French, which sounded as if it had been rehearsed, that she was surrounded by people who cared about her. If she got lonely or afraid, even in the middle of the night, someone would come and stay with her. He ended his little speech with an admonition: do not lose hope.

In English as halting as his French, she thanked him. "I do not have the despair," she told him. "I am stubborn. That is why, in my family, I am called 'the Mule.'"

He put a hand on each side of his head, and wiggled them back and forth like two long ears. "Hee-haw?"

"Hi-han," she nodded.

Their tension-easing laughter greeted Dr. Lerossi when he ducked into the tent. "What's so funny?" he asked.

After Barnes explained their merriment, the doctor frowned. "The 371st Fighter Group has never taken on a Mule before."

"A first, sir," the medic agreed.

"Sergeant, see if you can dig up a manual on the care and feeding of a Mule. We need to do it right."

"Very good, sir." The Sergeant saluted smartly, turned on his heel and marched from the tent.

When Barnes had disappeared, Yvette's smile faded. "I hope you'll excuse my behavior last night."

"I'm sorry I had to tell you but you needed to know."

She nodded. "Learning the bad news when the cast comes off would have been worse. Anyway, no more outbursts. I promise."

"Why not have one a day," he smiled. "They're good for you— like vitamins."

The cook's arrival with Yvette's breakfast ended their talk. For the first time since her injury she felt like eating. As she inhaled the aroma of bacon and coffee, she gave DiMarzo a blissful look. He, however, denigrated the abomination called powdered eggs. Yvette placated him with assurances that she would devour every mouthful. She puffed out her cheeks to show how fat she would become.

"Listen, sweetheart, when this war's over, you come to my family's restaurant in New York, and I'll fix you a meal that you'll never forget."

"That would be marvelous," she agreed. "In the meantime, you could tell me about some of the specialties of the house."

"You bet. Right now, you need to eat before the food gets cold."

"It smells delicious. I know it'll taste even better," Yvette replied.

Dr. Lerossi's glance followed the cook's reluctant exit. He shook his head. "Only two visits and you've got him wrapped around your little finger. Cut back on the charm, will you? Traffic in and out of here could get to be a problem."

She gazed at him wide-eyed. "I'm only trying to be polite."

"Hmmm," he grunted. Then he shoved his hands into his pockets. "While Davis helps you with your breakfast, I'm going to make arrangements with the barber."

Her stricken look was gone in a flash, but not before he noted it. "This is the only solution, Yvette."

She nodded. "Cutting my hair isn't the end of the world. Besides, it'll grow back. Won't it?"

"I promise," he answered.

"Then I'll be ready."

"Good girl," he said.

Davis arrived and the doctor left. Thirty minutes later, he was back, with the barber in tow. Yvette took one look at the soldier's hair and inwardly groaned: that's what I'm going to look like. "Meet Private Harrison," Dr. Lerossi introduced the blue-eyed, lanky blond.

She forced a smile. How apt a name! *Herisson,* the French word for porcupine, fitted the private's bristling crew-cut as if the term had been coined for him.

The barber placed his tools on the bedside table, propped the big pillows at her back, then ran his fingers through her hair. "I've never cut women's hair before," he offered cheerfully. "Lucky yours is curly, eh? It'll hide all my mistakes."

Yvette noted the grimace on Dr. Lerossi's face and knew he wanted to strangle his protege. "I'll be busy with sick call," he muttered. "After Harrison is finished, Davis will take over."

While he combed the tangles from her hair, Harrison kept up a steady stream of conversation—what a great guy Dr. Lerossi was, the pilots would be weathered in today, she was the first French girl he'd met, he's studied French in high school but, unfortunately, little of it had stuck. She surmised that his nonstop talk was designed to mask his shock at seeing her condition. By now, she'd encountered every kind of reaction: some talked too much, others didn't know what to say. She let him rattle on without interruption. Finally it wound down and he concentrated on his task.

As she listened to the snip, snip, snip of the scissors, felt unaccustomed coolness on the back of her neck, she told herself over and over that, given time, her hair would grow back. The cutting progressed from the back of her head to the sides, and with dismay she watched her dark locks fall to the sheet. In all too short a time, her ears were exposed. Harrison tilted her head and began to cut the top. Here's where I turn into a porcupine, Yvette decided, ready to weep. He and I will be twins! "It won't be long," the barber encouraged her.

It seemed just moments later that she heard him exclaim, "Voila, it's done." His comb and scissors clattered to the table. "Want to have a look?"

She didn't but she knew she owed him that. She nodded.

As he reached for the mirror, she shut her eyes. When she opened them again, she was looking at her own reflection. She gasped with surprise and pleasure. Layered from the crown of her head to the tops of her ears, her hair was a mass of ringlets. They spilled over her forehead, emphasized her high cheek bones, and displayed to best advantage, the slim contours of her neck. She admired his handiwork from all angles, then regarded Harrison with shining eyes. "I adore it! You are a marvelous *coiffeur!*"

He flushed with pride. "You are very pretty."

Accepting his compliment with a smile, she regarded his open, honest face. How could she have thought that porcupines were unattractive! While he removed the towel from her shoulders and gathered the fallen hair, she guided him with simple questions back through the French he thought that he'd forgotten. From what State did he come? How many brothers and sisters did he have? What were his hobbies, his plans after the war? He sat down in the chair beside her and they talked until Davis arrived with her medication. The medic whistled. "Holy cow! What a sight for sore eyes!" He turned her head from side to side to get an all-round view. Then he fixed the barber with a jaundiced eye. "Why can't you make the rest of us look as good you did her?"

"I could if I had the same raw material to work with," the barber retorted. He pushed himself to his feet. "I'd better get going or they'll have the M.P.'s after me."

"You'll come to see me again, won't you?" Yvette asked.

"You bet," he answered. He waved from the doorway and was gone.

The penicillin that Davis administered was for an infection in the stump of Yvette's right leg. The wound had begun to fester at the Pasteur Hospital. By the time she reached La Londe, red streaks had inched up her thigh. "Keep that bad news under your hat," Dr. Lerossi had instructed the medics. "God knows she has enough to worry about. Let her think the shots are vitamins."

The subterfuge had worked. To the periodic doses of "pepper-uppers," as Davis called them, Yvette attributed her feeling of increasing well-being. The inflammation had begun to recede, and she never knew how close she'd come to having to undergo re-amputation.

Davis lowered himself into the chair vacated by the barber. "I'll set a spell and keep you company," he said.

"'Set a spell and keep you company?'" Yvette repeated. "What does that mean?"

Davis smiled. "I'll visit awhile." He tilted back in his chair. "The part of West Virginia where I come from is mountainous, and isolated. We still use old-fashioned sayings which, we're told, were brought over by the early settlers. When you leave the state, you almost need an interpreter," he smiled.

"It is the same in France," she answered. "The country people of Brittany speak a *patois* that outsiders can't understand."

He wanted to know about her family; where she'd gone to school. He told her about his ambition to become a doctor when the war was over. By speaking a mixture of French and English, and using facial expressions, they managed to understand each other. She nodded toward the pictures on the opposite wall.

"Who is Frisky?" she asked.

Davis explained that, when flying missions, the pilots dropped their numerical identities and, in radio contact with each other, assumed the communications code name of their Group. "The code assigned to the 371st Fighter Group is 'Frisky.' The Crew Chief of one of the pilots drew these cartoons. When he showed them around, they were an instant hit. All the pilots could relate to this poor guy, and so they named him 'Frisky.'"

Davis took the cartoons from the wall and showed them to her one at a time. She smiled at a dejected Frisky being inspected through a magnifying glass held by a hawknosed General wearing an expression of distaste; a hapless Frisky whose P-47, loaded with bombs, fuel tanks, rockets and machine guns, was trying to lift off an airstrip axle-deep in mud; a terrified Frisky maneuvering to elude a swarm of ME-109s while his disabled plane was leaking oil and trailing smoke; a chastened Frisky forced to do laps around a parade field for an infraction of a rule. The last cartoon especially amused Yvette: Frisky asleep in a foxhole with rain dripping down his neck. In his dream he sips an *aperitif* in a Paris cafe. Across the table sits a gorgeous French girl gazing at him with adoring eyes.

"Poor fellow," she sympathized. "He's having a terrible time."

Davis returned the pictures to the wall. "It was Dr. Lerossi's idea to have them in your tent. He thought that seeing the pilots in their unheroic moments might entertain you."

He was right. For another interval, she'd forgotten her anxiety about her arm. The doctor had said the two weeks would fly. He was certainly doing everything he could to speed them on their way.

"He's ordered a nap after your lunch," Davis went on. "When you wake up, Barnes and I will carry your cot out to the salon. Since the field is weathered in, the pilots are grounded. Some of them might drop by to say hello."

"That will be very nice." She smiled at the medic. "Thanks for 'settin' a spell to keep me company.'"

21

Yvette felt refreshed from her long nap, and moments after she rang her bell, Davis appeared. Though still self-conscious about her body's more intimate functions, her embarrassment was lessened by the matter-of-fact manner in which the medics took care of them. After he'd combed her hair, the final step in her *toilette,* Davis stood back and inspected his handiwork. "Not bad," he decided. "If I can't get into med school when this war is over, I'll open my own beauty parlor. I'll make a mint if all my clients look as good as you."

He went to get Barnes and they lifted her cot out to the *salon* where they placed her facing the mess tent. Barnes lowered the canvas flap behind her to shield her from the wind but left the other two open to the view. Until her injury, she hadn't regarded fresh air as a luxury. Never again would she take it for granted. "Getting outside makes me feel so much better," she sighed.

"Ain't that the truth," Davis agreed. He straightened the parachute silk bedspread so it hung evenly to the floor. "There you are. All set?"

She nodded.

"I'm on duty for sick call, but Barnsey'll be around in case you need anything."

She looked from one to the other. "You're wonderful. What would I do without you?"

Davis jabbed Barnes with an elbow. "Listen to her butter us up. We know how women are. You'd take up with somebody else."

"Jamais!" she smiled, and bid them good-bye.

The steady morning rain had slackened to a drizzle, but dark clouds still lowered over the field. This was the kind of afternoon that Yvette had relished before the war. There had been time to sit at her bedroom window and read, or sew, or daydream over fashions she had sketched. How filled with expectations she had been. Now, none of her dreams would ever come true.

Her melancholy thoughts were interrupted by the sound of laughing voices. Through a gap in the tall thick hedge, a group of figures emerged. Mist blurred their outlines, but as they drew closer, she determined by their leather jackets and crushed caps that they were fliers. Now she would meet some of the pilots of the 371st Fighter Group to whom she owed her life. Were it not for their need of an airfield at Sainte Mere Eglise, she would surely be dead.

"Bon jour, Yvette," they called.

"Hello," she answered.

One by one, they ducked under the tent flap, and trying to mask their dismay with half-averted eyes, stood awkwardly holding their caps. She smiled, trying to set them at ease. "You will sit down, please," she said.

In the shuffle to settle around her on the grass, they regained some of their composure. How young they looked. They had not yet acquired the worn and watchful air of veterans hardened by too many brushes with death. German soldiers arriving in Coigny four years ago had had that same bloom of freshness on their faces.

"Bienvenue a La Londe," said a wiry pilot sitting cross-legged facing her. He had lively eyes and a puckish smile, and since he'd issued the welcome in her language, she supposed he was the spokesman for the others. "We're proud to have you join us, and hope you'll be comfortable here," he continued. "We were chosen to be your first visitors because all eight of us speak a little French."

"Merci beaucoup—" she squinted at the name tag on his jacket.

"Frank," he supplied.

"Francois," she smiled. *"Merci* to you and to your comrades. I'm grateful for this *salon,* the beautiful room that you've given me and your efforts—"

"Hold it," Frank held up his hand. "Don't give us much credit," he went on, as murmurs of agreement arose. "Maintenance and our crew chiefs did most of the work."

A redhead sitting beside Frank elbowed him and pointed to a wooden stake anchoring a tent rope. "O.K.," Frank conceded, "that one is mine."

"Almost nailed his foot into the ground along with the stake," the redhead said in a loud aside to Yvette. "How the guy ever gets a plane off the runway—" He shook his head.

"Out here in the country, these hay seeds have it over us more civilized types," Frank admitted to Yvette. "But wait'll we get to Paris." His eyes gleamed. "Then we'll see who knows his way around."

"Be careful, Tom," Yvette cautioned the redhead whose name she'd noted on his jacket. Her eyes widened in mock apprehension. "I've heard that Paris is even bigger than Sainte Mere Eglise."

"No kidding!" Tom exclaimed.

She gave him a solemn nod then joined the general laughter. The awkwardness had eased. Soon perhaps they would think of her first as a person, and then an amputee, instead of the other way around.

"The weather is boring for you. No?" she asked.

A happy refrain of "No flying today! No flying today!" answered her.

"What do you do when it rains?"

"Hit the sack!" A slim pilot sitting behind Frank spoke up. He had dark eyes, a cowlick, and a budding mustache, which only emphasized how boyish he looked. His name, she saw, was Andrew.

"Hit the sack." She shook her head. "I do not know that saying."

"Sleep," Andy explained. "When the weather's good, we're awake at three, briefed at four, and airborne by daybreak. Catching up on sleep is our"—he paused—"second most important aim."

She thought of the morning milking at La Hougue and nodded sympathetically. "What is the *most* important?" she asked.

Her question elicited a moment of silence, then a collective guffaw. She surmised that girls must be involved, and blushed.

"Oh, you know, to catch some more Messerschmitts in the air," Frank interjected quickly. "But they're getting scarcer all the time."

"That's because you Americans have driven the German airplanes away, thank God!" Yvette said.

"Right now, we're giving close support to our ground troops."

She was intrigued. "How can fighter planes do that?"

"Tell her about 'Cobra,'" Tom suggested.

Frank grimaced. "I'm not sure my French is good enough."

"Oui, oui, Francois," she insisted. *"Dites-moi."*

"O.K., I'll give it a try." He leaned forward, resting his elbows on his knees. "Our plane, the P-47, was designed for air-to-air combat. But it's so tough, and has such terrific firepower, it's become the major Allied plane for giving aerial support to our ground troops. This is a lot more dangerous, but it's paying off. When we're around, the Wehrmacht can't move without taking a beating."

He paused to draw the outline of the Cotentin peninsula on the grass.

"Until 'Operation Cobra' American troops were in control from here to here." He pinpointed Cherbourg in the north, and Carentan in the south. "The Germans wanted to box us in until their panzer reinforcements arrived from the east. So they threw everything they had into a line that stretched from Lessay to St. Lo." He placed his hand along the base of the peninsula.

"'Cobra' was designed to blast a big hole in their line. The 371st and other Fighter Groups divebombed and strafed everything that moved—tanks, trucks, staff cars, wagons—" he grimaced. "Killing the horses was the worst part. For five days, we hit them from sunup to sundown. When it was over, the hole was big enough for the Third Army to pour through. It cost us though. Five planes. The Krauts are tough."

Caught up in the experience, Frank had lapsed into English toward the end, and Yvette had understood only bits and pieces of the account. She had felt the tension build, however, as the listeners relived their part in the gigantic battle. She looked around the circle of faces. Were they afraid? They had returned

safely until now, but did they wonder every night: will I be here
this time tomorrow?

Her attention was drawn to a pilot who, at the far end of the
semicircle, stared through the open tent flap. A shock of blond
hair fell over his forehead; black lashes accented his smoke-gray
eyes. The flat plane of his cheek, his firm mouth gave his face a
lean, angular look. What was he thinking, she wondered. Was it
the terrors of "Cobra" that lent him such an introspective air, or
was he merely longing for home? As if sensing her regard, he
turned his head. Their eyes met and his somber expression gave
way to a smile.

Although disconcerted at being caught watching him so
openly, she managed to return his smile.

"—and now that 'Cobra' is finished, we can start chasing
planes again." Frank's voice drew her back into the conversation.
"That is, if the weather ever clears up!"

"Don't worry. It always does," Yvette assured him. She glanced
around at the dripping foliage, and frowned. "At least it always
has."

Tom groaned. "You sound like Captain Boles, our weather-
man."

A chorus of "Yeah," and "You can say that again," agreed with
Tom.

"We call him 'By-guess-and-by-gosh Boles,'" Frank explained.
"His forecasts are correct about half the time." He pushed himself
to his feet. "We'd better go. We were told not to stay too long on
our first visit."

"I'm feeling better all the time," Yvette said. "You'll come
again?"

"Of course," he answered.

"There are about a hundred of us," Andrew added. "You may
see more pilots than you really want to."

"Never," she smiled.

One by one, they told her good-bye. "Take care," Frank said.

As they straggled out of the tent, the pilot who had attracted
her attention lingered beside her cot. "I wish to improve my
French," he said haltingly. "I studied it in school and can read

pretty well, but my conversation is very," he waffled his hand, "limited. Would you mind just" —he shrugged— "talking with me now and again?"

As she looked into his clear gray eyes, an alarm went off in her mind. His gaze was direct, not pitying, yet his expression reflected that somehow he knew the depths of the trauma she'd endured. Like all fighter pilots, he carried with him an aura of danger that was exciting, and the physical attraction of healthy youth. This combination of virility and a gentle manner was a heady mixture, and so Yvette listened to the still, small voice inside her that cautioned: "Don't."

"You already speak French very well," she hedged.

He sensed her reluctance. "I shouldn't have asked. Listening to someone bumbling around in your language—all that correcting and repeating. It would be very tiring for you." He nodded. "I understand." He turned to leave.

Without meaning to, he had trapped her. If she refused the one thing any of them had asked of her, how ungrateful she would seem. Besides, just talking—what harm could come from that? The still, small voice was silenced. "I'm trying to improve my English," she said. "Let's help each other."

His face broke into a smile. "You're sure?"

"Bien sur," she answered.

"That's a deal. *Alors,* until we meet again." He set his cap at a jaunty angle, bid her *"Adieu,"* and hurried to join his companions.

She watched him stride away. He had an athlete's gait, smooth and effortless. Painfully aware now of balance and pace, she marveled at his grace. As he receded into the mist, his body seemed to shimmer, his feet merely to skim the ground. Her eyes strained to follow him, but suddenly as if he'd stepped into another world, he was no longer there."

"Are you O.K.?"

Dr. Lerossi's question startled her. She hadn't heard him come into the salon, and had no time to mask her feelings.

"A little sad," she answered. "The weather, I guess."

"A long siege like this does get one down," he agreed, though he knew her pensive expression had nothing to do with a rainy spell. Maybe arranging the pilots' visit wasn't a good idea. They were such an appealing lot, he'd hoped their conversation would cheer her. But perhaps their youth and vigor had only emphasized the gulf between what she used to be and her condition now.

He settled himself on the lounge chair. "You want to talk about it?"

"Maybe some other time."

"I'll be available."

"What did I do to deserve you?" she asked.

"Nothing. Just your lucky day."

"From now on, I'll try to be deserving."

He groaned. "Don't, please. I'd have to keep records—in triplicate—of when you were or weren't!"

She turned her head to smile at him. In the waning light, her skin had a translucent look beneath the dark halo of her hair. She reminded him of a portrait by Degas. If only he were an artist instead of a doctor! With paint and a few strokes of his brush, he could erase the shadows from her eyes.

22

The rumble of aircraft broke into Yvette's sleep. The bombers were coming! She must wake the others. She tried to get up, but a great weight held her down. Hurry! Hurry! she berated herself, or no one will have time to hide. "Maman! Papa! Gilberte!" she screamed.

A stir at the tent entrance revealed an anxious Dr. Lerossi. Buttoning a trench coat over his pajamas, he hurried to the cot and turned on the light. Yvette's face was white, her eyes filled with terror. "What is it?" he asked.

As recognition dawned, the terror began to subside. "The planes—" she shuddered. "They came almost every night. We never knew where they would drop their bombs."

"Those are our planes," he soothed her. "It's almost dawn. The weather has cleared and they're going out."

Relief washed over her.

"Crew chiefs are warming the engines while the pilots are getting briefed." He eyed her ashen face, her pupils still dilated with fear. "Would you like for me to tell you about a briefing?"

She nodded gratefully.

He settled into the chair beside her cot. "They're held in what used to be a milking shed," he began, "so the place smells more of cows than it does of planes."

She smiled.

"The pilots sit on benches facing a big map covered with a drape. On either side of the map there's a blackboard. One records takeoff times, directions to and from the target, and the emergency radio code. The other lists the names of the pilots going on the mission and numbers of their planes."

"Their numerical identities," she murmured.

"Correct," he smiled.

She felt herself relaxing into her pillows. How comforting it was to have him there.

"When the officer leading the mission arrives, the map is uncovered and lit with spotlights," the doctor continued. "The leader explains the mission, pinpoints the target, and gives compass headings. Sometimes details about the target or how the squadrons will coordinate need to be cleared up. Then the Meteorologist reports on weather conditions—" By-guess-and-by-gosh-Boles, Yvette recalled, "and the Intelligence Officer gives latest information on enemy aircraft and flak concentration. This usually sets off a round of groans, curses and bad jokes—a thin disguise for nerves. If the target is really dangerous, you can hear a pin drop. The first enemy a pilot has to confront is his own fear."

"That takes a lot of courage," Yvette mused.

"Indeed," Dr. Lerossi agreed.

They listened as the whine of revving engines accelerated to a roar. "What's happening now?" she asked.

"They're ready to go."

Yvette imagined the aircraft lined up like horses champing at the bit. Thunder rolled across the field as one after another they charged down the runway and hurtled into the sky. Sixteen in all, she counted. They circled high above the tent until the formation was complete, then set off on their awesome mission of destruction.

Yvette looked at the cartoons on the opposite wall. *"Bon voyage,* Frisky," she said.

"Bonne chance," Dr. Lerossi added. "And may you have a safe return." He stood up. "Both of us could use some more sleep. Will you be all right?"

"The nightmare is gone," she smiled. "Thanks for the briefing."

"Now you're an expert," he said, and turned out the light.

She awoke to full daylight and Davis calling to her from the door. "Wake up, Lazybones. The day's half gone." She told him about listening with Dr. Lerossi to the planes taking off.

"That was two hours ago," he answered. "Down at the flight line, they're sweating out the return."

"Who is they?" she asked.

"Crew chiefs, mechanics, pilots who didn't go on the mission. There's a mobile control tower waiting, along with fire fighters, and medics—just in case." He sat down beside her. "Crew chiefs joke about it being the plane they're worried about, but when their pilot doesn't make it back, they take it hard."

"How much longer will it be?" she asked.

"Soon, I think. The closer it gets, the less talk. Right now it's pretty quiet down there."

As Davis busied himself with her *toilette*, Yvette worried about her visitors of yesterday. Was Frank on the mission? Redhaired Tom? She thought of the pilot who had lingered behind the others. Was his crew chief one of those 'sweating out the return?'

"How about some chow?" Davis asked.

"That sounds good," she answered.

"I'll tell DiMarzo you're ready."

While she waited, Yvette regarded the whimsical figure in the cartoons. He returned her gaze with a baleful look. The cards are stacked against me, he seemed to be saying. With every mission I fly, the odds grow bigger that I won't get out of this war alive.

DiMarzo's arrival, followed by Davis, interrupted her silent conversation. She welcomed the cook with a smile. He strode to the cot and with his customary flair, swept the covering napkin off the tray.

"Ah!" she exclaimed. *"Les crepes!"*

"Pancakes," he corrected. "The American version of crepes." While Davis tapped his foot, the cook described the care needed to prepare the dish. "If they cook too long, they toughen. Not long enough, and they're soggy in the middle."

"These will be cold as a fish if you don't get out of the way and let me help her eat them," Davis complained.

DiMarzo yielded his place, but hovered at the medic's shoulder to be certain the right amount of hot butter and syrup was applied. Yvette's reaction was all that he could ask for, and glowing with satisfaction he left the tent.

Her medical checkup following the meal was encouraging. The red streaks inching up her thigh had all but disappeared, the doctor and medic were pleased to note. "Did you eat all your breakfast?" Dr. Lerossi asked.

"Licked the platter clean," Davis reported.

"DiMarzo's pancakes deserve a shrine," Yvette sighed.

"I haven't noticed he's that creative in feeding the rest of us," the doctor observed.

"Me either," Davis grumbled. "It's disgusting! She rolls her eyes at him and he grovels."

"Try rolling your eyes," Yvette suggested.

The medic's answer was a sour look.

"C'est la guerre," Dr. Lerossi sighed. He put his medical tools back in his bag. "Do you want to see the planes come in for landing?"

"Oh, yes," she answered eagerly.

"I'll get Barnes," Davis said, following the doctor out of the tent. "Be back in a sec."

As the medics set her cot in its usual place, a distant drone carried to them on the hazy August air. "They're on their way," Barnes said. "Keep your fingers crossed that they all got back."

The drone grew louder. Barnes pointed above the mess tent. "There they are."

Yvette, too, caught sight of the four aircraft flying in tight formation. They were not sleek like the German fighters she had seen. The cowling that housed the enormous engine gave the nacelle a thick-bodied look. Yet as they streaked across her field of vision, they had a powerful grace. The P-47 Thunderbolt! An appropriate name for a weapon that had struck such terror into the enemy's heart. As they rotated out of sight around the field, another flight came into view, and soon all sixteen planes had been accounted for.

"Wonderful!" Yvette breathed a sigh of relief.

"Watch this," Davis said, when the first flight had reappeared. Suddenly the leader peeled off from the other three. He seemed to hang suspended on a wire, one wing tip pointed toward the earth, the other at the sky. Then gently as a mother rocks a cradle, he leveled the fuselage, and rapidly losing speed and altitude floated out of sight behind the hedge. The rest of the planes followed the pattern, and soon the whines, roars, rumbles and drones that heralded the Group's departure now verified its return.

The final flight swung in for its approach. The leader and his wingman landed safely, but as the third plane hung vertically in the sky, its engine sputtered, coughed then suddenly was stilled. The appalled spectators watched the aircraft plummet to the earth and heard the silence rent by a deafening explosion. Beyond the hedge a thick black column of smoke arose. Yvette stared at the medics in disbelief. "What happened!" she cried.

They shook their heads, their faces grave.

"I've seen pilots climb out of wrecks you wouldn't believe, but never when the plane caught fire," Barnes said in a somber voice.

Yvette's flesh crawled. She'd always had a fear of fire. No farm was safe from its devastation. A barn, a stable, a whole house could be demolished while the family looked on helplessly.

"Here's hoping the poor devil died when he crashed," Barnes said.

The wail of racing firetrucks and ambulances carried to them across the field. "Go check it out," Davis suggested to Barnes. "I'll stay with Yvette."

"No, no. Both of you go," she said. "I'll be all right."

"You sure?" Davis asked.

"Of course. Hurry."

She watched them disappear through the gap in the hedge, then waited in a fever of suspense. Thirty minutes later, Davis returned with the grim details. The aircraft was destroyed. The fuel tank had exploded on impact, and the plane had turned into a fireball. The reason for the engine failure would be forever unknown.

"Who was the pilot?" Yvette asked.

"A guy named Bradley," Davis answered. "I'd seen him around. Likeable, slow-talking, kind of country. Redheaded. His first name was Tom."

"Mon Dieu," Yvette cried.

Davis looked at her in surprise.

"He was one of the pilots who visited me yesterday." She saw again the infectious grin, heard the good-natured gibes. She'd thought of him as a kindred spirit since they'd both grown up on farms.

"It's tough on these guys," Davis mused. "They never know from one mission to the next which of their buddies will still be around."

Yvette stared out of the open tent flap. The grass was still green, the sun shone. A life had been snuffed out, yet life went on. Cooks prepared lunch, mechanics readied planes for the next mission. Suzanne, Gilberte, Tom. How many killings did it take before one became immune to violent death?

23

As the days passed, Yvette's health steadily improved. Proper medical attention, good food, and fresh air heightened her color, and the stream of visitors that passed through her salon boosted her morale. After watching a gaggle of maintenance men take their leave one afternoon, Davis shook his head. "There may be some guys in the 371st Fighter Group who've never heard of Colonel Kleine but, by golly, they all know you."

Yvette looked at the bedside table where the departing guests had left a tin can filled with marigolds, a couple of comic books, three chocolate chip cookies and a hair ribbon. "Everybody is much too kind."

Davis stuffed his hands into his pockets. "You're a good influence, Yvette."

She pretended to brace herself for the dig she knew would follow, but for once the medic's face was serious. "An all-male outfit like this can get pretty raunchy," he said, "but with you around, we clean up our talk, we care about our behavior, and we don't gripe as much." He stared across the field. "We look at you and say: she's had a rough go, but she never complains. If she can take what's been dished out to her, we ought to do the same." He cleared his throat. "So it's a two-way street. Whatever we've done for you, you've paid back many times over."

Her tears blurred his stocky figure silhouetted against the evening light. "What a nice thing to say."

"Don't let it go to your head," he grunted.

The old Davis was back.

Her daily schedule fell into a pattern. Her toilette preceded breakfast; her physical exam followed it. A woman from the community of La Fiere did her laundry and cleaned her room. Yvette was never left alone. Either Dr. Lerossi or one of the medics was always within reach.

"I've got a surprise for you this afternoon," the doctor told her one morning after her checkup.

"What is it?" she asked eagerly.

He gave her a patient look. "If you knew, it wouldn't be a surprise."

She ignored his logic. "Just a hint?"

He shook his head. "Not a peep. You'll find out after your nap."

She knew she'd never be able to close her eyes, but after a busy morning and her lunch, her strength ebbed as usual, and she fell asleep. Two hours later, she awoke to see Dr. Lerossi ushering her parents into the tent. "Maman! Papa! What a lovely surprise."

Dr. Lerossi withdrew, and her parents hurried toward the cot. Her mother's eyes filled with joyful tears. She kissed Yvette and stroked her hair. "It's so good to see you, my sweet," she said.

"You look like a different girl from the one that Dr. Glocker and I brought here from Cherbourg," her father marveled.

"I'm getting stronger all the time," Yvette answered. "In five more days the 'monster' will be gone."

She saw the apprehensive look her parents exchanged. "I know the problems. Dr. Lerossi explained."

"The signs so far are good," her father said.

"We pray for you, my child. Have courage." Her mother stroked her hand. "Can we bring you anything?" she asked.

Yvette shook her head. "I'm getting terribly spoiled!"

Alice gazed around the tent. "Papa tried to describe it. He didn't do it justice."

"Everybody had a hand in it." Yvette's words tumbled over each other as she repeated Dr. Lerossi's account of the tent's erection. Then she went on to tell them of the visit of Colonel Kleine and his two adjutants.

Her parents stared at each other. "Two thousand dollars!" her mother exclaimed. *"Mon Dieu!* These Americans are generous!"

Antoine sighed as if a great weight had been lifted from him.

He leaned over and stroked his daughter's cheek. "You'll learn to walk again. I don't know how we could have managed without their help."

"Colonel Kleine is going to keep the money until the 371st Fighter Group moves on," Yvette said. She told them of Dr. Lerossi's kindness, the gentleness of the medics, and of the many people who had been to see her. "It's like living in a fairy tale," she finished.

As usual, she was hungry for news of home. "Michel is getting married—to Juliette Bouvier from Pretot," her mother told her. The banns would be posted in the fall.

"Dear Michel," Yvette said. "I hope he'll be very happy."

Her father nodded. "She comes from a fine family. They will be good for each other."

The *Comtesse* had returned to Coigny. She had stopped by La Hougue yesterday and shared a glass of wine. Damage inflicted by the Germans quartered in the Chateau would take a long time to repair, but she was glad to be home. The Abbe Giard was working too hard as always. He and many others in the town asked often about Yvette. As soon as it could be arranged, Claire and the rest of the family would come and visit her. The mention of Gilberte's name brought tears, but now at last, they could talk about her without restraint. All too soon, the jeep arrived to take the Hamels back to Coigny. Scarcely had she bid her parents good-bye than the medics appeared.

"It's time for your *soiree* in the salon," Davis announced and, again, Yvette saw the fine hand of Dr. Lerossi scheduling activities to leave no interval for brooding.

The medics placed her cot so she could overlook the repair depot near the mess tent. In good weather, mechanics tuned engines, changed tires, fixed minor damage to vehicles belonging to the Group, and the activity diverted her before her visitors arrived. The mechanics kept a lookout for her and called out greetings.

Barnes walked to the edge of the tent and inspected the work in progress.

"They either killed or cured those two 4x4's they were working on yesterday," he told Yvette. "Today you'll have to make do with a jeep."

"Some comedown," she grumbled.

Barnes nodded. "The level of entertainment around here has certainly deteriorated." He turned to Davis. "I think we ought to speak to the Colonel."

"I agree," Davis answered. "First thing tomorrow."

Barnes plumped up the bed pillows; Davis straightened the bedspread. They stood back and nodded approval of the results. "Holler if you need anything," Davis said.

"Try to behave yourself," Barnes admonished.

She rolled her eyes. "Nag, nag."

She smiled as they walked away. The change in Barnes had been fun to watch. His reticence had hidden a lode of humor which she and Davis had successfully mined. She'd welcomed his reserve during their first encounters but now that the tension in their relationship had eased, she could enjoy his banter.

She turned her attention to the mechanics in the repair depot. The mutter of the jeep engine formed a backdrop to their talk. She noticed the one called Hal glance toward the adjacent hedgerow, and heard him say, "Hi, Lieutenant." Yvette's pulse quickened when she recognized the airman who appeared through the gap. She watched him stroll along the dirt track leading to her salon.

In the interval since she'd first encountered him, she'd alternated between hope that seeing him in the context of the danger of the "Cobra" mission had blinded her to unattractive features he undoubtedly possessed, and dread that he would look as handsome as he did right now. He stood just outside the extended tent flap, his back straight, shoulders squared. He swept off his cap, planted an arm across his waist, bowed. *"Bonjour, Mademoiselle,"* he said. *"Je suis enchante de vous voir. Si cela ne vous derange pas, vous permettez-moi entrer?"*

His ludicrous formality released some of the tension that had built during his approach, and she giggled. He looked downcast. "That bad, huh?"

"Come in," she said in a mollifying voice, and nodded toward the lounge chair. "Make yourself comfortable."

He stuffed his cap into his pocket and took a seat. He shook his head. "And after all that practice!"

"It was—great. Just not quite the way we greet people nowadays. Maybe back in 1910—"

"Our high school French teacher was kind of old," the pilot conceded, "and she wasn't French," he added. "Bringing me up-to-date may be more work than you bargained for."

"I wish my English was as good as your French—" she paused.

"James," he supplied.

Yvette tried to copy his pronunciation, but after several attempts, the name still sounded like "Djahmes." She shook her head. "I don't think we have the equivalent in French."

"My mother was set on names from the Bible. She saddled my older brother with Bartholomew. The younger one escaped with Luke, but I got tagged James—one of the Apostles—as in James, the son of Alpheus."

"Your mother sounds like mine," Yvette smiled.

"She wanted to call me Alpheus. Thank God my Dad put his foot down."

"Alpheus," Yvette repeated. "I like that. It sounds better in French than Djahmes. I'll call you Alpheus."

"Not in front of people, you won't," he threatened.

She smiled. "See—your French is already better. You don't sound stilted any more."

"It's easier if you're not embarrassed by your mistakes. You make me feel comfortable," he added.

The contrast of his soot-black lashes and gray eyes was startling. His fine textured complexion would be the envy of any girl. Yvette tried not to notice the tanned column of his throat rising from the open collar of his khaki shirt. "The weather has been clear lately," she said hastily. "That's kept you busy?"

He nodded. "The Group is flying cover for General Patton's army in Brittany. It's a new kind of maneuver for us. We radio to the ground troops where a buildup of enemy tanks and troops are lying in wait, so they won't be taken by surprise." He relaxed against the back of the chair. "I'm off today—a nice break."

"What did you do?" she asked.

"Slept late, then wrote some letters home."

"Where is home?"

"A state called Montana. It is in the western part of our country."

"Then you are a cowboy!" she exclaimed.

He smiled. "You might call me that. My family owns a cattle ranch."

"We have something in common," she said. "I grew up on a farm. We raise pigs, chickens, geese, horses, and I, myself, have helped milk our seventy cows."

"I've done a little of that," he nodded.

"How many cows do you have on your farm?"

"Hmmmm. Let's see. I'm not really sure," he answered.

She frowned. "You do not know how many cows you have?"

"I haven't been home since last August," he hedged.

"It takes nine months to drop a calf. They don't multiply like rabbits."

He grinned. "About fifteen thousand."

Her mouth dropped open. He was making fun of her.

"It isn't the same kind of farm as yours, Yvette. We raise beef cattle to ship by rail to eastern markets. You need a lot of cows to make it pay."

"Fifteen thousand," she murmured. She could not imagine the number of hectares it would take to feed such a herd. "Who takes care of all these cows?"

"My brothers and I, our father, a cousin, and some hired hands."

"Everybody lives together?" she asked.

He shook his head. "It's hard to explain our life-style because you have no words for 'bunkhouse,' 'chuckwagon,' 'cow pony,' 'grama grass.' It's a different world." As he stared through the open tent flap, she wished that she could see what he was looking at— an icy torrent gushing over boulders, a vast plain milling with cattle, a sky that went on forever.

"You are homesick?" she asked.

"We all are. One of the many curses of war. I suppose the German soldiers occupying Normandy were homesick, too." His expression became grim. "With all the bombing, they will not have much to go home to."

"They never should have left," she answered tartly. "I have no sympathy for them."

He looked at her and nodded. "Nor I."

They were silent a moment, then he pushed himself from the chair. "I'd better shove off. I'm flying the first mission tomorrow, and I need to talk to my crew chief. My engine is running a little rough." He smiled, nodding toward a group approaching the row of tents behind her. "You're about to have your usual crowd of visitors." He took his cap from his pocket. "May I come back and talk some more?"

The warning voice was louder, but she paid it no heed. "Do," she answered. "I must learn more about this Montana."

"Adieu, until then." At the edge of the tent he paused and looked over his shoulder. "What grade did I get today?"

"You go to the head of the class," she answered.

"You tell that to everybody."

She shook her head. "Only cowboys."

He laughed and settled his cap on his head.

The August haze blurred his outline as he retraced his steps to the gap in the hedge. Before he disappeared, she was already longing for the next time. Why had she let him come!

24

For the next three days, as the 371st Fighter Group lent support to Patton's rapidly moving troops, the air around La Londe vibrated to the sound of airplanes taking off and landing. On the fourth day, bad weather closed the field. Rain fell steadily and gusts of wind billowed the walls and ceiling of Yvette's tent. "I'm afraid you'll be stuck inside this afternoon," Barnes commiserated with her when she awoke from her nap. "The salon is a mess."

"I can put up with anything today," she answered. "My cast comes off tomorrow."

The medic's eyebrows lifted. "Has it been two weeks already?" He examined the penicillin syringe he drew from his pocket as if it were different somehow from all the others he'd ever seen. "Where has the time gone?"

She studied his averted face. "It's going to be O.K., Barnes. I'm scared," she acknowledged, "but—"

He looked up and met her eyes. "We're all pulling for you."

"I know. That helps," she said. "A lot."

She tried not to wince as he administered the shot. She'd had so many, she imagined her backside looking like a pincushion. But thank God for the "pepper-uppers." They'd done a good job.

After he'd tended to her needs, the medic hurried away. When he returned, he sat in the chair beside her cot, and Yvette assumed he was "settin' a spell to keep her company." But as they chatted, he had a watchful air as if waiting for something to happen. When he heard a scrape of shoes at the tent entrance, he broke off mid-sentence, and hastened to the door. He held the tent flap open. "Finally," Yvette heard him say. "I was about to send out the frogmen."

170

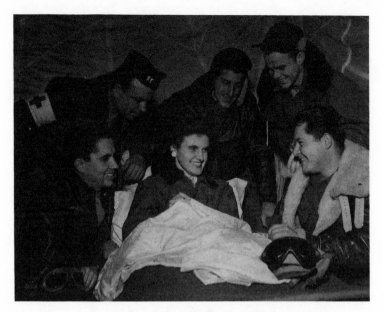

In the parachute-tent at La Londe.

She smiled at DiMarzo's answer: "I could have used somebody with webbed feet. What a day!"

Dripping rain, he came into the tent. One hand held a raincoat suspended over his head to protect the large, round tray he balanced on the other. Barnes rescued the tray from its precarious perch, while DiMarzo hung his raincoat over a tent rope. When he'd retrieved the tray, he crossed the room to the cot.

"Greetings from your friendly, neighborhood *patisserie,"* he addressed Yvette.

Barnes followed the cook. "A tea party this afternoon seemed a good idea," he said.

A tea party! One final distraction to keep her from worrying about tomorrow. "I think it's a wonderful idea!" she said.

She watched the cook slide the tray onto the table. His hair was matted, his apron mud-spattered and, from his knees down, his pants were soaked. "Cows love this kind of weather, eh?" he grinned. "Good for the grass."

She marveled at his lack of complaint. "But it's hell on wheels to get around in," she sympathized.

The medic and the cook exchanged a startled look. "Who taught you that?" DiMarzo demanded.

"I overheard it," she answered, pleased that she'd remembered the phrase so readily. "Is it not correct?"

"It's perfect," Barnes laughed.

"Cussing!" DiMarzo bristled at the medic. "Next thing you know she'll be shootin' craps."

"I don't want to shoot anything," she answered. "I just want to see what's on the tray. I'm starving! Take the cover off."

"Shut your eyes," the cook ordered.

Yvette closed her eyes and turned her face to the wall.

"You, too, Barnes," DiMarzo added.

The clump of the medic's shoes as he rotated toward the door, the cook's tuneless whistle while he busied himself at the table brought a lump to Yvette's throat. Such a to-do. Just for her.

"Voila!"

"Mon Dieu!" Yvette breathed.

A rose in a bud vase decorated the center of the white-clothed table. Around it were arranged cups and saucers, cream and sugar, a steaming teapot, wedges of cheese, fresh fruits and a plate piled high with sugar cookies.

"Who did you rob?" Barnes exclaimed.

DiMarzo airily dismissed the accusation. "One has one's ways and means," he answered.

"When they throw you in the brig, I'll come visit. I promise."

"It's beautiful," Yvette breathed, "but where—?"

DiMarzo held up a hand to silence her. *"'Noli equi dentes inspicere donati,'"* he intoned.

Barnes pondered the cook's reply. "I can live with that." He lifted his eyebrows at Yvette. "O.K. by you?"

"D'accord."

"So," DiMarzo surveyed the table, "on with the party."

"I'll get the other chair," Barnes said.

As the medic left for the salon, Yvette inspected the crockery. "Why the extra cups?" she asked.

"Somebody may drop by," the cook shrugged.

As if on cue, they heard running footsteps brushing through wet grass. "Whew! I'm glad I'm not flying in this stuff!" came a familiar voice from the other room. Yvette held her breath to listen to Barnes's reply, and the rustle of a raincoat being shed. Moments later, James stood framed by the doorway. Raindrops glistened on his hair, and his face was flushed from exercise. His hesitant smile crumbled the defenses she'd tried so hard to erect. "May I come in?" he asked.

"Entrez, Lieutenant," DiMarzo welcomed him.

He crossed the room and stared at the food-laden table. *"Sacre bleu!"* he murmured. Then he eyed the cook suspiciously. "I'm not even going to ask," he said.

"It's better that way," DiMarzo agreed.

The airman offered the package he carried. "These just arrived from home. I hope they'll add a little something to the festivities."

"Any donations gladly accepted." The cook inspected the contents of the box. "Brownies!" He looked the Lieutenant up and down. "For an officer, you're O.K."

"God knows we try, DiMarzo," James sighed. He turned to Yvette. *"Ca va, Mademoiselle?"*

The interval of banter had given Yvette time to adjust to the pilot's unexpected visit. *"Ca va bien, merci,"* she responded. "And you?"

"A little tired. Lots of flying lately," he answered.

"So we've heard!" she nodded. "You're glad for the rain, eh?"

"You bet!"

Barnes's entrance carrying the lounge chair was followed by the appearance of Dr. Lerossi. He greeted the pilot and the cook, then crossed the room to Yvette. "How's it going?" he asked, sitting in the chair that Barnes put beside her cot.

"You planned this, didn't you?" she smiled.

"Let's say it was a joint effort. I had the idea; DiMarzo carried it out. I felt that was a fair division of labor."

"It was a lovely idea," she said. "Thanks."

"Holy cow!"

Davis's exclamation from the salon entrance interrupted their exchange. The medic tiptoed toward the table as if afraid the culinary largesse was a mirage and might vanish if he startled it. He beamed at the cook. "Since you're a thief, thank God you're a good one."

DiMarzo shrugged off the compliment. "It was nothing."

"Brownies!" Davis persisted. "Where in Normandy can you steal brownies?"

"They're courtesy of the Lieutenant," the cook explained.

"Jeez, I'm glad we invited him," Davis breathed.

"How great to be appreciated just for oneself," James murmured.

"O.K., everybody. Take your places," DiMarzo directed.

James and Davis sat cross-legged on the floor; Barnes took the other chair beside Yvette's cot. DiMarzo poured the tea, and passed the delicacies around. He accepted the praise that rained down upon him with his usual poise. Whatever bribes, threats, or 'you-owe-me-one' debts he'd employed to accumulate such abundance remained undisclosed. When the last crumbs had disappeared, the group lingered over a final cup of tea. Barnes leaned back in his chair and patted his stomach. "You've done it again, DiMarzo. This party ranks right up there with the Bar-B-Que."

"Ain't that the truth," Davis agreed.

James looked at Yvette. "That's when we heard about you. During the Bar-B-Que, Colonel Kleine announced that you were coming to stay with us."

Yvette looked puzzled. "What is the Bar-B-Que?"

In a few words he explained the outdoor picnic.

"But where did one obtain the cow?" she asked.

"We owe it to the Lieutenant." Davis gave the pilot a smart salute.

DiMarzo crossed himself. "May I live long enough to forget that night."

"I was only trying to help Doc Roberts," James insisted.

"Please!" Yvette interrupted. "Tell me about the Bar-B-Que."

James leaned forward and rested his elbows on his knees. "Doc Roberts is the Flight Surgeon for my squadron. His French is good, so he's our liaison with the town. Frisky was one year old on July 15th, and Colonel Kleine decided we ought to celebrate. He told Doc to organize a party. When Doc asked for suggestions, I proposed a Bar-B-Que."

DiMarzo rolled his eyes.

James ignored the cook's pained expression. "Everybody thought that was a wonderful idea so Doc put out some feelers, and located a farmer near La Fiere who was willing to sell us a steer."

As the story progressed, Dr. Lerossi translated for Yvette the slang expressions he thought she might find difficult. Yvette was surprised at how well she understood the pilot who spoke slowly for her benefit.

"The hitch was," James continued, "the farmer said he couldn't deliver the cow—we'd have to pick it up. The only vehicle we could round up was a jeep."

"Impossible!" Yvette murmured.

James shrugged. "It was that or walk the beast back to the field tied to a rope. For some reason that I've forgotten, it was late afternoon by the time we got started."

His voice had taken on a kind of lilt, much like that typical of the country people of Normandy when they launched into a tale such as this. As Yvette listened, she imagined him sitting around a camp fire with other cowboys spinning yarns. She watched him gesticulate with strong, big-knuckled hands. Probably they used to be calloused from hard work. Now they were smooth and supple. "I sat beside DiMarzo who drove the jeep," she picked up the story's thread, "while from the back seat, Doc directed us to the farm which, after the Calvados we'd drunk, was pretty hard to find. We got there just as night was falling. The farmer led out the cow, I looked it over, and Doc paid him what he asked." James shook his head. "Doc Roberts is pretty good with sick folks, but he ain't worth a durn when it comes to wrestlin' a steer onto the hood of a jeep."

"I don't imagine the cow enjoyed the experience either," Dr. Lerossi smiled.

"That was part of the problem," James conceded. "Anyhow,

we persuaded Doc to stand out of the way and, by the time the dust had settled, DiMarzo, the farmer, and I had tied the steer right snug—"

"—with its head facing front, and its hindquarters next the windshield," DiMarzo interrupted. "Big, brave Tom Mix here couldn't stand to look at the cow's mournful eyes on the way back to the airfield and know that when we got there, he'd have to kill it." He scratched his head. "Funny. At the time, that made sense."

"Apple brandy does that to you," Davis spoke up.

"The farmer and his wife waved good-bye and we drove off. God knows what they were thinking," James smiled. "Anyhow, we got up to the road O.K., but the night was black as the inside of a cave, and those regulation cat's-eye headlights didn't make a dent. After we almost drove into a ditch, DiMarzo switched onto full beam. The jeep purred along, the cow seemed to have settled down for the ride, so we had another nip of doc's Calvados and belted out a ditty or two. Then it began to rain, which called for the windshield wiper. That was when I began to have second thoughts about the position of that cow."

The cook shuddered.

"The problem was that every time the wiper crossed the windshield, it nicked the cow's hind leg," the pilot explained to Yvette. "And each time it got nicked, the cow flicked its tail back across the windshield that the wiper had just cleaned."

Yvette smiled.

"It's surprising how much dirt, leaves, and crawling things one tail can pick up from a barnyard. For awhile the contest between the tail and the wiper was a draw. It was kind of like watching a ping-pong game, and we even laid bets on which would win. But," the pilot grimaced, "the cow finally reached the end of its tether, and lost control of one of its major bodily functions. Needless to say, the windshield wiper wasn't equal to the task."

"*Quelle horreur,*" Yvette said.

"*Quelle horreur,*" James agreed. "DiMarzo couldn't see a thing, so I stood up to give him directions. Just when I was beginning to feel like General Patton leading the Third Army across France, we heard this shout behind us: 'Halt!'"

"No!" Yvette exclaimed.

"'We've crossed the German lines,'" Doc yelled. "'Get the hell out of here!' So DiMarzo floored the gas pedal, and we careened down the road. 'Faster!' Doc hollered. 'They're gaining on us!' Trees blurred together, the rush of wind nearly took our hats off but still they bore down on us like a hound after a rabbit. Doc stood up mad as a hornet, shook his fist at them and nearly fell out of the jeep. With that, shots rang out and dirt kicked up in the road ahead. Above the bawling of the cow and the ricochet of bullets, suddenly we heard: 'Turn those damn lights off!'"

Yvette's eyes widened. *"Les Americains?"*

James nodded. "DiMarzo screeched to a stop and a jeep with two military police pulled up beside us. God, they were mad! 'Douse the light!' one of them yelled. 'You trying to get yourselves killed? These woods are crawling with Krauts.'"

"Mon Dieu," Yvette murmured.

"It took awhile to explain the cow, but Doc's a good talker. They agreed not to press charges for trespassing in a restricted zone if we high-tailed it back to the field and stayed there. DiMarzo and I thought that was mighty nice, didn't we?" James looked at the cook.

"Yeah, but Doc was really miffed," DiMarzo answered. "'What kind of war is this when your own side is more dangerous than the enemy?'" he grumbled.

"The next day I slaughtered the cow." For a moment, the pilot looked doleful. "I felt like I was doing in a buddy after all we'd been through together. My maintenance crew rigged up some grills out of used oil barrels, and DiMarzo outdid himself with the food. Some of the guys put on skits, we had a baseball game, and Doc had rounded up a comedian from Special Services who did a show."

"It sounds like the Bar-B-Que was a great success," Yvette smiled.

"A party we'll remember for a long time," James agreed.

Yvette looked around at the circle of faces. "This is a party I'll never forget."

A chorus of "Hear, hear," "You bet," "Right on," answered her.

James pushed himself to his feet. He looked at Yvette. "I'll try to stop by tomorrow to see how you're doing. Is that O.K.?"

"That would be nice," she answered.

His face which moments before had been animated, now was sober. "Good luck."

She nodded.

He told the others good-bye. "Thanks for a great time," he said. They watched him leave. "Nice guy," Davis said.

"One of the best," DiMarzo agreed.

25

When Yvette awoke, the rain had stopped. Today was the day. With mingled fear and anticipation, she eyed her cast gleaming in the dim morning light. How wonderful to be free of its confinement, yet as long as it was there, she had hope. Once it was gone, she must face the secret that it hid. Would she have an arm that functioned—one that would help her gain a life of her own? Or one that didn't, which would insure her dependence from now on. The specter of a wheelchair brought tears to her eyes.

A stir at the entrance cut short her painful reverie. *"Bonjour, Mademoiselle."* It was Davis.

She blinked quickly. *"Bonjour, Monsieur,"* she answered.

He crossed to the cot and turned on the light. He looked at her a moment in silence. "You've been awake awhile," he accused her. "Why didn't you call?"

"It's still so dark, I thought it might be very early."

"That's no excuse."

She smiled. "I can be awake and alone for five minutes. It won't kill me."

"There are twelve hundred of us. Isn't that enough? Someone is always available to stay with you."

"But I hate to bother—"

"Godamighty! Will you get this through your hard head. You," he pointed a finger at her, "are not a burden to me," he jerked a thumb at his chest, "or anybody else," he whirled his arm in a circle, "on this whole damn airfield. Do I make myself clear?"

"Yes sir," she answered meekly.

"How many times have we had this conversation! I'm getting sick of it." He turned away to make preparations for her bath.

"My! We are grumpy this morning, aren't we? It must be very early."

"No, it's not early. The sky is overcast." He began to wash her face. "I hate it when you cry. I want so much to help you and I can't."

She swallowed painfully. "No more tears. I promise."

He was silent a moment. "Dr. Lerossi will take your cast off after sick call," he volunteered. "About ten o'clock."

"What time is it now?"

"Eight."

Do I want it to be a short two hours, or very long, she wondered.

Finished with her toilette, he gathered his utensils. "I'll tell DiMarzo that you're ready."

She watched him cross to the door. In this short time, he'd grown as close to her as one of her brothers. Perhaps he was most like Michel, who felt other peoples' hurts more than he felt his own. Yet there was some of Henri in him—the joking and the good camaraderie. But a worker, too, like Georges. As his list of virtues grew, Yvette smiled. He would never recognize himself.

The cook had fixed pancakes for her, but as he slid the tray onto the table, his usual verve was missing. "How are you doing?"

"Keep your fingers crossed," she said.

"Along with my eyes, toes and ears, if it would do any good." He went through the routine of the right amount of syrup and butter with Davis, but after a couple of mouthfuls, she shook her head.

"I'm sorry you went to so much trouble. Maybe after it's over, I'll be hungry."

"I understand." He picked up the tray. "I'll check back with you later."

Davis stayed with her while well-wishers came and went. For once, she wished she could be without company. The effort of talking with them was wearing, and the pretense that everything would come out all right was getting on her nerves. The steamy August heat made her irritable, hot and sticky. She longed to close her eyes; to lie still and silent, with a cool cloth covering her forehead. Davis glanced often at his watch. Finally, "It's time," he said.

It had been a long two hours.

"Will you be here?" she said.

He shook his head. "I've got sick bay duty. Barnes is going to help Dr. Lerossi."

Moments later, they filed into the tent. The medic carried a black leather bag.

"How's my favorite patient?" the doctor asked.

"Ca va," she answered.

He noted her strained expression. "You look tired, Yvette. We could put it off until later."

"No, no," she said. "I'm O.K."

"All right," he stroked her hair. "We'll get started."

The medics moved her cot away from the wall. While Barnes took instruments from the black bag and arranged them on the table, Davis folded Yvette's bed-sheet down to her hips. He smiled encouragement, and gave her a thumbs up gesture. "I'll be back," he said, and hurried from the tent.

Dr. Lerossi motioned Barnes to the other side of the cot, then picked up the foot-long cast cutter. "All set?" he asked.

She nodded. She stiffened when the cold metal touched her stomach. The crunch of the thick, serrated blade into the plaster sounded like a sheet ripping. "Let's get the spreader in there," Dr. Lerossi said. Barnes inserted the wedge into the opening and forced the two sides apart. "Good. Now I've got a beachhead," the doctor grunted.

Step by slow step, the cutter and the spreader leapfrogged up the front of the cast. It was a tedious process, done at an awkward angle. The plaster yielded reluctantly. As Yvette regarded the two intent faces above her, she wondered if they'd forgotten her. She scarcely breathed, fearing to distract them. When they approached her neck, the doctor took a hook-nosed knife from the table. "Turn your head to the side," he instructed her, "and keep still." He winked. "I didn't contract to take out your tonsils, too."

His bit of humor released some of her tension and, as the last segment of the cast parted under the knife, she sighed with relief.

The doctor straightened. "Now it gets a little difficult. This is called a bivalve procedure because we open up the cast like you would an oyster. We need to prop you over on your left side so we can get to your back."

It was easier said than done. Without the use of her legs to act as stabilizers, she had nothing to counterbalance the weight of the cast on her right arm. As a makeshift, they wedged her all around with pillows. The army cot had none of the rigidity of an operating table, and offered no resistance to the force needed to cut the cast. The result was that her body was in constant motion. The swaying made her dizzy, and her neck ached from her uncomfortable position. The heat in the tent had become suffocating. Yvette felt frustrated at being powerless to help. She listened to the grunts and muttered expletives of the other two and knew that, like herself, they must be bathed in sweat. She lost track of time. An eternity later, she heard Dr. Lerossi say, "Here we go," and the cast loosened at the back of her neck.

"How are you doing?" he asked.

She could only nod.

He looked at her exhausted face. "We'll rest a little before we tackle your arm."

Gently, he and Barnes eased her onto her back. She took a deep breath, filling her lungs. "After two months in a straitjacket, breathing is going to be a new experience," Barnes smiled. He wet a cloth and bathed her face.

"Oh, that feels so good."

He held a glass of water to her lips, and she emptied it without pause. "I'm ready now," she said.

The tedium of cutting, slicing and wedging began anew, starting at the back of her right hand and working up her arm. The bend at her elbow momentarily slowed the progress, and separating the cast at her shoulder required patience and care. Finally, it was done and, like squires removing plates of armor from their feudal lord, the doctor and the medic freed her body from its plaster prison. The stench made her gag.

"Mother of God!" she gasped.

"I should have warned you," Dr. Lerossi sympathized.

"I reek like a dead goat," she wailed.

He laughed. "The good news is that the reek isn't permanent. Once you've had a bath, it will only be a bad memory."

She sank into her pillows and reveled in her new freedom. "My skin feels so cool. I want to scratch, and scratch, and scratch."

"Not yet." The doctor covered her with a sheet. "Your skin is very fragile now, and with rough treatment, it might bleed. We must treat it gently for awhile."

Her left arm had no muscle definition, and was weak. Still, the collar bone was mended and the flesh wounds in her upper arm were well healed. Gingerly she flexed her elbow, then rotated her stiff shoulder. Dr. Lerossi waited patiently. Finally, she looked up at him.

"And now my right one. I guess I can't put it off any longer."

"Whenever you're ready," he answered.

In apprehension, she watched him loosen each of her fingers from the plaster; held her breath while he and Barnes pried open the severed cast. It yielded with a snap. Yvette recoiled as her arm, thin and shapeless as a stick, lay exposed. The dark hair had grown long and was matted with flakes of dead skin. At the junction of wrist and forearm, there was a bony protuberance below which her hand jutted at an oblique angle to the left. Above her elbow, a crater yawned as if a vicious animal had torn out a piece of the flesh. The skin around the wound was as puckered as the mouth of a drawstring purse. A red, angry-looking scar wrapped around her shoulder.

She was too stunned for words. Barnes removed the cast and, in a daze, she watched Dr. Lerossi take the stick in both his hands. He examined all its wounds. "Thank God, they're clean," he murmured to the medic. Gently, he manipulated the wrist, then little by little, worked his way up to her shoulder testing to see if there was "give" to any of the bones. Satisfied that they had knitted properly, he placed the arm on her lap. "For the moment, I want you to forget its appearance," he began. He looked up, and his eyes narrowed as he noted her blank expression. "You felt a change in temperature on your arm when we opened the cast, didn't you?"

She gazed at him vacantly.

He pointed to her hand. "Try to move it."

She stared at the stick lying inanimate as a dead bird on the sheet. It did not belong to her. Why should she move it?

"Yvette," Dr. Lerossi said sharply. "I said to move your hand!"

She was tired of his badgering. She wished he would go away.

"You're not trying. Pay attention when I speak to you!" He snapped out the words in a staccato voice. "You're still disturbed about how it looks. I want you to concentrate on whether it will move."

She frowned, peeved at his tone of voice.

He leaned toward her. "Did you hear me!"

Yvette shrank away from his insistence. Her mouth quivered, and she began to sniffle.

He threw up his hands in disgust. "So now we're going to cry. That's a big help! God damn it!" he suddenly yelled. "Stop acting like a spoiled rotten little brat."

She jerked upright as if he'd slapped her across the face. Her eyes blazed, and in her rage her fingers curled upward as if her hand were trying to form a fist.

"Hey, Doc! You did it!" Barnes shouted.

"Whew," Dr. Lerossi shook his head.

As if awaking from a dream, Yvette looked from the doctor to the medic. Then wonderstruck, she examined her hand. "It works," she whispered.

"It works," the doctor repeated. "Time, effort, patience—you'll need all three, but you can walk again."

26

The reek that had so appalled Yvette became, as Dr. Lerossi predicted, a memory. After Barnes had bathed her, he rubbed her with a lanolin cream. Dressed in a clean hospital gown, she lay back on her pillows, and sighed with pleasure. "Now I smell like a rose."

Her good news spread rapidly, and her tent became clogged with well-wishers. She welcomed them all. Finally Dr. Lerossi called a halt. "Yvette's had a busy day. She needs to rest."

Lunch was a messy affair. She insisted on feeding herself with her weak left hand. As often as not, the food missed her mouth, and dropped to the towel which Barnes had placed across her chest. She was not deterred and, when she'd finished, she looked at the medic with triumphant eyes. "What do you think of that!"

"I think you're about to do me out of a job," he grumbled.

When she awoke from her nap, the medic brought her a parcel wrapped in brown paper and tied with string. Attached was a note which she translated aloud to Barnes.

"'Dear Yvette,

"'I've thought of you often, and get news of you through relatives of yours in St. Jores. You were the most talented pupil I ever had. Hang on to your dreams. With your determination, they could still come true.

"'I'm sending you this bundle hoping its contents will cheer you. The material is courtesy of those brave American paratroopers who not only brought us our freedom, but also supplied us with clothes!

"'Kindest regards,

"'Madame DuBois'"

"What dreams?" Barnes asked.

Yvette shook her head. "Nothing."

"What dreams?" he persisted.

"I'd hoped to become a clothes designer," she muttered.

"Why do you put it in the past tense?" he asked.

"Why do you think?" she snapped. "Because it's in the past."

"Oh? There are lots of people with two good legs who can't design clothes. Is something the matter with your head? I thought that's where ideas came from."

"It's not that simple. First you must study in a school of design, then apprentice in a *maison* in Paris. The competition is intense, it takes a lot of time and—"

"Well," he interrupted, "like they say—you have to really want something to make it happen." He shrugged. "I guess it wasn't that important to you."

"How can you say that?" she bristled. "It's been my dream ever since I can remember!"

Startled by her own vehemence, she stared at the medic. Wasn't the dream dead? She thought it had been buried under the debris of that exploding shell. Perhaps it was only biding its time—waiting for the right moment to reappear. "Barnes, do you think that it's possible?"

"For anyone who has pulled through what you have," he nodded, "Yes!"

She wanted to throw her arms around his neck. By the time she had finished her rehabilitation, the couture school would be back in operation again, and she would enroll. With her handicap, she would have to work twice as hard as everyone else, but hard work was nothing new to her. She would— She saw him smiling at her. "You can daydream later," he said. "Let's see what's in your package."

He untied the string, and from the brown paper bundle spilled three bed jackets made from different colored parachute silk. The medic held up the white one for her inspection. "How pretty!" she exclaimed. "Look!" she pointed to the ruffled collar. "That's like the flower I embroidered the first day I joined her class. Imagine her remembering!"

"Which one would you like to wear?" he asked.

She studied the three colors. "The blue."

He helped her slip the jacket over her hospital gown. After he adjusted her right arm into a sling, he tied the ribbons at her throat into a bow. He stood back to look her over. "That's your color," he agreed. He held up the mirror.

He was right. Her skin had come alive, and the blue was the exact shade of her eyes. She smiled at her reflection.

"O.K., that's enough." Barnes slid the mirror onto the table. "You'll be so stuck up, none of us will be able to stand you."

"We can't have that," she agreed. "Now, may I go out on the salon."

"Hmmm," the medic glanced toward the entrance. "The weather has changed. It's getting chilly."

"But I have my new jacket to keep me warm."

"Dr. Lerossi will have my head if you catch cold."

"I never catch cold. Please, I'm dying for some fresh air."

"All right," he relented. "Let me find someone to help me move your cot."

Although the sky was leaden and the ground soggy, being outdoors lifted her spirits. Ordinarily, the air in late August was redolent with the smell of hay. But this year, danger from unexploded shells and hand grenades had kept the farmers from their fields. She thought of her father watching in dismay as crops withered where they stood. The coming winter would be as hard as any since the German invasion. Autumn was almost here. When September arrived, the war would be five years old.

"Mademoiselle, forgive me if I interrupt your thoughts."

James's voice startled her. She stared at him over her shoulder, her face reflecting her surprise. "I didn't mean to frighten you," he apologized. "I thought you heard me coming."

He stood under the elongated tent flap, his back to the light. His broad-shouldered silhouette took her breath away. "You— you usually come through the gap by the mess tent," she stammered. *Mon Dieu,* how silly that sounded. As if she sat here all the time waiting for him.

He didn't seem to notice. "Today I stopped by to see Doc

Roberts. It was quicker to come the other way." He walked toward her pulling off his cap. "I heard the good news. I thought I'd let everyone else congratulate you first, then you'd have time just for me."

Her pulse hammered in her ears. "Have a seat,' she said. "Your French gets better all the time," she hurried on as he moved the lounge chair so the foot was at right angles to the cot.

"That's because I've got the best teacher around." He sat down facing her. His leather jacket was open down the front, his khaki shirt unbuttoned at the throat. She saw the faint mark on his forehead where his cap had been. Though he was an arm's length away, she felt his nearness pressing on her.

"Dr. Lerossi and I had lunch together," James propped his elbows on his knees. "He told me about how you moved your hand."

"I won't forget *that* scene for quite a while."

"He said you get mad real good. I like that."

She looked to see if he were teasing, but his face was serious. "I don't like pouting," he went on. "I'd rather people blow up and clear the air."

"The air in the tent was very clear," she assured him.

He smiled at that, then tilting his head, he eyed her new jacket. "That's parachute silk, isn't it?"

She told him about Madame Dubois.

"If I meet any paratroopers from the 82nd or 101st Airborne Divisions, I'll tell them how pretty you look."

Her face flushed under his gaze. To divert his attention, she told him of standing with her family at the upstairs window early on the morning of D-Day, and watching the parachutists landing in the fields. She tried to convey their awe at realizing that the long-awaited Allied invasion had begun.

"I flew the first mission that morning," he said. "From the buildup in traffic going by our airfield the night before, we knew something unusual was happening. When they woke us, we were told: 'This is it.'" His eyes narrowed. "Those thousands of ships, as far as you could see. We were supposed to protect them from enemy aircraft, but no German planes showed up. We had the skies to ourselves. I didn't envy those poor guys on the landing crafts. Seasick, packed in like sardines. They knew that even if they made it to shore, a lot of them would die on the beaches."

He grimaced; shook his head. "I didn't come to talk about the war." He took an envelope from his pocket. "I got a letter from home today. I want to show you some pictures of my family."

"I'd like that," she answered.

His expression softened as he handed her the first snapshot. "My younger brother. He's your age—sixteen."

Yvette looked at the boy leaning against a split-rail fence. One of his arms was draped over the top log of the fence, a boot-clad foot rested on the bottom rung. The shock of sandy hair, the smile, the unselfconscious pose was that of a younger James.

"You're sure that isn't you?"

"People do say we favor."

"Then it's Luke," she smiled.

"What a memory you've got." He leaned forward to look at the photo over her shoulder. She smelled his leather jacket, heard his breathing. The place where his arm brushed hers felt on fire. "My mother had wanted a girl," James went on. "It took awhile for her to get reconciled to another boy. Even though I'm four years older, Luke and I have always been real close." His face clouded. "I hope to God the war is over before he turns eighteen. I couldn't stand it if anything happened to the guy."

She'd scarcely heard his words. She'd listened only to the sound of his voice. "My older brother, Bart," James went on, handing her another snapshot, "teaching his little girl how to ride."

Yvette forced herself to concentrate on the young man in work clothes wearing a cowboy hat, and the little girl dressed in a ruffled smock. She sat astride the pony that he was leading by the reins. Her head was thrown back in a carefree laugh while her hands clutched the pony's mane. The picture struck a chord in Yvette's memory. "How old is she?"

"Five. Her name is Melinda."

"I was five when I rode my first pony," Yvette mused. "Michel led it past the kitchen window so Maman could see."

"Michel?" he asked.

"My brother. I have seven older brothers."

"Then you must be very spoiled," he smiled.

"Yes, indeed."

"I spoil my niece and, if she'll turn out like you, I'll go on spoiling her."

He said it matter-of-factly, without embellishment.

At a loss for words, she watched him flip through the rest of the photographs as if looking for a special one. "Here it is." He handed her the snapshot. "My family."

She looked at the group sheltered by the branches of a giant fir. They were gathered in a two-row semicircle around a seated man. Yvette recognized Luke, Bart and Melinda. James pointed out his mother, father and Bart's wife.

"Who are the others?" she asked.

"Cow hands, wranglers, the cook, trail bosses, the foreman," James answered. "The foreman was like an uncle to us boys— taught us how to ride, rope a steer, and lots of other things." He waited a moment. "Aren't you curious about my father?"

"Should I be?" she asked.

"He's sitting in a wheelchair."

Jolted, she examined the photograph more closely. Where before, the wheelchair had faded into the shadows under the tree, now it leaped out at her. "What happened?"

"Four years ago, he was thrown from a horse into a ravine. We searched for twelve hours before we found him. Pinned under the horse, he was almost dead."

"How awful," Yvette sympathized.

"He pulled through, but both legs had to be amputated." James slid the snapshots back into the envelope. "Ever since the accident, he's wondered why he lived."

"I know the feeling," Yvette said.

James laced his hands together. "Living with his bitterness has shown me what an unusual person you are."

"Don't give me too much credit," Yvette shook her head. "I was bitter. I wanted to die."

"At the beginning—of course," James agreed. "But now, you're moving on—making plans. Every day, my Dad feels sorrier for himself."

"It's easy to judge," Yvette answered. "Unless you've been there—don't."

"I haven't. I'm too much like him," he said. "I would be judging myself."

She thought of the agonizing weeks, the closeness of death. What *had* kept her alive? "There's no predicting how you'll act until it happens."

"I know I couldn't be like you," he countered, "and that's one reason I joined the Air Force. I wanted to survive this war intact or else buy the farm."

"What does that mean?" she asked.

"You don't see many mutilated pilots because very few walk away from a crash," he answered.

As she looked at the symmetry of his face, the interplay of bone on muscle, she saw superimposed on that perfection the bandaged, motionless head of her "Professor." She heard Michel's voice: "They say he'll never see again," and gave an involuntary shudder.

"You're cold." His voice was concerned.

Before she could think of an answer, he'd shed his jacket. He draped it around her shoulders and its warmth enfolded her as if he'd taken her in his arms. A stillness settled on her. The struggle to keep him distant was over. Was this new contentment in his nearness good or bad? She no longer knew—or cared.

"Is that better?" he asked.

"Much better."

"With a pair of goggles and a white silk scarf, you'd make a hell of a pilot," he smiled. "I'd trust you to fly my wing any time."

27

A shout awoke Yvette from her afternoon nap. "The Germans have surrendered Paris!" A moment later, Dr. Lerossi entered her tent on the run. "General von Cholitz has capitulated to General LeClerc at the Prefecture de Police."

Blinking, Yvette pushed herself to a sitting position. "Not so fast!" she protested. "Start at the beginning." Her face clouded. "Did they destroy—"

"No, they gave up the city intact."

"Thank God."

He sat on the edge of the chair beside her cot. "Patton's troops were at Fontainebleu, the French Underground had come out of hiding, the Police were on strike. The Germans knew it was hopeless." He got up and paced the room. "At Le Mans, General Eisenhower received word that they were ready to come to terms. The streets are jammed, everybody's gone wild." His eyes glowed. "I spent a year in Paris as a student before the war. How I'd love to be there now!"

"In 1940, the Boches had a victory parade past the Arc de Triomphe. Today," Yvette gloated, "they're marching to a different tune."

"August 25th," Dr. Lerossi mused. "A date to remember."

"What happens now?" she asked.

"If the German military had any sense, they'd hang Hitler and end the war before their country is obliterated. But—no such luck." Dr. Lerossi stopped his pacing to face her. "The further east the Germans retreat, the longer distances our pilots must fly. Soon, we'll have to move closer to the front."

Leave La Londe! She held her breath.

"You still need care and medication that a French civilian

hospital can't provide. What would you think of going with us?"

She stared at him. "Go with you? How?"

"There's always room in a cargo plane. You'd be flown to the new location, along with your tent—lock, stock and barrel."

How simple he made it sound. She could only imagine the complications that moving her would entail. "Where would we go?" she asked.

"St. James has been eliminated—it's already too far behind the lines. Le Mans is under consideration."

"But the Colonel—? What would he say?"

"It was his idea. 'We can't get along without our Mascot,' he said. For classification purposes, you've been labeled: 'Morale Booster.' The Transportation guys didn't blink an eye."

"Morale Booster," she smiled. "I like that. And am I?"

"As if you needed to be told." He shoved his hands into his pockets and walked slowly toward the cot. "It's against all the rules. Military regulations prohibit involvement with civilians. Colonel Kleine thinks you're worth the risk." His eyes softened. "So do I."

She shook her head. "I'll never be able to thank—"

He leaned over and put his finger across her lips. "Your getting better is thanks enough. Now," he continued briskly, "let's have a look at that arm."

The sight of it was no longer repugnant to her, though she marveled that such a rigid, misshapened appendage could ever function again. Since the removal of her cast, it had seemed to Yvette that either Barnes or Davis had been at her side unwrapping its bandages, massaging it, manipulating her fingers, wrist and shoulder, applying warm compresses, then rewrapping the bandages. They were gentle, but every move was painful. She gritted her teeth and gripped the edge of the bed with her other hand in order not to cry out. Her efforts and the medics' care had paid off. Now she was able to flex her fingers slightly, and raise her arm slowly from lap to shoulder height.

"Steady improvement," Dr. Lerossi gave a satisfied nod. "Soon, it'll be time to start more vigorous exercises. Good muscle tone in your upper body will be a must when you learn to walk." He pursed his lips. "A metal bar suspended over the cot would do it. I'll stir up one of the mechanics to get to work on it."

"When will we leave?" she asked.

"No one knows. Tomorrow I'll go to Coigny to get your parents' permission for you to accompany us. Don't worry," he added, seeing her anxious look. "Our medical unit will be the last to leave. You'll have plenty of time to see them."

"Another good-bye," Yvette murmured when Dr. Lerossi had departed. She recalled her parents' farewell on the evening she was wounded. Their anguished looks as she was carried from the kitchen had convinced her that she would never return. And then there was her father's good-bye kiss at La Fiere. Little did either of them know that, by mistake, she would be taken to the Pasteur Hospital. The coming separation would not be traumatic like the other two. Still, any change carried with it its own uncertainties. At La Londe she felt secure, knowing that her family was readily available. To no longer see the dear familiar faces or hear the news of home—

And James. Would the new locale change everything? The distance between his quarters and her tent might be too great for the visits she anticipated more eagerly with every passing day. Despite the incessant air activity of late, he'd found odd moments to drop by for a chat. She never knew when to expect him, and if he came during one of her exercise sessions, he waited patiently until she was finished. Although he seldom spoke of his air exploits—where he'd been or how dangerous the mission—they talked of everything else. He told her of the house where he'd been born.

"Not as old as yours, of course, but the foundation was laid by my great-grandfather. Three generations of cattle ranchers have added to it. The chimney was built of granite boulders washed down by glaciers from the high peaks." She reminisced about Christmas Eve candlelight processions to the church at Baupte, and excursions with her mother to visit the *Comtesse*. He described the excitement of a cattle roundup; she the rigors of milking ten cows in the predawn cold of winter.

The moments they spent together were her reward for the

hours of painful exercises she endured when they were apart. Every time he left her tent, she prayed for his safe return.

"Bonjour, Mademoiselle."

As if in answer to her latest prayer, he stood at the door, waiting to let his eyes grow accustomed to the dimmer light. "I just passed Dr. Lerossi. He said you're doing great."

"The man has no mercy," she groaned as, hands in his pockets, the pilot strolled toward the cot. "He's starting me on another round of exercises. Soon I'll have muscles like a weightlifter."

James braced himself. "I'll remember to keep a safe distance," he said, then sat down in the chair beside her. "He also told me that, with your parents' permission, you'll go with us when we leave La Londe."

"That was a surprise!"

"It makes good sense."

"I don't need convincing," she assured him.

He looked at her intently for a moment, then shook his head. "I heard about the Pasteur Hospital. Do those memories still bother you?"

"Not lately." She pretended to be piqued. "Dr. Lerossi doesn't give me any time at all to mope."

"Good for the old Slave Driver," James replied. He took a small package from the pocket of his flight jacket. "My mother sent you a present," he said.

"Me?" Yvette exclaimed. "How did she know about me?"

"From my letters. She's very interested in your progress."

Bemused, Yvette gazed at the parcel he handed her. It was wrapped in white tissue paper and tied with a yellow ribbon. That it had come such a distance, from someone she'd never met, filled her with wonder. She untied the ribbon and, without thinking, wound it carefully around her finger. Feeling his eyes fixed on her, she looked up and met his smile. "Force of habit," she flushed. "On the farm, we saved everything."

"That's exactly what my mother would have done," he answered.

From the folds of the tissue paper, Yvette lifted two lace-bordered handkerchiefs, and a pair of silver earrings fastened to a flowered card. She looked at the pilot with shining eyes. "They're lovely. How kind of her to think of me."

"She wrote you a note." James showed her the other side of the card.

As Yvette read aloud the message of good cheer, and hope that her progress would continue, a lump caught at her throat. "She must be a wonderful person."

"She is," James replied. "She's had a rough time with my Dad, but she never complains."

Yvette touched the lacy filigree of the earrings. "Every time I wear these, I'll think of her."

"Would you like to put them on?" he asked.

She examined the tiny screws which served as the clasp. "I can't manage these quite yet. I'll wait for Davis."

"Well, I've roped a steer, shoed a horse and flown a plane. I think I could handle two of those," he answered, taking the card.

He removed the earrings and set the card aside. "Turn your head," he said.

As she looked into his clear gray eyes only inches from her own, her heart pounded and she could scarcely breathe. Intent on his task, his teeth caught at his lower lip. With a few deft twists of the screws, both earrings were soon in place. The procedure lasted a bare ten seconds, but the touch of his hand against her cheek was sweeter than any caress she'd ever dreamed of.

"How's that?" he asked.

She managed to swallow. "Perfect," she answered.

He dusted off his hands. "Piece of cake."

She lifted her eyebrows. "What is the piece of cake."

He smiled. "Slang for something that's easy. I'll write my mother and tell her how pretty you look."

She was saved from having to answer by Davis's appearance. James pushed himself to his feet.

"No need to shove off, Lieutenant," the medic protested.

"I need a couple of hours sack time before my next flight," the pilot answered.

"They're really putting it to you guys, but it's sure brought results, hasn't it?" Davis eyed the pilot admiringly. "General Patton doesn't hand out TAC commendations just for looking good."

"The old boy went all out," James agreed.

"Say, Lieutenant, you heard any rumors that we'll be leaving soon?" the medic asked.

"About every hour on the hour," James laughed. "Let's see—the latest is that at 0700 day after tomorrow, we head for Stuttgart."

"I heard it was Brussels."

"Your rumor is as good as mine," James shrugged. "By tonight, it may be Berlin."

"Berlin!" The medic shook his head. "That'll be the day!"

James looked at Yvette. "I'll be seeing you."

"Thanks for—everything," she answered.

He nodded, then headed for the door. "See you in Berlin, Davis," he called over his shoulder.

The medic smiled. As he slid the compresses for her arm on the bedside table, he eyed her earrings. "Something new has been added."

Yvette told him about the presents and note from James's mother. "And she doesn't even know me."

"She must be a very fine person. Like mother like son, eh?"

"Ain't that the truth," Yvette imitated the medic's accent.

Davis nodded approvingly. "Spoken like a native."

She watched him unwrap the bandages from her arm. "How does a Group as big as this pack up and leave?"

"It takes lots of planning. This time, thank God, we won't get seasick!" He applied the warm cloth to her elbow. "The Colonel scouts out the region that WING has selected, then the engineers go in and prepare the landing strip. The Service Squadron sets up whatever kind of bivouac we'll occupy. The pilots fly the planes and everything else from tents to hypodermic needles is hauled on trucks."

As the steps involved in the undertaking grew more detailed, Yvette marveled that Colonel Kleine would consider adding her transportation to the complicated process.

"Dr. Lerossi told me that, with my parents' permission, I'm going with you," she said when he'd finished.

The medic waited a moment, then frowned. "So?"

"Well—I mean it was a surprise. You know, I, I"— she fumbled. "I didn't expect—"

Davis let her flounder. Finally, he eyed her suspiciously. "Stop beating around the bush. You want to get rid of us." He nodded, knowingly. "You got a better offer—those wimps in the tanks. You think they're handsomer than us Air Force types."

"Crazy!"

"Of course you're going. The outfit would come unglued if you didn't." His face sobered as he put his joking aside. "It'll be tough on you—leaving your folks. But you'll be with us. We don't know any more about where we're going than you do. We'll all be in the same boat."

The fall of Paris had triggered a flood of speculations and, by late afternoon, Yvette felt that she'd been told every single one: Hitler and Mussolini were dead; the Russians had taken Poland; the German army wanted to surrender. Of more immediate concern was where and when the 371st Fighter Group would move. Ruminations on the possibilities were endless. When DiMarzo came to pick up her dinner tray and informed her that positively it would be Metz on Thursday, she wanted to shout: enough!

The morning after her new exercise program began, Barnes came to inform her that someone wanted to see her. "He wouldn't give his name. 'Just tell her it's her brother,'" he quoted.

Yvette stared at the medic. Only one brother would be reluctant to identify himself. How often, during her weeks of pain and hopelessness, she'd imagined this confrontation. Now it would come to pass.

"Yvette, shall I show him in?" Barnes prodded.

She nodded.

He gave her a puzzled look, then disappeared, and moments later Henri was at the door. Red-faced, avoiding her eyes, he shuffled toward the cot. Like a child who knows that nothing he says will make any difference, he stood cap in hand, staring at the floor.

"You finally came." Her voice was cold, without inflection.

"I didn't have the courage to face you," he answered.

"*Mon Dieu!* took courage!"

"The first of July will always haunt me." He blinked. "I never thought anything like this would happen to you—I just wanted to get the damn chore over with!" He shuddered. "In my nightmares, I see the shell explode, and hear you cry."

She was crying now. "I hated you. I never again wanted to hear your name."

Numbly, he nodded.

"When Papa told me that Gilberte had died, I thought: she is the lucky one."

In anguish, he turned his face away.

"You have nightmares? I'll swap yours for mine any time."

He stood rigid as if frozen to the spot.

Silence stretched between them until, with a hopeless gesture, he dropped his hands to his side. For the first time, he looked her in the eye. "Everything you can think of to say to me, I have already said to myself. What more do you want of me?"

Yvette stared at his red-rimmed eyes, the sweat beading on his forehead. What indeed? He'd already endured his share of pain. Did she want him to suffer even more? As she regarded his dejected figure, childhood memories flooded back: Henri binding up her scraped knees and elbows, riding her around the driveway piggyback; hanging a swing for her from the branches of an apple tree; playing games of checkers on winter evenings by the fire. Would she let one July day blot out all the years that had gone before?

Yet, how hard it was to let go of her resentment. As she turned away from the misery on his face, her glance fell on the present that James had brought her from his mother. "She's had a rough time with my father, but she never complains." In her mind's eyes, Yvette saw the blond hair, faded now, the calm expression that had looked out from the photograph. His mother had accepted her lot. She didn't demand a pound of flesh in exchange. Yvette looked at the empty space at the foot of her cot. Her legs were gone. Making certain that her brother never forgot he was in a sense responsible would not bring them back.

"The past is past, Henri," she said. "Neither of us can change it. Two months ago, I wanted to die. Now, I care about the future. You have a future, too. I don't want you to live it saddled with guilt."

A sob tore at his throat. As Yvette watched the tears of release stream down his face, she felt as if a burden were lifted from her. In unshackling Henri, she had set herself free also.

"Every day I'm getting better. Look," she said.

Slowly she raised her right arm. As she inched it across her body, he leaned over and, meeting her halfway, took her hand in his.

28

Yvette watched the khaki-clad figure step through the hedge. His progress along the dirt track raised the dust left by three hot, dry days. Collar open at the throat, sleeves rolled up above the elbow, his skin glowed amber in the sun. She'd grown accustomed to the way he moved, yet the seamless motion of his stride still stirred her. He stopped at the edge of the salon and smiled. "How's it going?" he asked.

"Fine. *Entrez,*" she answered. *"Ca va?"*

"They're keeping us on the run. Another flight in a couple of hours."

"So soon?"

"It's been crazy—trying to keep up with Patton. You head out in one direction, and before you get there, the objective has been captured. So they switch targets on you."

He sat on the grass and stretched his legs in front of him. He propped himself against the corner guy ropes so that the sun warmed his back. "This is the best I've felt all day," he sighed, and closed his eyes.

"You remind me of a calico cat we had at the farm," she said. "He could sleep draped across the top rail of a fence, the branches of a tree—anywhere."

"I learned early to catnap," he answered. "Riding herd, I could doze in the saddle."

She was silent, thinking he really might like to doze. Even without talking, it was comforting to have him near. She forced herself to look away from the perfect relaxation of his muscular physique. It would never do for her to be caught watching him.

"You have two freckles underneath the angle of your jaw."

Startled, she turned to find him watching her.

"I never noticed them before," he said.

"They're pretty old—been there all my life."

"Ancient," he agreed. "Your birthday's in November, isn't it?"

"Yes."

"Seventeen! When the day arrives, we'll have a party." He laced his hands behind his head. "I'm glad you're going with us. I'd miss you."

"You speak French so well you don't need a tutor any more."

"You know that isn't what I meant." He studied her a moment. "It's hard to believe we met such a short time ago. I feel like we've been talking like this for years. Sometimes your thoughts are as clear to me as my own."

How often she'd felt the same.

"Maybe we knew each other in another life," he said.

She smiled. "And what were we in that other life? Elephants? Kangaroos?"

His eyes narrowed. "Wild horses."

She considered his suggestion.

"You should see a herd of them on the run. They go like the wind. My cow pony and I try to keep up with them, but they lose us in their dust. Flying a plane is as close as you get to being that free."

"Wild horses it is," she agreed.

"When this war is over, I'll take you flying."

"Ohh," she sighed. "I would like that. It must be wonderful—"

The rattle of a jeep speeding toward the tent interrupted her. James glanced at it over his shoulder, then rose in one motion to his feet. "It's Andy."

The jeep shuddered to a halt a few meters from the salon. "Hi, Yvette," the driver called.

She waved at the pilot dressed in his olive drab flight suit. His mustache had filled out somewhat, but that and the cigar stuck in the corner of his mouth made him look as if he were still playing at being a grown-up.

"What's happening?" James asked.

"The schedule's been changed. We're up next," Andy replied.

As James sprinted toward the Jeep, Andy winked at Yvette.

"You break a guy's heart in that blue thing you're wearing."

She shrugged. "A little something a parachutist gave me."

"Whoever designed that color had you in mind."

"You're dangerous," she smiled. "They shouldn't let you out alone."

He jerked a thumb at James. "Ol' Dad here looks after me. So far, he's kept me out of trouble."

James rolled his eyes. "It hasn't been easy!"

"Be careful, you two," Yvette called.

The jeep spun around and, in a swirl of dust, headed back the way it had come. Her smile faded. 'Be careful.' As if they were going on a little jaunt in town!

Watching the vehicle grow smaller in the distance, a sense of foreboding settled on her. It persisted through her exercise and massage session, lingered while she composed a letter to Madame Dubois. She was morose with Barnes, and even her father's morning visit could not lighten her gloom.

"Is something special bothering you?" Dr. Lerossi asked after her father had left.

"Yes, but I don't know what." She shrugged her shoulders as if to rid them of some constraint. "Do you believe in premonitions?"

"I like hard facts better. Hmmmm. I suppose so. Why?"

"I've got the feeling that there's going to be—" She sighed. "Maybe it's the humidity. It's depressing."

"How about a game of checkers?"

She forced a smile. "Great idea. Beating you always makes me feel better."

"Oh? Who won the last time?"

"You cheated."

"I was merely trying to teach you to be alert."

"Humph!" she growled. "This time I'll watch you like a hawk."

As he brought the checker box from a stack of games against the wall, they heard the rumble of approaching planes. Their eyes held a moment. Silently, they arranged the pieces on the board. "You're black. Go ahead," the doctor said. Neither of them remarked that they'd dispensed with their usual argument over who moved first.

The shiny red and black disks blurred together as, in her mind's eye, Yvette saw the airstrip with the mobile control tower, the waiting ambulances and the fire trucks. She imagined silent crew chiefs searching the sky for the first glimpse of that special plane; medics poised for quick action. She went through the motions of playing, but lost track of each move after it was made. He, too, was abstracted, and as they listened to the planes circle for landing, they stopped the exercise in futility, and began to count. When the last reverberation was stilled, of the twelve planes that had left on the mission, three had not returned.

"I'm going over to see what happened," Dr. Lerossi said. His face was glum. "I'll be back as soon as I can."

In growing alarm, she waited. It seemed an eon before there was a stir at the door, but it was DiMarzo with her lunch. The look on his face sent a chill down her spine. He placed the tray on her lap, and while the food grew cold, she listened to him relate the reason for the losses. Burdened by rockets, belly tanks and bombs, they had been jumped by 109's before they could jettison their load. Three planes had taken direct hits. "Two pilots bailed out, but Lieutenant Markham wasn't that lucky."

"Not Andy!" she cried. "But I saw him just before the flight."

"You won't see him any more," DiMarzo said grimly.

Dr. Lerossi brought more details. Of four enemy aircraft destroyed, James had accounted for three. "He was holed up pretty bad, but managed to get back."

Weak with relief, Yvette offered a silent prayer of thanks. She would mourn for Andy later. All she could think of now was that James had returned. Absorbed in her own thoughts, she scarcely heard the two men discuss the costly aerial battle. A stark statistic, however, caught her attention: in less than six months overseas, the Fighter Group had lost 21 pilots and 25 planes.

The afternoon was endless. During her rest period, sleep eluded her. She kept seeing Andy, dressed in his flight suit, flirting with her from the jeep. On every visit, he'd kidded her, always lifting her morale. How could anyone so alive suddenly be dead?

Another massage, more exercises, the maid's appearance to

clean the tent and, finally, the day was almost done. Like everyone else, the medics were subdued by the Group's losses, and there was little banter when they moved her to the salon. Yvette flipped unseeing through the pages of a *Yank*. Unable to concentrate, she put the magazine aside, leaned her head against her pillows and stared at the dirt track leading to the hedge. As if she'd willed him to appear, James stepped through the gap.

Gone was the spring in his step. She waited for him to duck under the entrance, cross the room and lower himself to the chair before she spoke. "I heard about Andy," she said.

"He never had a chance." James leaned forward and rested his elbows on his knees. "If only I'd been able to see into the sun better! Blue Flight really let us down. That damn Taylor again!" He clasped his hands together. "My orders have come through. I'm leaving for Le Mans."

Everything inside her froze. "When?"

"Early in the morning. I've been assigned to the advance formation. The rest of the Group will follow."

"When?" she asked again.

"Nothing's definite. All I've heard are rumors. Plenty of people will still be around so you won't get lonely. Frank says he'll stop by as often as he can. You can count on B. J., too, as well as— God! I can't believe it was Andy!" His mouth trembled. "I did look after him, you know. But when he needed me the most, I wasn't there."

"You can't blame yourself!" she said.

He didn't hear. His eyes were glazed. "They came at us before we knew they were there. That never would have happened if someone hadn't had their head up and locked. I managed to take out three, but that doesn't make up for Andy."

A lump rose in her throat. She saw again the rakish wink, the jaunty tilt of his head.

"*C'est la guerre!*" James's voice was harsh. "None of us know how long we'll be around." His eyes met hers and in their bleak depths she read his message to her: "You must not care too much."

She fought back tears. You're telling me too late, she longed to say. From the moment I first saw you, it was too late.

He pushed himself to his feet and walked to the edge of the tent. "So—it's good-bye to Normandy." He gazed around at the darkening landscape. "Better landing strips in our future, I hope, but we'll never forget the sunsets, the smell of apple blossoms, or the way we were welcomed, even by people whose towns were leveled." He shook his head. "Maybe when it's over, someone can make sense out of all this."

Her throat ached and she scarcely breathed. In the fading light, his profile stood out in sharp relief against the dark green foliage. Yvette etched each curve and angle, every line and facet of it into her memory.

He turned back to the cot. "We don't know where our new quarters will be, but Dr. Lerossi will get word to us when you're settled. It's good they're taking your tent. At least you'll be in familiar surroundings."

She nodded, afraid to speak.

"Alors," he bowed from the waist. *"Au revoir, Mademoiselle."*

His reminder of his formal behavior when they'd first met was meant to amuse her. It only made her yearn to be back where they had begun. His expression softened. "Andy was right. Blue is your color."

She watched his departing figure grow dim. A truck approached him, paused, and he jumped aboard. With a grind of gears, it moved on. Before it disappeared, she saw the white blur of his hand wave farewell.

Dry-eyed, she stared as the dust raised by the truck slowly settled. The shock of his departure preempted tears. Spoiled by his frequent visits during the past three days, she'd been living in a fool's paradise. She'd known that it had to end—that abandoning La Londe was drawing closer with each passing hour, yet she'd pushed that eventuality from her mind. She would not let herself think ahead, but had given herself over completely to the present.

Now the present was past, and he was gone.

29

Frank, B. J. and other pilots came often to see Yvette. Unlike James, they enjoyed talking about missions they had flown. She never tired of listening, for James figured in many of the accounts.

"What a pilot!" Frank said during one such report. "He was my flight leader on a mission to the marshalling yards in Brest. We'd been briefed about 20mm guns protecting the place, but we were already into our dive when 88s opened up. Flak bounced us all over the sky. He kept right on going, and we blew the place apart. It was rough." Frank winced. "You see those black puffs coming at you and you know there's not a damn thing you can do. He was scared like all the rest of us, but I'll never forget his voice on the radio—steady as a rock. He's the kind you hope to God is covering your tail if you get jumped."

September arrived, the warm weather continued, and Yvette spent as much time in the salon as her schedule allowed. Here she was surrounded by reminders of James. Sparrows wheeling above the mess tent recalled his tales of chasing birds in his Stearman trainer. Sea gulls skimming the tree tops suggested his aircraft circling to land. Fields carpeted with daisies and buttercups brought memories of the bouquets he'd gathered for her. Sunsets always included his figure silhouetted against the evening sky.

Some member of her family came every day to visit. It might be her father or one of the brothers riding a bike, or her mother, Claire and Marguerite arriving by jeep. Though her parents dreaded Yvette's departure, they knew her recovery depended on medical care that only the Americans could provide.

On the morning of September 10th, while Yvette was doing her exercises, Dr. Lerossi entered the tent. "I've just come from

Colonel Kleine's headquarters," he told her. "We're not going to Le Mans."

She stared at him, her mind rejecting what she'd heard.

"We're headed for an airfield that's just been captured in the east," he went on. "At Perthes—in the Champagne district near the town of St. Dizier."

"But—but what about the others?" she asked.

"They never should have been posted to Le Mans, but when the orders were given, no one knew that. The front is changing so rapidly—"

"What will happen to them?"

"They're leaving Le Mans on the 12th and will take the southern route through Orleans and Sens. A contingent from here leaves the 13th, and travels the northern road via Paris. Both echelons should converge on St. Dizier around the 18th. The rest of us, God willing, will depart La Londe the 23rd."

The separation from James would be only temporary! Then she realized how far from home the new bivouac would be.

"All the way across France," she murmured. "Cherbourg is the longest distance I've ever traveled from Coigny."

He sat beside her. "By plane it's not so far. And you'll still be surrounded by people who care about you. There's no other way," he said gently. "It's us, or back to Cherbourg."

"I know. It'll just take some getting used to."

"That's my girl," he smiled.

As the days passed, evidence of the departure of the 371st Fighter Group grew more and more apparent. From her salon, she watched trucks being readied for the long trip; heard the increased rumble of traffic on the road. Friends stopped by to say good-bye, and C-rations replaced the meals that DiMarzo had so carefully prepared. She was left for longer periods by herself. Amidst the bustle came the welcome news that British and American armies had crossed the frontier into Belgium, but the loss of two popular pilots struck the Group a terrible blow. Major Rockford Gray died in a crash a hundred yards short of the La Londe runway—cause unknown—and Lieutenant Colonel William J. Daley, Jr., was killed in a landing accident in the town of

Coulommiers. Yvette was especially saddened by the latter's death. On the day she'd arrived at La Londe, he was one of the two young officers who'd accompanied Colonel Kleine when he'd visited her tent. The Deputy Commander was twenty-four years old.

Frank came to tell her he was leaving. "We're heading out tomorrow. Some of the guys get to stop in Paris on the way. I wasn't among the lucky ones. Maybe later. When I see James, I'll tell him you're doing fine."

"And looking forward to seeing him again," she answered. "Have a safe flight."

Activities at La Londe dwindled until, on the morning of September twenty-second, the last flight of P-47s roared down the runway. Dipping a wing in salute, they bid good-bye to the airfield where, soon after D-Day, they had arrived as greenhorns. Today, they were leaving as veterans. Only a skeleton crew remained to fill in foxholes, strike the last of the tents, and burn what was left of gliders that had served as offices.

"Everything's all set," Dr. Lerossi told her. "We're leaving in the morning."

At eight o'clock, her parents and Claire arrived to say good-bye. Claire carried a little suitcase. "I put in your favorite blouse, ribbons for your hair, some books." She leaned over and pinned a tiny French flag to Yvette's bed jacket. "I made this so you won't get too Americanized," she smiled. Then, with brimming eyes, she slid her arms around her sister and held her close.

"We know you will be well-cared for," her father's voice was hoarse. He kissed her. "We'll miss you sorely, *ma petite.*"

Yvette gazed at his weathered face. So many lines, now; so many worries had put them there. She managed to smile. She had to smile, or dissolve into tears.

Alice gathered her daughter in her arms. Still in mourning for Gilberte, she'd worn a light gray shawl over her black dress to soften her somber appearance. Yvette rested her head on her mother's breast. She closed her eyes to better savor the sweet aroma, to be comforted by the steady heartbeat. "My dear, dear child," her mother murmured, caressing her daughter's hair. "I wish this separation were not necessary, but it is. Have courage."

Yvette nodded, unable to speak.

A commotion at the door announced the arrival of Dr. Lerossi and two soldiers carrying a stretcher. "It's time," the doctor said.

"We'll see you at the airstrip," her father called as Yvette was carried to a waiting ambulance. Through its rear window, she saw soldiers dismantling the shimmering haven which for eight weeks had been her home. How she would miss La Londe!

Her parents and Claire awaited her at the airstrip. They hurried forward for final kisses and words of encouragement. No tears marred the good-byes, but the forced cheerfulness wore on Yvette's nerves. She longed to tell them how afraid she was; plead to be taken home. Instead, she pressed her lips together and smiled an *"Au revoir."*

After the soldiers lifted her stretcher into the fuselage and fastened it into brackets against the wall, she caught a glimpse through the eye-level porthole of Claire and her parents standing beside the jeep. Their brave facade had evaporated. Huddled together, they waited silently, staring at the plane. Panic seized her. What if something happened and she never saw them again!

"All set?"

Absorbed in her misery, she hadn't heard the doctor's entrance. She nodded, blinking quickly.

"As soon as the medics get here and your tent is put aboard, we'll be on our way."

Again she nodded, afraid to speak.

He studied her face, then hunkered down beside her. "Cry, Yvette. Homesickness is something we all understand."

The words released her constraint, and she began to cry. He waited with her, smoothing her hair until her tears were spent. Then he dried her eyes with his handkerchief.

"You always know what to do." Her voice was shaky.

"I get lucky sometimes," he answered.

Moments later, her tent was added to the equipment loaded into the front part of the fuselage. The medics got on board and the heavy door clanged shut. Barnes looked around at the drab, bare walls with their rows of bucket seats, the metal floor scarred by much usage. "All the comforts of home!" he sighed.

"Better than five days on the road in a truck convoy!" Davis strapped himself into one of the seats opposite Yvette.

"I ain't complaining," Barnes imitated his fellow medic's accent. He sat beside Davis and patted the aircraft's aluminum shell. "I love you, old Gooney Bird."

Yvette's eyes grew round as the starboard engine sputtered, then sprang to life. While it rumbled, the port engine caught, and the thunder of the two drowned out all other sound. Dr. Lerossi settled into the seat beside Yvette, the C-47 shuddered, then began to move. Through the porthole, Yvette caught sight of her father, his arms upraised in a V-for-Victory salute. The triumphant gesture lifted her spirits. She held her breath as trees marched past in ever-quickening tempo, then suddenly she felt a gentle lift. They were airborne. Rays from the morning sun glanced off the wings, the sky was cobalt blue. She was unafraid. What was there to fear? She was flying in an American plane, piloted by an American. She trusted both—without doubt and with no reserve. In her experience, nothing was too difficult for these amazing people to undertake, and what they attempted, they accomplished without fail. She felt at ease, marveling at the miracle of being borne so effortlessly through the sky.

Dr. Lerossi signaled for her to look down. "Utah Beach," he called.

She pressed her forehead against the window to survey the vestiges of the gigantic struggle which had erupted on the Normandy coast. She saw the German guns aimed out to sea, barbed wire protecting the dunes. Burned out tanks and trucks littered the sand, and boat hulls lay upended in the water. "I didn't envy those poor guys in the landing crafts," James had said. "They knew that even if they made it to shore, a lot of them would die on the beaches." He'd told her that it was the C-47s that had transported the parachutists when the invasion began. This very plane might have been one of those she'd seen from the upstairs window at La Hougue.

The aircraft veered inland and, as the seacoast receded, Yvette remembered James's promise that when the war was over he would take her flying. How she wished that he were with her now. He'd flown this route many times before, and could have named the villages and towns, the meandering rivers; pointed out radio towers and church steeples that he'd used as landmarks. Suddenly, as if he'd touched her shoulder, she had a feeling of his presence. "It's hard to believe we met such a short time ago," echoed in her mind. "Sometimes your thoughts are as clear to me as my own." She closed her eyes and conjured up his broad-shouldered silhouette etched against the darkening sky.

"Yvette!"

Reluctantly, she turned her head.

"Are you all right?" the doctor asked.

She nodded.

"I've been calling you. I didn't want you to miss Versailles."

As she looked obediently out of the window, she felt a terrible sense of loss. Her mind's-eye picture of James was gone, and masking her indifference, she inspected the vast gardens and palace that unfolded below. Over the noise of the engines, Dr. Lerossi described the Hall of Mirrors, the salons with their works of art. "I've been there half a dozen times and only scratched the surface."

She summoned a smile. "I'll put that on my list of places to visit."

"The pilot told me we're being routed around Paris," he said. "Too bad you'll see so little of the city, but there will be other times."

She nodded.

"Everything O.K.?" Davis called to her.

"Fine," she answered. "I love flying!"

"Me, too. When nobody's shooting at you," he added.

She tried not to think of the flak, the air battles that Frank and the other pilots had talked about, but in spite of her efforts, her imaginary conversation with the cartoon "Frisky" came to mind. "The cards are stacked against me. With every mission that I fly, the odds grow slimmer that I'll get out of this war alive." The inevitable question followed: what were James's odds?

She didn't have time to dwell on that depressing thought. Her ears popped as the plane began its descent. Their arrival at St. Dizier was imminent and wonder about their living conditions there occupied her mind. She watched ribbons become roads again, and doll houses return to their true size. She heard the wheels lock into place, felt a jolt as they touched the runway. Rolling toward a hangar, she saw many different kinds of aircraft, and soldiers everywhere. Finally, the C-47 came to rest, and the engine sounds were stilled.

Dr. Lerossi smiled at her. "It looks like we've arrived."

30

Yvette awoke to the rumble of aircraft engine and daylight seeping between flaps of the tent. Parachute silk shimmered above her head, the bedside table stood within easy reach, and the chair that had held so many visitors at La Londe was in place beside her cot. Even the cartoons of Frisky had been pinned to the opposite wall.

The only difference that marked her new quarters was the squat, black gasoline stove. Fall mornings and evening in this region were chilly.

She thought back to the events of yesterday.

As soon as her stretcher had been lifted from the plane, she'd been surrounded by familiar faces. Dr. Cohen was there—what memories the lounge chair that he'd woven from parachute shrouds evoked—Doc Roberts of Bar-B-Que fame, Herisson, DiMarzo, and others. Dr. Glocker had extended her a welcome on Colonel Kleine's behalf. Promises to come and see her followed her to the waiting ambulance.

"This was a French Air Force Base and depot when the Germans took it over," Dr. Lerossi had explained after they'd gotten under way. "When the Americans captured it, the Germans had to bug out in a hurry. They left tons of equipment stored in warehouses. The air base has hangars, as you saw, and permanent barracks. Since it's being used by four Groups, it's crowded and there isn't room for us here. Our medical unit will be set up at St. Eulien, a village not far away."

"Oh? Then the pilots will be staying in the barracks?"

"Yes. They're delighted. For the first time since being overseas, they won't be sleeping in foxholes or pup tents. Don't fret now," he'd hurried on, seeing her anxious look. "You'll have lots of company. They'll have access to jeeps. You couldn't keep them away!"

But what if a jeep wasn't available when James was free, she'd worried. With the fighting so intense, there would be more important demands on his time than calling on a war-wounded girl.

The dirt road was narrow and deeply rutted. As the ambulance lurched to avoid a rock, Dr. Lerossi had steadied her stretcher. "I'm sorry it's such rough going. We have to travel the back roads because the highway is restricted to military traffic." By the time the ambulance had shuddered to a stop, she was exhausted. Not only had the trip been arduous, but the move from St. Dizier to St. Eulien had filled her with misgivings.

Outside the ambulance, she'd looked around at the wide expanse of field, bordered on one side by the village, and on another by a thick forest. Beyond the forest lay the highway, from which the muffled sound of moving trucks was audible. Her tent had been waiting for her. It was the first one the airmen had erected. The others would be positioned in a row, the doctor had told her, with his next to hers as at La Londe. She'd cocked her head to listen.

"Yes, you can hear the planes from here," Dr. Lerossi had assured her. He'd pointed in the direction opposite the forest. "The airfield is over there." Sure enough, she'd been able to distinguish from the myriad of other sounds the familiar stutter of P-47 engines.

She listened to it now, and was comforted.

Her morning began as had those at La Londe with a stir at the door and the appearance of one of the medics. This time, it was Barnes. "Well, Miss," he switched on the light above her head, "You finally decided to wake up."

She yawned, stretched. "How's the weather?"

"Perfect. At home, we call this Indian Summer."

"And here, it's *l'ete de la Saint Michel.* There will be lots of flying, I suppose."

"Beaucoup." He turned away to prepare her bath.

His cryptic reply puzzled her. Barnes usually enjoyed discussing the fliers and their latest missions. "DiMarzo wants to know if you'd like anything special for breakfast," he said.

"How sweet of him. Tell him anything he fixes is special to me."

Her saccharine answer drew from the medic a sickly look. "Tell him."

"I do," she smiled. "All the time. You fellows just don't know how to handle the cook. Any news from the airfield?" she persisted in a casual tone.

He busied himself with getting a clean gown ready to slip over her head. "It's been pretty hectic around here—the move and all. We haven't heard much from Operations."

When Dr. Lenocci came to check on her, she asked him the same question and received an equally evasive answer. He went on to apologize for the loss of her salon. The tent was needed for other purposes, he explained. "On days like this, we can roll up one of the sides so you can get the feel of being outdoors."

"I'd like that," she agreed.

And so an airman came to turn off the fire, and raise the tent wall opposite her cot. As she looked out at the golden color of the sun-dappled field and the dark green of the forest beyond, as always nature worked its magic on her. Exercises, meals, massages, followed their usual timetable. She had lots of company after her nap. Some of the airmen called out greetings as they passed her tent, others stopped in for a chat. None of the pilots came, however, and her fears of yesterday were confirmed. Despite the doctor's assurances to the contrary, the distance between the medical unit and the base would render drop-in visits rare. In truth, communications between the two seemed all but disconnected. Not once during the day's activities had anyone even mentioned the airfield.

When the sun had set, the wall of her tent was lowered, and the fire relit. Bored, she decided to amuse herself by playing solitaire until supper. As she reached for the cards on the bedside table, a movement at the entrance attracted her attention.

"May I come in?"

Her face lit up at the sound of Frank's familiar voice. He would be bringing word of James! *"Entrez, s'il vous plait!"* she gaily called.

She waited expectantly to welcome the cocky pilot who would strut into the tent, but the figure who hesitated at the door had no relation to the Frank she knew. His eyes were dull, his shoulders slumped and, as he walked toward her, every step seemed to require an effort. A chill went down her spine.

"Mon Dieu! What's the matter?" she asked.

Mute, he looked down at her, then shook his head. "I had the speech all planned. Now that I'm here, I've forgotten it."

"Speech for what!" she demanded. Then suddenly the evasive answers, the abrupt switches in conversation, the absence of flying talk that had bothered her all day took on meaning. They weren't just her suspicions; something terrible had happened. Desolated, she watched the pilot lower himself to the chair.

"Yvette," his voice rasped. "James is—dead."

'NO!" The cry exploded from her.

He nodded. "Yesterday morning."

Incredulous, she stared at this evil bearer of false news. Impossible! she wanted to shout. Yesterday he was with—

"We were headed for Zweibrucken, looking for trains caught by daybreak between towns. Sure enough, we spotted one. James was leader, Red Flight. He blew the locomotive away, and we set up the gunnery pattern to strafe the cars."

The words floated toward her as if carried on a wave. Each was distinct, had meaning, but the sum of them strung together was beyond her comprehension. She heard another voice instead. "It's hard to believe we met such a short time ago," it said. "Maybe we knew each other in another life." She thought of that moment on the plane when his presence was as real to her as the touch of his hand. He couldn't be dead!

"It was a milk run until James made his second pass on a boxcar." Drawn against her will, Yvette listened. "There was a tremendous explosion, and he never came out on the other side. I tried to raise him on the radio, but—nothing. Then we circled and saw some of the wreckage of his plane."

The fire hissed, a moth sizzled against the light bulb. Frank stared at his clasped hands. "He couldn't get over Andy's death. For some stupid reason, he felt responsible. Now, he's gone."

Numb, unable to respond, she gazed at the pilot.

"Back at gunnery school, we used to play follow the leader among the big cumulus clouds. He always could outfly the rest of us. The sky seemed to be his natural element. He was happy there—so caught up in the thrill of piloting a plane, he said he could always leave his troubles on the ground. Yet he never shied away from troubles—his own or those of people he cared about."

Go! she longed to say. I can't listen any more.

As if he'd heard her silent plea, Frank pushed himself to his feet. "I'm leaving in the morning. I've got to do my two weeks as an Air-Ground Controller at the front."

She struggled to show concern. "Is it dangerous?"

"Not really—I guess." He leaned over and covered her hand with his. "Good-bye, Yvette." His eyes brimmed with tears. "We'll miss him, too."

She nodded. "Take care, Francois."

He gave a final wave from the door.

She sank into her pillows and stared at the ceiling. Gone. Like the tolling of a bell, the word echoed in her mind. James was gone. Not just to Le Mans, but forever. He would not walk into her tent again, nor smile at her in that special way. The voice that had thrilled her was silent now. His laughter stilled.

"Yvette."

She listened to the footsteps cross from the entrance to the cot. "You knew," she said without looking at him.

"Yes, we knew," Dr. Lerossi answered. "Frank felt that he should be the one to tell you."

"Why did it have to be James!"

He sat beside her. "I wish I had an answer." He shook his head.

"What will I do?" she murmured.

"We want to help you, Yvette. Please let us."

Vacant-eyed, she nodded. "Yes, I must do that," she answered, and turned her face to the wall.

31

She studied the tray on her lap, and tried to remember who had brought it to her, and how long ago. "Come on, Yvette, you gotta eat," DiMarzo urged.

"I did eat," she said. "It was—so good."

The cook hunkered down beside her cot. "You don't like this? I'll fix something else. *Crepes suzettes?* I might have to steal a few ingredients but—"

"Tomorrow," she promised. "I'll feel like eating."

Reluctantly, he picked up the tray. "Today is Halloween. That's why I carved your apple like a jack-o-lantern."

She frowned, puzzled.

"I guess you don't celebrate Halloween in France." His expression brightened. "Would you like for me to tell you how we do it at home?"

"Yes, you must do that," she answered. "Tomorrow."

He nodded and gave up further attempts to cheer her.

After he left, Yvette stared again at the ceiling. The cook had interrupted James's story about the Bar-B-Que. The pilot had just gotten to the part where the MP's were chasing their jeep. She watched the gestures of his strong, big-knuckled hands, saw the smile that started in his eyes spread in its lazy fashion over his face.

Then the irritating murmur of voices outside the tent again broke her concentration. She couldn't hear what was being said. It was the worried tone that distracted her.

"It was that same old crap about 'Tomorrow,'" DiMarzo reported. "Doc, when is she going to snap out of this? My God, it's been over a month."

"I know," Dr. Lerossi sighed. "Severe depressions are the devil to treat."

"I wish I could—"

"You're doing everything you can. We all are. She's strong-willed, stubborn. That makes me hopeful. We'll just have to give her more time. James's death must have seemed the final blow."

Mercifully, the voices ceased and she could get back to James's account of the Bar-B-Que. But moments later, Dr. Lerossi entered the tent. "How about a game of checkers?" he asked.

She glanced at him in irritation. Another interruption! Why were they always pestering her! "Maybe later," she retorted. "I'm tired after my exercises."

Her flash of annoyance made the hair prickle on the back of his neck. After five weeks of numb acquiescence, a change! "You haven't done your exercises," he countered.

"Oh? Well—all right."

The contest took longer than usual. In other checker games since James's death, Yvette had merely responded by rote to her adversary's maneuvers. But twice during this rivalry, he watched her hesitate to plan the move ahead. Again, he began to hope.

Her eyes followed him as he put the game away. "Is the sun shining?" she asked.

The question almost stopped him in his tracks. "No," he answered in an even tone, "but at least it's not raining like it has been lately. That's a plus. We can roll up a side of the tent," he went on. "It'll be a mite chilly but—you're tough," he smiled.

He watched her struggle. Not since the tragedy had she allowed a side of the tent to be raised. Only if completely enclosed in her silken cocoon had she felt secure. Was she ready now to emerge? He longed to say "Do it!" but knew that he must not interfere. She, herself, had to decide. She gave a tentative nod.

He stifled a sigh of relief. "While I find someone to raise it, doing some exercises would be a good idea," he said smoothly.

News of her budding recovery spread, and her tent again had a parade of visitors. There were nights when she cried herself to sleep, and days when life without James seemed not worth living. Gradually, however, she took an interest in her surroundings. The capture of a band of German deserters in the forest brought the war very close, and rumors circulating that once again the 371st Fighter Group would have to move set her wondering about her future.

The 13th of November followed its usual course until her afternoon nap was done. Then Herisson came to wash and trim her hair, Davis insisted she don her blue bed jacket, and Barnes brought in a folding stand and extra chairs. Bemused, she watched the bustle.

"General Eisenhower is coming to call?" she asked.

Davis nodded. "Something like that."

As he finished speaking there was a commotion outside the tent entrance. "What is going on!" she demanded.

A loud whistle from the medic brought the noisy confusion to a sudden end. He yanked the tent flap open. "This!" he exclaimed.

Yvette's eyes widened. Framed by the doorway, a group of servicemen, old friends now, stood stiffly at attention. At a signal from Barnes, they broke into song: "Happy Birthday to you!"

She clapped her hand to her forehead. She had forgotten!

When the singing ended, they filed by her cot, offered her their congratulations, and left the little bundles they carried. When the ritual was completed, Davis held an imaginary trumpet to his lips: "Ta-ta-ta-ta ta-ta!"

DiMarzo came though the door carrying the most enormous cake she'd ever seen. The tantalizing aroma of cinnamon and vanilla filled the tent, and cries of "Attaboy, DiMarzo!" and "Bravo!" set the parachute silk above their heads to quivering. "A mere *bagatelle,*" the cook shrugged, but as he made his slow progress toward the cot, the grin he wore stretched from ear to ear. Speechless, Yvette stared at his creation. It was four layers tall, and its sides were decorated with candied fruit, half-buried in the snowy icing. Around the top, seventeen lighted candles illuminated the single word, YVETTE.

She looked from the cake to the waiting company and her eyes brimmed with tears. "What can I say?"

"You don't have to say anything, sweetheart," DiMarzo's voice was hoarse. "Just give us a smile."

She beamed, her face radiant. The group broke out with "Hooray!"

"We were afraid you'd forgotten how," DiMarzo said. He placed the cake on the folding stand. "Make a wish and blow out the candles," he instructed her.

She filled her lungs, and when the last flame flickered out, another "Bravo" arose. DiMarzo cut the cake and offered her the first slice. "Here's to your health and happiness, with time to enjoy both," he toasted her.

She took a bite, and officially declared that it was "Groovy!" a word that she had learned the day before.

While slices of cake were passed around, Yvette opened her presents. She admired the scarves, handkerchiefs, earrings, gloves, and barrettes for her hair and gave the donors her heartfelt thanks. The last present was a narrow, oblong box. Dr. Lerossi helped her unfasten the safety catch. She lifted the lid, and caught her breath. On black, velvet matting lay a silver bracelet fashioned into small, interlocking medallions. She looked for a card, but there was none to be found.

"Maybe something is written on the back," the doctor suggested.

She turned the bracelet over and on each of the medallions was inscribed a word. "To the most gallant person that I know. 11/13/44. Lerossi," she read.

"Will you help me with it?" she asked in a shaky voice.

As he placed the bracelet on her wrist and fastened the clasp, she looked up at him with glistening eyes. "It's there forever. I'll never take it off," she said.

By ones and twos the servicemen departed. Even after the last of them had told Yvette good-bye, Dr. Lerossi noted that her face was not dejected. Instead it reflected a quiet contentment. The broken heart had begun to mend.

As the days passed, rumors of the Group's departure multiplied. That Dr. Lerossi hadn't spoken to her about their plans seemed odd to Yvette. One morning after her medical checkup, she asked him why he'd been so reticent. He put his medical instruments back in his bag and sat down in the chair. "Because there's something that I have to tell you and I didn't know if you were ready. Unfortunately, we're running out of time."

His sober expression set off an alarm in her mind. She braced herself.

"When your legs were amputated," he began, "there wasn't time or opportunity to prepare them to accommodate prostheses. Before you undergo rehabilitation, your wounds will need revision: scar tissue removed, bones tapered, skin flaps formed." He hesitated. "In short—more surgery."

Yvette cringed as nightmare memories of La Fiere flooded back. "This operation won't be as traumatic as the first," he hurried on, "but it's equally as necessary. Can you be brave one more time?"

Could she? How much bravery did she have left. Just meeting the demands of every day took a toll. Yet, what was the alternative? A wheelchair—like James's father.

"Where will it take place?" she asked.

"That's still uncertain. Colonel Kleine is working on some possibilities. We'll know in a couple of days."

The two days dragged by on leaden feet. She filled them with extra exercises, her English studies, letter writing—anything to keep her mind from thoughts of La Fiere.

Finally, the afternoon of the second day, Dr. Lerossi hurried into her tent. "Colonel Kleine is on the way."

Moments later, his tall, familiar figure, accompanied by Dr. Glocker, appeared at the entrance. "I'm glad to see you're looking so much better," the Colonel said.

"Thanks to yours and everyone else's kindness and generosity," she answered.

His hazel eyes crinkled at the corners. "Mine's the easy part. I just give the orders. It's people like Dr. Lerossi that get things done."

He tucked his floppy pilot's cap under his arm, and took a couple of paces back and forth. "I'm sure you know that the 371st Fighter Group will soon be on the move again. Dr. Lerossi has informed me that you've made such progress, your condition requires treatment that we're not equipped to give."

He spoke slowly, giving Dr. Glocker time to keep up a running translation. Yvette held her breath.

"Two options are available," the Colonel continued. "Now that Paris is secure, you could enter a French civilian hospital there or," he paused, "go to the United States."

Open-mouthed, she stared at him.

"You'd fly in a plane equipped to handle wounded, and be treated in a military facility which specializes in cases such as yours. There, you would learn to walk again."

Her thoughts were in turmoil as the impact of his offer became clear.

"I know you can't make a choice right now," the Colonel went on. "However, our departure is approaching. As it won't be safe for you to travel with us, and bad weather will necessitate giving up your tent, Dr. Glocker has arranged for a temporary stay in an advanced surgical unit set up by the army in the town of Vittel. While you're there, you'll have time to reach a decision." His expression softened. "Be assured, Yvette, that you would be most welcome in our country."

Overwhelmed by his offer, she stumbled through her thanks. As always he made little of his part in the matter. "I wish you the best, whatever you decide," he finished.

Still stunned, she watched the two officers make their exit. The United States! It seemed as far away as the moon. She looked at Dr. Lerossi. "Would you go with me?"

"That was the original plan," he said, sitting beside her. "When we left La Londe, General Patton was racing across France so fast, oil had to be rushed by cargo plane to keep his tanks supplied. We thought the Germans were done for—" he gave a short laugh, "— and that we'd all be home by Christmas. But that was eight weeks ago, and the closer we get to 'the Fatherland' the deeper they dig in their heels. There's even speculation now that they plan a counterattack. It's going to be a long, hard winter," he added grimly, "and the medics and I will be needed here."

Her eyes were bleak. "Then I would be surrounded by strangers."

"We were strangers to you once. But not for long. Actually, the medics and I would only be in the way. We did such a good job on you that you've outgrown us."

His attempt at a light touch was lost on her. "That would never happen!"

"It's happened, Yvette. We're trained for the battlefield. You need long-term rehabilitation."

Paris? or the United States? The familiarity of her own language and customs, or the foreignness of that distant land. It would be so easy to decide if Dr. Lerossi would go with her; how difficult it was because he couldn't.

As she gazed at the face that had become so dear to her, she was suddenly aware of how tired and drawn he looked. The lines that bracketed his mouth had deepened, dark circles shadowed his eyes. Pangs of remorse swept over her. Engrossed in her own feelings, she'd ignored the trials of those around her. He, like his fellow soldiers, was far from home. The war to liberate her country dragged on. The way ahead was uncertain, and losses mounted every day.

"I've been so selfish." Her eyes brimmed with tears. "Please forgive me." She reached for his hand. "Whatever decision I make, I'll be grateful until I die for all that you have done for me."

He raised her fingers to his lips. "Davis called it 'a two-way street,' remember."

She nodded. "It's worked both ways."

Davis had called it a two-way street. She smiled. So it had been.

32

On the morning of November 30, airmen from all over the field gathered at the cargo plane. Though they shivered in the cold raw wind, they waited patiently to tell Yvette good-bye. Rank held no precedence. The Corporal who had tended her fire stood in front of a Major who was Team Commander of the Service Squadron. In her language still foreign to so many of them, they stumbled over expressions of good will. Eyes filled with tears, she replied in English as best she could. Accompanied by Dr. Lerossi, the two medics carried her into the aircraft. They adjusted her stretcher, straightened the pillows, fussed with her blankets. Finally, there was nothing left to do. They stood awkwardly in a row, looking at her.

"Dr. Glocker will let us know how you're doing," Dr. Lerossi said.

She nodded, afraid to speak.

"Who am I going to play checkers with, or talk to about my troubles?" Davis grumbled.

"No more tea parties or birthday celebrations." Barnes's voice was hoarse. "The 371st will just come apart."

Yvette smiled. "Somehow I think you'll muddle through."

"We'll miss you."

"I'll miss you, too."

With such inadequate expressions and brimming eyes, they left each other.

The engines rumbled, Dr. Glocker climbed on board and, assured that Yvette was comfortable, strapped himself into the seat beside her. As the plane began its journey down the runway, Yvette waved through the window to the crowd of men. With arms held high, they bid her farewell. She watched them grow smaller in the distance and suddenly in the angle of the plane's ascent, they were lost to her view.

Gradually her thoughts turned from her bereavement to wonder about her destination. "Vittel was a fashionable health resort before the war," Dr. Glocker had told her on one of his visits to her tent. "Since the town has little military value, it escaped the destruction inflicted on Nancy and Metz." Parks, hotels, casinos and, of course, the famous mineral springs had attracted vacationers for years, he went on. "During the occupation, the Germans set up facilities to care for their wounded submariners. One of the big parks was surrounded by barbed wire and used as a holding camp for Allied prisoners. When the Americans took over the town, they converted one of the hotels into a hospital to care for soldiers and civilians injured in the fighting at Strasbourg. That's where you'll be staying."

She looked down at the gently rolling countryside. To the east, the foothills of the Vosges bit into the sky. Forests gave way here and there to villages laced together by narrow roads. A series of canals linked the Marne, the Meuse and the Moselle Rivers into a giant waterway. How often had the French and Germans fought for possession of Alsace-Lorraine. The Maginot Line was supposed to be France's ultimate protection of these border provinces. She thought of her brother, Michel, captured when the Germans attacked through Belgium and rolled up the Line from the rear. American blood was being shed here now. Would their efforts be as disastrous as that struggle four years ago?

Dr. Glocker's touch on her arm interrupted Yvette's gloomy thoughts. He directed her attention out the window to a plateau-like elevation barely visible from the plane. "Tantonville," he said.

Eagerly she tried to pinpoint the town near which the 371st Fighter Group would set up its next encampment, but the distance proved too great to make out any details. A change in the engine sounds indicated the plane's descent. The brief flight was almost over.

In the ambulance, Dr. Glocker's comments on points of interest that they passed kept her mind occupied until they reached the Hermitage Hotel. But the sights, sounds, and smells of the lobby crowded with wounded dispelled any aura of "fashionable resort" the rest of the town might give. Clerks, corpsmen, and nurses looked worn and harried, and when it came her turn to be admitted, no time was spent in chitchat. As she looked around the bare cubbyhole to which she'd been assigned, a feeling of deja vu came over her. The beautiful hiatus at La Londe and St. Eulien was over. Once again, she was one patient among many, some of whom had suffered injuries even more devastating than her own.

The time for Dr. Glocker's departure drew near. How she dreaded to see him go. She'd known he would have to leave, but when he'd told her several days ago that he would be going on to Tantonville on business for the Colonel, she'd had no idea how deserted she would feel. "I've spoken to the doctors and nurses about you. They'll give you good care."

She tried to smile. "Thank you for all you've done."

He took her hand. "You saw from the plane that Tantonville is just a hop, skip and jump from here. I'll be back in a few days. You concentrate on getting better. Meanwhile, we're trying to reach your parents but," he grimaced, "communications between here and there are still a mess. So far, no luck, but we'll do everything we can."

She nodded.

"Alors, good-bye for now, Yvette. I'll see you soon." With a final squeeze of her hand, he was gone.

She was alone. The fears that had been building since her arrival overwhelmed her. Was the Hermitage any better than the Pasteur? So many wounded; so few to look after them. She was unwanted and would be forgotten. If she died here, who would care? Tears of self-pity streamed down her face and she fell into an exhausted sleep.

When she awoke, a corpsman was standing beside the bed. "Are you all right?" He wet a cloth and bathed the tears from her face. "Don't be afraid. You're safe here. It's just that," he nodded toward the hall, "it's been a mad house."

"I understand," she said.

"Are you hungry?"

She wasn't, but she nodded anyway.

"I'll bring some soup."

When he returned, he laid the tray across her lap. "I'm sorry I can't stay. Can you manage by yourself?"

"I can manage," she answered.

She tried a little of the soup but its glutinous texture stuck in her throat. She thought of DiMarzo's creations, and fresh tears arose. She pushed the bowl away. A lassitude crept over her. She should do some exercises, read, or write letters to occupy her mind, but everything seemed beyond her strength. She dozed again and awoke to the sound of voices at her door. Yvette recognized the doctor who had seen her on admission, and the nurse who had settled her in her room. Both of them looked exhausted. The nurse shook her head. "Shortages—bandages," was all that Yvette understood.

"My God, what next?" the doctor exclaimed.

"Don't ask," the nurse advised him. She consulted the chart she carried and read off some figures while the doctor looked at Yvette. When she finished, he nodded. "Let me know of any change," he said, and the two of them disappeared.

The days dragged by. Hurrying footsteps and muffled voices in the corridor never ceased. Though she was bathed, fed and given medication, no one had time to monitor exercises, massage or apply hot compresses to her arm. Her strength began to ebb, and as time passed and she heard nothing from her parents, her apprehension grew. When was Dr. Glocker coming back?

On the morning of December 10th, a flustered nurse hurried into her room. "Yvette!" she cried, "you're about to have a visitor."

Yvette sat up, her torpor forgotten. Dr. Glocker! With news of her parents.

"We must make you presentable, my dear." Mrs. Manning snatched Yvette's brush from the bedside table, and with rapid strokes fluffed out Yvette's hair. "He's come to visit the wounded soldiers, and has asked especially to see you."

Yvette regarded the nurse with a puzzled frown. "Dr. Glocker?"

"No! No!" the nurse exclaimed. "General Eisenhower!"

Yvette stared at her in disbelief. "You joke!"

"It's no joke. He wants to see you. Now!"

As if in a trance, Yvette watched Nurse Manning smooth her hospital gown, rearrange the pillows, straighten the bedcovers. "Why?' she asked.

The nurse stood back to inspect the results of her efforts. She gave a nod of satisfaction. "That'll do. I don't know why," she went on, "but you'll find out in a minute." She lifted her head to listen. "They're coming."

The hospital noises to which Yvette had grown accustomed had suddenly ceased. Instead, she heard the measured tread of what sounded like a small army moving down the hall. With eyes riveted on the doorway, she waited. Moments later, incredibly, there he was. In his army great coat, he looked enormous and, with the smile that charmed everyone he met, he stepped into the room.

"Bonjour, Mademoiselle," he said in an accent she would have recognized anywhere as that of an American. Dr. Glocker walked in behind him along with several officers she'd never seen.

"Monsieur le General. C'est un honneur," she managed to say.

"Mine is the honor," he replied, inclining his head. "I regret that I speak little of your language, but with the good doctor's help, we'll get along." He moved a couple of steps closer to the bed, giving the members of his staff a chance to come into the room. Despite the ready smile, his face looked tired and drawn. "I've been aware of you for some time and—" he raised his eyebrows "—looked the other way." His eyes twinkled. "A French girl traveling with an Air Force Fighter Group does bend Army regulations just a bit."

There were nods and grins behind him, and Yvette smiled also.

"However," the General continued, "I've heard nothing but good reports about that Group's morale, and Colonel Kleine gives you a lot of the credit."

Her face flushed at his compliment.

His expression became serious. "The military situation in this sector has rapidly deteriorated, I'm afraid, and it's no longer safe for you here. I thoroughly endorse Colonel Kleine's proposal to fly you to the States. All of your immediate medical needs will be taken care of, and we promise that your future will be secure." He paused and cleared his throat. "We hope you will accept this offer. It comes not only from an officer in the United States Army, but also from the heart of someone who has been deeply touched."

Scarcely breathing, Yvette listened to the rapid translation. Fumbling for suitable words of thanks, she gazed into the General's wide-spaced eyes. She was astounded to see that even the leader of the world's most powerful military organization still could shed tears. He shifted his weight, laced his hands together. "There's not much time. This afternoon, a planeload of wounded leaves for the States. Can you be ready?"

"This afternoon! *Mon Dieu!*" she gasped.

"It is sudden," the General agreed, "but the circumstances call for an instant decision."

Yvette's eyes searched Dr. Glocker's face. "Have you reached my parents?' she asked.

"Unfortunately, no," he answered. "We have tried to get through many times."

"Then they wouldn't know."

"Not until you're there."

She tried desperately to sort out the thoughts racing through her mind. Another world, America, that vast continent three thousand miles away. Helpless and alone, she would leave behind everything with which she was familiar. Family, friends— the ties would be broken. She would be dependent on the charity of strangers.

"I appreciate your offer more than I can say," she began, "and will always remember the kindness that has been shown to me." Her eyes brimmed with tears. "But it has been twelve weeks since I saw my parents. I'm sorry. I must refuse."

After a moment of silence, the General nodded. "I understand. We won't urge you." He turned to Dr. Glocker. "You'll make the arrangements with the Paris hospital?"

"At once," the doctor agreed.

"We wish you well," the General said to Yvette. He smiled. "We'd hoped to make an American of you. *Au revoir.*"

The officers opened a path for him. As he walked out the door, they bid her good-bye and followed him. Dr. Glocker remained.

She looked at him with anxious eyes. "Did I make the right choice?"

"I don't know, Yvette," he answered. "Only time will tell."

33

I t was ten o'clock and bitter cold the following morning when Yvette and Dr. Glocker left Vittel. The sense of urgency that gripped the hospital following the Eisenhower visit had now invaded the town. A trickle of what would soon become a flood of refugees pushed carts piled high with household goods along the streets. The *Gendarmerie* were much in evidence, and shoppers seeking last-minute supplies hurried along crowded thoroughfares or gathered at street corners to discuss the latest rumors. Their expressions of disbelief mingled with dread reminded Yvette of the look on peoples' faces when advanced units of the German army reached the outskirts of Carentan four years ago.

"It's incredible!" Dr. Glocker exclaimed as the ambulance slowed to allow an American troop transport to pass. "The Germans suffered tremendous losses when they were driven back to the Siegfried Line. By all rights, they should be done for. But they've regrouped for a counterattack—with no air cover and in the dead of winter!" He shook his head. "Hitler has pulled rabbits out of a hat before when he needed them. God knows what he's up to this time."

Wherever the assault came, whatever its outcome, many wounded would result. Yvette knew that hospital beds would be at a premium at the Hermitage, and she was glad to relinquish hers. But as the plane lifted into the leaden sky, she wondered again whether she had made the best choice. How much easier it would have been if she'd had no options—if someone had told her, "This is the way it's going to be; you must make the best of it." But there'd been no "someone," and she'd had to choose. Right or wrong, her decision had been final. The C-47 on which she could have traveled to the United States left yesterday.

She saw little of the countryside on the trip to Paris for they flew above a thick layer of clouds. An ambulance awaited at Bourget Airport, and soon after their arrival she and the doctor were on their way to the Rothschild Hospital. She should have been excited at her first view of the capital, but four years of German occupation had robbed it of the gaiety and exuberance for which it had been famous. The unkempt air of neglected buildings, and tattered clothing of pedestrians; the shuttered windows of famous cafes, litter blowing in the wind revealed a city gripped in the throes of deprivation.

"It's a step up from La Londe, eh Yvette?"

The doctor's comment announced their arrival at the Rothschild Hospital. When Yvette was lifted clear of the ambulance, she agreed that the edifice was an impressive one, "but I doubt that the care that I'll be given here can match what I received in an army tent," she smiled.

"Welcome, Mademoiselle Hamel. We've been expecting you." The Administrator wore a dark blue suit, and had brown hair sprinkled with gray. His blue eyes smiled at her through gold rimmed glasses. He turned to Dr. Glocker. "Everything is ready."

As the two men shook hands and exchanged pleasantries, Yvette hoped they would keep the amenities to a minimum. She was tired from the trip, the jostling in the ambulance, and no matter how gentle stretcher bearers were, the constant swaying when they walked was painful to her. She was grateful to the nurse who came up and interrupted their conversation. Monsieur Duval introduced the newcomer.

"Madame Laconte is the Supervisor on the floor where you'll be staying," he told Yvette. Though the nurse's face was neither weathered nor lined, it was hard to tell how old she was. Tall, spare, she wore a long white apron over her uniform, and her hair was hidden by the customary *voile*. Her pale blue eyes seemed remote until she smiled, and her austere expression softened. "Would you follow me, please?" she said.

The trip across the vestibule, up the flight of stairs and down the long corridor seemed endless. Finally, she was settled in her bed. While the nurse and Dr. Glocker conferred at the door, she looked around at the spartan furnishings of the white-walled room. A large armoire stood against the opposite wall. Above an armchair beside the armoire hung a watercolor of a farmhouse scene. Her bedside table held a basin, pitcher and a glass, and a second chair beside the bed held the little suitcase that Claire had given her.

Madame Laconte departed, and Dr. Glocker walked toward the bed. Yvette dreaded to hear what she knew was coming.

"It's time for me to leave," he said. "I need to check the medical supplies that they're loading on the plane. The pilot is anxious that we get to Tantonville before dark." He grimaced. "These short winter days are stingy with good flying hours."

"I understand," she answered, fighting tears.

The doctor patted her hand. "Don't think that you're rid of the 371st Fighter Group. We fliers have a habit of turning up when you least expect us," he smiled.

"I do hope so," she pleaded.

"You can count on it," he assured her. "I've urged Monsieur Duval to try to make contact with your parents. Communications are still a shambles, but he should have more luck reaching them from Paris than we have from Tantonville. God knows what we'll have thrown at us in the next few days," he added glumly.

"I'll be so worried," she said.

"We can only hope that if they counterattack, it will be the last gasp of a dying regime."

She nodded.

"So, adieu for now." He leaned over and kissed her on the forehead. "You will not be forgotten. I promise."

She blinked quickly. "A thousand thanks for all—"

"No need for that," he broke in gruffly. "You're in good hands here, and we wish you the best."

She listened to his hurrying footsteps fade away. "You will not be forgotten," he had promised, but how could that be possible? During these turbulent days, her friends would have little time to think about her. If the counterattack was repulsed, the 371st Fighter Group would be moving east; if it were not— She cringed.

She gazed at the bracelet that Dr. Lerossi had given her. 'To the most gallant person that I know.' Feeling anything but gallant now, she pulled the sheet over her head and burst into sobs.

"Mademoiselle!"

Yvette recognized the voice of Madame Laconte. "Leave me alone, please."

"No." The answer was firm but kind. Yvette felt a tug on the sheet, and realizing the nurse was determined, she let her tear-streaked face be uncovered. "Dear child, don't be afraid. You're going to be all right."

Her gentle manner sent Yvette into gushets of fresh tears. Murmuring words of comfort, the nurse sat on the side of the bed and gathered Yvette into her arms. Her calm voice, her woman's touch reminded Yvette of her mother. She rested her head on the nurse's shoulder, and gradually her sobs diminished. Madame Laconte eased her onto her pillows, then bathed the tears from her eyes. "I think you'll be able to rest now, won't you?"

"I'm very tired," Yvette agreed. Before the nurse had left the room, she was asleep.

Two days after her arrival at the Rothschild, Yvette heard the news of the commencement of the German counterattack: a massive artillery barrage on the Belgian front stretching from Malmedy in the north to Bastogne in the south. Madame Laconte brought her a map, and with news from the daily paper, Yvette followed what came to be called the Battle of the Bulge. She sympathized with troops fighting in the aching cold, grieved over mounting numbers of dead and wounded. Bad weather kept the Allied air forces on the ground, and she imagined the frustration felt by her pilot friends at being powerless to lend support. The plight of the 101st Airborne Division trapped at a road junction in Bastogne filled her with distress. She wondered if some of the parachutists there had been among those who had dropped into the fields of La Hougue. Alarming, too, were reports that Panzers had broken through the Allied line at Hagenau, and were headed directly for the town of Tantonville.

In the midst of this flood of discouraging news, Christmas Day arrived. Yvette awoke to weather that matched her mood—dark and gloomy. Not only was this to be her first Christmas away from home, but the prognosis for her right arm was not good. The rigors of her recent journey and lack of care during her stay at Vittel had frozen the joints at shoulder, elbow and wrist. Efforts by the Rothschild's masseuse, a hard, unsmiling woman, to loosen the rigid nodes had caused Yvette such exquisite pain that yesterday, the doctor had discontinued the treatments. She gazed at the limb which, for the rest of her life, must serve her as an arm. Though the crevice which yawned between shoulder and elbow was no longer raw-looking or streaked with red, it was unsightly enough to make her wince. Her wrist jutted to the left at the same awkward angle as before, and her fingers reminded her of the witch's claws in the Hansel and Gretel fairy tale. How could such an arm help her learn to walk?

Her morning started as had all the other mornings since her arrival at the Rothschild: *toilette, petit dejeuner,* a visit from Madame Laconte. The doctor made his rounds. Examining her arm, his face was glum. "We haven't done it any good. Why don't you try your own *reeducation?* Massage and flex your fingers, rotate your wrist, squeeze an orange, a ball—anything you can get your hand around. You know better than anyone how much pain you can endure."

And so she set up a schedule. An hour passed and then another as, with mindless repetition, she massaged, and flexed, rotated and squeezed. By lunch time, her arm was as rigid as before, and felt on fire from fingertips to shoulder.

Her lunch tray was decorated with a paper cutout of Pere Noel, an effort in the face of shortages to make this meal different from the rest. After her tray had been removed she dozed, dreaming of the holiday of former years. How she'd loved the ritual of assembling the creche for the Coigny church, the excitement of exchanging simple homemade presents. The aroma of the chocolate Yule *buche* in the making, the turkey basting on its spit had filled every corner of the house. And finally when all else was done, came the best part of the celebration—the family dressed in Sunday best, gathered at the table for the festive dinner.

She awoke to the cold reality of her surroundings. The season used to be the highlight of her year. This Christmas had been just another day.

A stir in the hall distracted her. She waited listlessly for the nurse bringing her afternoon medication. Instead, there was a shuffle of feet, a whispered conversation. Her curiosity piqued, she lifted her head from the pillow. A knock sounded on the door.

"Entrez," she called.

Laden with packages, Frank and B. J. shouldered their way into the room. She must still be dreaming! "Is it really you?" she cried.

"Bad pennies," B. J. answered. "Always turning up."

Her eyes never left them as they crossed to the bed, afraid that if she blinked, they might disappear. "What—? How—?"

"We were getting a little flak-happy," Frank explained. "Doc Roberts decided it was time we took a couple of days leave."

"When the guys found out we were coming to Paris and planned to see you, they loaded us down with all this stuff," B. J. continued. "We requisitioned a light weapons carrier and, voila, here we are."

As always where she was concerned, they made the complex sound simple. Dazed, she watched them pile the gifts on the bedside table. "Would you look at this!" Frank exclaimed, un-wrapping an oblong pound cake sprinkled with powdered sugar. "Now how in the hell in Tantonville could DiMarzo dig up stuff to make a cake!"

"It's beautiful," Yvette breathed. "I'm starved for some of DiMarzo's cooking. Let's eat it—right this minute."

"I just happen to have a pocketknife," B. J. smiled.

Frank crossed the room to get the other chair, and the next two hours flew as the cake disappeared and the pilots brought Yvette up to date on what had happened to them since they'd seen each other. As members of the squadron detached to Dole to support the Seventh Army, they'd made contact with American fighting men with whom they shared no memories and no experiences. Invading southern France by way of Africa, Sicily, Italy and the Riviera coast, the Seventh Army soldiers marked their vehicles and dressed differently from those the airmen had been accustomed to. Their talk was of Anzio, Kasserine Pass, Palermo, and Cap Bon, not Utah Beach, St. Lo, Falaise and Caen. "It was almost like fighting alongside a foreign ally," B. J. smiled. At Dole, too, they met for the first time members of the French Air Force who had trained in the United States. "What a surprise when we saw French markings and *Ma Petite Cherie* painted on P-47s landing on the runway," Frank laughed.

The city was fantastic, he went on, with crooked cobblestoned streets, canals lined with mills, and arches of an old Roman bridge over the Doub. "We were quartered in town, and got to know our neighbors. When the weather closed in, we went to movies, church a few times in the Cathedral—even took in an opera. There was a French kid—about thirteen years old, I guess—whose name was Paul. His family lived on the perimeter of the airfield. Every morning when the crew chiefs began warming our engines, he'd come racing across the field. We asked him if it was all right with his parents for him to be out so early. He'd grin and shake his head. 'They lock my door. I climb out the window.' He'd wish us 'Bon voyage,' and watch us taxiing out toward the runway." Frank's expression softened. "It gave us a good feeling to see him standing there—hoping we'd make it back O.K."

B. J. nodded. "He loved everything about the P-47, from the roar of the engine to the smell of gasoline. I guess we were just enough older to be heroes to him. I miss the little guy."

"Then came the flood." Frank shook his head. "The Doub went on a rampage, overflowed its banks, washed out the airfield. We had to move operations temporarily to Dijon, then back to Dole again. All that was a picnic compared to Tantonville."

"I saw the town in the distance from the plane," Yvette recalled.

"That's the best way to see Tantonville," B. J. assured her, then proceeded to catalog the misfortunes that had beset them: an airfield floating on a sea of mud, snow covering the pierced-planking runway, dripping tents, wet C-rations, cold that chilled to the bone, and "red alerts" at night that interrupted sleep. "You can put up with all of that—they don't promise you the comforts of home when you join the Air Force—but the pressure from higher command to get the planes in the air, no matter what the weather, really wrecks morale."

Frank nodded grimly. "'If you can see the end of the runway, take off,' was the order of the day."

As she sympathized with their woes, Yvette thought back to the first time that she had met them. Along with Tom, Andy, James and the others in Dr. Lerossi's handpicked group, they'd sat at ease in the lush grass beside her cot. They had joked with each other, and made her feel welcome.

How young they'd looked. So eager to test themselves against the enemy. Six months later, three of the eight were dead, and the drawn, gray faces and weary eyes of these two made them look older than their years.

"—and you can tell by all this griping how much we miss you. We didn't grouse like this with you around because you never complained."

B. J.'s apology brought her back to the present. "I've had my moments," Yvette assured him. "I was feeling pretty down before you came."

His dark eyes filled with concern. "DiMarzo told us how worried they were about you at St. Dizier—that you might not come around. Yet even after James's death, you didn't knuckle under." He was silent a moment. "James would have admired that," he added, bemused.

"I wrote his mother and told her about our last mission." Frank's voice was husky. "Her answer almost broke my heart. She asked to be remembered to you." He stared at his hands clasped together between his knees. "Some people you never stop missing. James is one of them."

She nodded, unable to speak, while tears streamed down her cheeks. Daylight had faded from the room, but engrossed in thoughts of their lost friend, they didn't notice. They shared an unconstrained silence until an orderly paused in the doorway. With a *"Permettez-moi,"* he crossed the room and turned on the light above her bed. The pilots blinked in its harsh glare, stirred, then pushed themselves to their feet.

"I guess we better shove off," Frank said.

"Thanks for coming, for the gifts, for everything." Yvette looked from one to the other. "You made my Christmas."

B. J. shook his head. "You got that backwards."

"You've made ours," Frank smiled.

34

Clearing skies unleashed American planes and the resulting havoc wrought on enemy food supplies, ammunition dumps, and oil depots brought the enemy to a standstill. The 101st Airborne Division, holding out at Bastogne, was relieved and by the end of the year, the Germans had retreated to positions behind the Seigfried Line. Nazi efforts to capture the port of Antwerp and cut Allied supply lines had failed, and hopes arose that Hitler's gamble had indeed been the last throw of the dice.

In the days that followed, other pilots on leave in Paris came to see Yvette, and one mid-January afternoon, Nurse Laconte ushered Dr. Lerossi into the room.

Smiling, the nurse watched the happy reunion, then left them to themselves.

"You look tired," Yvette said as he sat down beside the bed. "I know it's been rough."

"They had us worried, but they can't replace men and materiel like we can." He shook his head. "Sickening—the needless loss of life. When will it end!"

She asked about the people she knew.

"B. J. had a close call last week. When he came in to land, his plane slid off the icy runway and cracked up. Moments after they dug him out, it caught fire. He was lucky to escape with only cuts and bruises."

"Thank God," Yvette murmured. "And Frank?"

"Sick to death of the cold, rain, and snow, like we all are, but otherwise O.K. My news is that I'm being transferred."

"Really!" she exclaimed. "Where? And when?"

"To an Army Hospital in Luxembourg. They're swamped with wounded right now. I've been with the 371st Fighter Group since it was activated in the spring of '43. It'll be really tough, leaving those guys."

"They'll miss you terribly," she said.

He shifted in his chair. "I talked to your surgeon, Dr. Leveque. Your operation is set for the 21st."

"Yes. He told me." She didn't add how much she dreaded the ordeal. He already knew.

"I plan to be here to scrub in."

Her eyes lit up. "Really?"

"Dr. Leveque said it would be O.K. Since it's scheduled for early in the morning, I'll come by to see you the night before."

"Having you here will make it so much easier."

"I hope so," he said.

"And after I've recovered, I'll be ready for the big plunge—learning to walk again. Do you really think it's possible?"

He nodded. "For someone stubborn as a mule."

Though she noted that his smile came readily, it seemed forced. In fact, his conversation since he'd arrived had been—strained. She frowned. "Is something the matter?"

He got to his feet and, with hands shoved in his pockets, he crossed the room and stared out of the window.

"What's bothering you?" she insisted.

He turned to face her. "Why did you reject General Eisenhower's offer?"

The unexpected question caught her off-guard.

"I would have *made* you get on that plane if I'd been there!"

"But you weren't," she reminded him, "and I had to choose. America is so far away, and I hadn't heard anything from my parents since—"

"I know! I know! but," his hand swept the scene beyond the window. "It's chaos out there. The transportation system is wrecked, communications are nonexistent, there's a shortage of everything. The few rehabilitation centers that function are already jammed with military amputees. God knows how long it'll be before they take civilians!"

Her shocked expression brought his outburst to a halt. Wearily, he rubbed a hand over his face. "I'm sorry. I was so disappointed when Dr. Glocker told me you hadn't gone!" He came back to sit beside her. "I want to help you, Yvette, but my transfer to the Army will end my contacts with the 371st Fighter Group. The staff at the Luxembourg Hospital won't have time or the clout to intercede for a wounded French girl. After the war in Europe is over, we still have to fight the Japanese. A lot of us will be shipped direct to the Orient."

His catalog of reasons why she should have gone to the United States enveloped her in a fog of hopelessness. For the first time, she truly realized what she'd lost. With so many wounded needing help, that General Eisenhower had made such an offer seemed beyond belief. Yet the miracle had happened—and she had rejected it. She looked at the doctor with bleak eyes. If only he'd been with her at Vittel. At his command to "Go!" she would have gone. The operation would be over and, by this time, she'd be on the mend. Six months from now, she could have been walking!

He saw her anguish and stroked her hair. "It would have been quicker in the States, but France will recover. By that time, your surgery will be done with and you'll have regained your strength. When the rehab centers open, you'll be ready."

"I'll be ready, but it may be years before they are," she said bitterly.

As if conceding that to raise false hopes was unjustified, he slumped back in his chair and let his arms drop to his sides. His words had dismayed her; his uncharacteristic gesture of defeat touched her to the quick. How much she owed this man! He had helped her in more ways than she could count, and she had returned so little. Now was not the time for self-pitying tears.

"Mules never give up, do they?" she asked.

His eyes met hers. He shook his head.

"I'm an unusually stubborn mule."

"They're the best kind," he answered.

"Then I'd better go on being one."

"We miss you," he said. "Things aren't the same since you left."

"For me either. I'll take an army tent and twelve hundred men any time."

He smiled. Then he leaned toward her and his expression sobered. "We're concerned that no one has been able to reach your parents. Colonel Kleine asked me to try while I'm in Paris. I'll do my best, though I doubt that I'll have any better luck than the French authorities. If Coigny were a market center or even on a major highway, we Americans would have a better chance of getting in touch with them. But since the town is so small and off the beaten track—"

"Coigny has two Chateaux," she answered defensively. "One of them is the ancestral home of deFranquetot, a *Marechal* of France. The church's altar is listed in the national registry—"

"The Church!" Dr. Lerossi broke in. "Why didn't I think of that before! Who was the priest who came with your father one day to visit you at La Londe?"

"Father Giard. He is our Abbe, but he lives in Baupte. Baupte," she repeated, her voice rising with excitement, "is on the main highway between La-Haye-du-Puits and Carentan."

"Right. Fighting took place all around the town for control of the road. If we could get word to Father Giard—" He crossed the room to the armoire and got his coat. "Even in times like these, the hierarchy must have ways of keeping in touch with its parish priests. I'll hustle around and see what I can find." As he shrugged into his overcoat, he eyed her glowing face. "Now don't get your hopes up."

"I won't! I won't!"

He rolled his eyes at her less than convincing promise. With assurances that he would see her the following week before her surgery, he said good-bye.

No matter that she told herself not to be impatient, she soon began to listen for different sounding footsteps in the hall. But days ticked by, and no one from her family appeared. What if Dr. Lerossi failed, as had everyone else who had tried? If her parents could not be reached, where would she go when she was discharged from the Rothschild? As if that worry were not enough, Dr. Leveque announced that he'd advanced her surgery two days. Dr. Lerossi would therefore be unable to scrub in.

"But he is a dear friend and is going to a lot of trouble to get here," Yvette protested.

"He is a military physician," Dr. Leveque replied. "He'll understand that schedules sometimes must be changed. I thought you would be pleased to have it over with sooner," he added smoothly.

He never explained the reason for advancing the date. Was it a family problem, a trip out of town, or a deliberate slight to Dr. Lerossi, Yvette wondered. In any event, there was nothing she could do about it.

The evening before her surgery seemed interminable, and though she was given medication to help her sleep, she tossed and turned all night. It was still dark when, early the next morning, the nurse came to prep her. Fearful and lonely, she welcomed the anesthetic that sent her into oblivion.

As if from a great distance, she heard a knock on the door. *"Entrez,"* she answered weakly.

Dr. Lerossi came into the room. "You're awake?" he asked softly.

She nodded. The effort made her dizzy.

"How are you feeling?" he asked.

"Ca va," she answered listlessly.

He sat down in the chair. "I'm sorry I wasn't here when you needed me. The surgeon never told me why he changed the date. I was mad as hell. Maybe he doesn't like Americans, or maybe I came on too strong. Who knows? We doctors are a touchy lot!" He shook his head. "I wanted so much to be with you."

Though she kept her eyes fastened on his face, Yvette felt her concentration slipping. That Dr. Leveque had moved the date of her surgery did not interest her. All that mattered now was that the operation she'd dreaded so much was over, and she had survived.

"But that's water over the dam," Dr. Lerossi echoed her thoughts, "and you're going to be all right." He took her hand. "I've got good news. Church officials reached Father Giard. He contacted your parents. As soon as your father can make travel arrangements, he's coming to see you."

She wanted to shout her joy; all she could produce was a

smile. "Thanks a million."

He nodded. "I'm being transferred this week, but I'll come back whenever—"

Her eyes closed. Her lashes were the color of soot against her stark white face. How fragile she looked. The amount of blood she'd lost was worrisome. Damn Leveque! Even digging that bit of information out of the sonovabitch was like pulling teeth. Poor Yvette. Better that she not be told what a long convalescence she faced. He'd discuss that with her medical doctor. He checked her pulse and breathing. Thank God, Madame Laconte was so competent. She'd keep a close watch.

35

Though her recovery was glacially slow, the prospect of seeing her father buoyed Yvette's spirits. Each afternoon as visiting hours approached, she wondered: will be come today? It was not until the second week in February that she heard the footsteps she'd listened for so long.

"Papa!" she cried.

He hurried across the room and took his daughter in his arms. "At last!"

Mute, Yvette clung to him. The feel of his rough tweed coat against her cheek, the smell of his tobacco, the tone of his voice crooning endearments could best be savored in silence. Finally, she let him go, and he sat in the chair beside her bed. It had been four and a half months since she'd seen him, and she searched for changes. He looked tired—as did everyone these days—and his hair was grayer than she remembered. "It's so good to see you. I was beginning to wonder if I ever would!"

"We were crazy with worry," he answered, "and then, out of the blue, Father Giard brought us the message."

"Ever since St. Dizier, the Americans have been trying to reach you."

"I'm not surprised they couldn't. All of France is bouleverse! Nothing works!."

"How is everyone? Start with Maman."

As he began the recitation of family activities that she loved to hear, she settled herself against her pillows. Her mother was doing well, he told her, untiring in her efforts, as always, to keep the household in good running order. "She sends you her boundless love."

Claire had taken over Gilberte's duties in the *cremerie*, he went on. Marguerite was contemplating marriage to a farmer in Appeville. Henri, Etienne and Edouard were busy with customary winter tasks. Michel was happy in his marriage. A child was on the way. No word from Georges.

Although German prisoners were being used to clear fields of artillery shells and hand grenades, the effort had come too late for the grain harvest. Thus, due to lack of fodder, milk production was lower than usual at this time of year. On a happier note, he informed her that the Renault had had a miraculous resurrection.

She smiled, remembering the night four years ago that she and her father had outwitted the Germans.

"Amazing recovery," Antoine said. "As soon as the Boches packed up and left, it ran like a top."

"That's wonderful!"

He made a rueful face. "Now all it lacks is gasoline. I hope it won't be four more years before *that* becomes available."

Yvette asked about the *Comtesse*.

"She's busy trying to put the Chateau in order," he replied, "but she can't get building materials and there's no labor to hire. The 'Goose-Steppers' almost wrecked the place—" he shook his head in dismay "—stabling their horses in the classrooms of the seminary!"

"Cochons!" Yvette agreed. "And Father Giard?" she asked.

"His bicycle gave out months ago. Now he walks between Coigny and Baupte." Her father frowned. "He never complains, but he just—doesn't look well. Perhaps it's fatigue. He asked me to give you his love. By the way," her father added, "everybody's wondering how the Abbe got wind of your whereabouts?"

"Dr. Lerossi got the process started here in Paris." Yvette shrugged. "That's all I know."

"That good, good man. How is he?" her father asked.

"Weary of the killing and the maiming." She told of the doctor's visits, his anger with Dr. Leveque, his disappointment that she hadn't gone to the United States.

Astounded, her father stared at her. "What do you mean?"

Yvette told of the nurse rushing into the room to tell her she had a visitor; of her frenzied efforts to make her patient look presentable. "Suddenly everything got quiet. Then we heard the sound of footsteps marching down the hall. Moments later, there they were—General Eisenhower and members of his staff, standing at the foot of my bed. I could hardly believe my eyes. You can imagine my topsy-turvy thoughts when he extended his invitation."

A look of incredulity spread over her father's face. "And you *refused?*" he demanded.

"But Papa," she explained, "America is so far away. I hadn't heard from you and Maman. Dr. Lerossi couldn't go with me and—"

She paused, watching his knuckles whiten as he gripped the arms of his chair. "And you refused?" he repeated as if the thought were beyond his comprehension. He sat immobilized, his eyes glazed.

Stricken, she tried again to explain. "Everything happened so fast. The plane carrying the wounded was leaving that afternoon. How could I—"

His head sank to his chest. "If I'd only known."

Tears streamed down her cheeks. "Maybe I'll get a second chance."

"Miracles like that seldom happen in twos." His voice rasped in her ears.

A strained silence settled between them. She had never seen him so upset, but as she gazed at his expression still frozen in disbelief, a sudden anger gripped her. How easy it was for him and Dr. Lerossi to castigate her—after the fact. If she'd possessed their knowledge of existing conditions, and the time to examine all possibilities, she could have chosen wisely. But she'd had neither. She'd been lonely and frightened, pressed by events to commit herself. That she'd made a mistake was all too evident to her now. She did not need them to keep reminding her of it.

As she looked away from this parent whom she had so sorely disappointed, her glance strayed to the painting on the opposite wall. When she was perturbed, she seemed to seek out instinctively its depiction of cows grazing beside a stream, a kitchen garden at the back door of a farmhouse, a girl scattering seed for chickens pecking in the dirt. If only she could go home! How she longed to escape the confines of this room, the stultifying boredom of routine, and most of all the memories of her unfortunate choice.

"Yvette."

"Yes, Papa."

"It's going to be all right."

His expression had softened. He reached for her hand. "It was such a surprise. The offer. If it caught me unawares, I realize how you must have felt."

Through her tears, she saw the blurred image of his face. How worn it looked. His journey to see her had exhausted him. With railway terminals destroyed, bridges out, and sections of the roadbed missing, there must have been delays all along the way. Yet he'd never mentioned that.

"I'm sorry, Papa," she said.

He squeezed her hand. "That decision is behind us now. We can't do anything about it. So—we'll think of tomorrow."

A voice from the corridor announced the end of visiting hours. He pushed himself from the chair, leaned over and kissed her good-bye. She put her arms around his neck. "I love you."

His three-day visit ended all too soon. He had stayed, as he usually did on his trips to Paris, with the *Proprietaire* of La Hougue. "He has invited me to his home whenever I come to see you," Antoine told Yvette. She loaded him with messages for the rest of the family, and with an "I'll see you soon, my sweet," he was gone.

She scarcely had time to feel bereft after his departure when that afternoon she had another visitor—a law student from the Sorbonne. Jean-Louis had been intrigued by her story which he'd heard from Madame Laconte, his mother's cousin. He brought a couple of classmates with him, and the four young people had a lively chat. The newcomers described conditions in Paris during the Nazi occupation, and the riotous celebration when the city was freed. She told of watching the parachutists landing in the moonlit fields of La Hougue, and amused them with the tale of the red Renault's rejuvenation. The fifteen-minute courtesy call stretched to an hour, and when good-byes were said, the students promised to come again.

Visiting hours soon became the focal point of her days. Sometimes her new friends came as a group; other times Jean-Louis came alone. He brought her presents: books, sprays of daffodils, ribbons for her hair. She learned about his family, his preferences in literature and music, his ambition to become a judge. He was a clever mimic and regaled her with imitations of his law professors. She found him an amusing companion, someone who speeded up the otherwise slow passage of the hours.

One afternoon, however, he was uncharacteristically sub-dued. Her efforts to carry on a one-sided conversation became wearing, and she asked what was troubling him. He stared at his hands clasped in his lap, then looked at her with soulful eyes. "I love you, Yvette," he blurted.

She stared at his thin, earnest face. "You don't know what you're saying!" she exclaimed.

"I know very well!" His dark eyes shone. "I want to spend my life taking care of you."

Revulsion swept over her. "I don't need your pity! As soon as I learn to walk, I can take care of myself." Her hollow boast sounded as ridiculous as his declaration of love, and she dissolved in tears.

He was instantly at her side, and took her hand. "I'll be your feet, Yvette, your messenger, your contact with the world—"

"Stop!" she shook her head. His protestations grated on her nerves, but their absurdity helped her regain a measure of composure. "It's out of the question. I don't want you—or anyone—to give up everything for me. You are kindhearted, and I appreciate that. But the answer is no."

He pleaded with her to reconsider—to take time to think over his proposal. She shook her head and held up her hand to terminate the conversation. When that failed to stem the tide of his entreaties, she turned her face to the wall. Finally, she heard his footsteps drag across the floor, and then the finality of the closing door.

She stared at the ceiling. What a romantic he was. He envisioned her languishing Camille-like on a graceful *chaise* while the two of them sipped wine and talked on a lofty plane. The reality of their life together would not only appall him but send him packing in three days. The more she thought about his proposal, the more depressed she became. Until now, the possibility that she might not walk for years had made her feel sorry only for herself. But his offer to spend his life taking care of her brought home a harsh, unpleasant truth: when she returned to Coigny, she would be a tremendous burden to her family. The thought became a constant worry.

Shortly after that episode, Dr. Lerossi came to see her unexpectedly. Though she welcomed him as warmly as always, thanked him for his part in reaching Father Giard, and plied him with questions about his transfer, ten minutes into their conversation, he asked, "What's the trouble, Yvette?"

Her pretense at being puzzled by his question made no impression on him. "You can save the lifted eyebrows, the wide-eyed look for others. I know you too well."

"You've already heard more than your share of my problems," she retorted. "Enough is enough."

He sat back in his chair and yawned. "This is shaping up to be a very boring visit because I'm not planning to talk either."

Reluctantly, she described Jean-Louis's proposal and how it had crystallized her fears of becoming an encumbrance to her family. "As if they didn't have enough to do already!" She gave him a rueful look. "At La Hougue there won't be twelve hundred men at my beck and call."

He'd listened through to the end and, as usual, didn't waste time on soothing words that accomplished nothing. "There may be a solution right here at hand. It would only be a stopgap, but better than none. Madame Laconte."

Yvette frowned, intrigued.

"During our discussions of your case, she's told me bits and pieces about herself." He went on to relate that the nurse had worked throughout the war without leave. She wanted now to take a month's vacation, but being a widow and childless, she had no place to go. "I think she would be very pleased to spend the time at La Hougue taking care of you," the doctor finished.

"Really!" Yvette's eyes lit up. "I like her so much. She's been wonderful to me."

"She's quite fond of you."

"It wouldn't be a very exciting vacation for her," Yvette mused, "but perhaps a month in the country would be a welcome change."

"Ask your parents to send her a written invitation."

"Of course," Yvette replied. "At once."

"By the end of her stay, you will have settled into a routine. Then something else may work out."

She sighed. "You have answers for everything. How will I ever get along without you?"

36

rrangements for Yvette's departure from the Rothschild fell into place. Nurse Laconte accepted the Hamels' invitation, and at Colonel Kleine's behest, an ambulance, driver and mechanic were provided to make the trip. From their new bivouac area outside of Metz, a delegation from the 371st Fighter Group came to tell Yvette good-bye. Frank, B. J., Barnes, Davis and DiMarzo brought going-away presents, and hopes for a brighter future. With brimming eyes, she bid them farewell. Now, only the parting with Dr. Lerossi remained.

He stood by her bed. "We've said good-bye so often, we should be experts at it by now."

"It doesn't get any easier," she answered.

"No, it doesn't," he agreed.

"Will I ever see you again?"

"Maybe after the war is over, I'll come back to Normandy to visit."

"What a wonderful idea!" she said. "I'd love that."

He took an envelope from a pocket of his jacket. "Colonel Kleine asked me to deliver this. It's the money the guys in the outfit collected."

Misty-eyed, she gazed at the envelope and shook her head. "I wish there were some way I could tell the Colonel how grateful I am."

"He knows, Yvette. He also asked me to convey his hopes that your rehabilitation won't be delayed too long."

"I guess for the rest of my life I'll regret not taking his offer."

"Don't think that far ahead," he advised. "Concentrate on getting your strength back. Your arm will need a lot of work. Exercises, massages, and more exercises."

She inspected her still-rigid fingers. "No change yet," she grimaced.

"It will come. It may take months, but it will come. I promise."

She looked up at him. "So be it. You've never been wrong."

"I'm selective about promises," he smiled. "But you have my word on this." He leaned toward her. *"Au revoir,* my mule."

She put her arms around his neck and wordlessly, they clung to each other. When she let him go, he gripped her hand. "Have courage," he said hoarsely. At the doorway, he turned for a final look, and then was gone. The tears she hadn't shed while he was there, spilled down her cheeks. He had been everything to her: Doctor, good companion, Father Confessor. How *would* she get along without him?

By eight o'clock, March 20, everything was ready. The envelope was packed in Yvette's suitcase, she had thanked the Administrator and the staff for their good care. Nurse Laconte followed the two orderlies carrying Yvette's stretcher to the ambulance and made sure that she was comfortable. Yvette noted that the driver and the mechanic had trouble hiding their curiosity about the statuesque nurse in the royal blue, ankle-length cape, and the French girl wounded so grievously. Did they wonder why Americans had been ordered to take the two from Paris to a little town in Normandy or, like all soldiers, had they long ago decided that the military moved in mysterious ways and theirs not to reason why. Whatever lay behind the mission, they doubtless counted themselves lucky that this assignment took them west and would delay for a little while their having to head east.

Robert, the driver, and Joe, the mechanic, had decided on the southern route through Dreux and Argentan, hoping the roads might be less congested than the more direct highway through Evreux and Liseux. Also, they would avoid Caen. The pivotal city had been all but destroyed during the bitter fighting soon after D-Day between German and English-Canadian forces.

Considering the condition of the roads, they made good time to Dreux. As they approached the main crossroads of the town, Robert slowed. "I'll never forget coming through here in August of '44," he said. "I was attached to Patton's forces then. It looked like the whole town had turned out to welcome us. They pelted us with flowers, and offered us wine. We stopped only long enough to find out the shortest route to Rouen, then full steam ahead. Those were the days!" he mused. "We were sure the war was almost over. Then winter came and the Battle of the Bulge!" His grim tone reminded Yvette of Dr. Lerossi's comment: "We thought we'd be home by Christmas. Now we're bracing for a counterattack." So many soldiers and civilians killed; so many lives wrecked by Hitler's final, insane stand.

A bombed-out bridge over the Eure forced the ambulance onto a detour. The dirt road was rutted and narrow, and the ambulance slowed to a crawl. As best she could, Madame Laconte steadied Yvette's swaying stretcher all the way to Verneuil. Here they joined the main highway and picked up speed. As they neared the town of Argentan, the scars of war were everywhere apparent. Yvette had heard the pilots talk of the Battle of the Falaise Gap, and now she saw firsthand the result of the debacle. Slaughter, they had labeled it. Eight German divisions had been trapped in a triangle bounded by Falaise to the north, Mortain on the west and Argentan in the south. Obedient to Hitler's command, they had refused to surrender, and had tried to escape. Strafed by planes, attacked by tanks and infantry, the eight divisions had been annihilated.

At Vire and further on St. Lo, she viewed what remained of once-thriving communities. Buildings which had survived saturation bombing were later devastated by door-to-door fighting. The sun was setting when they arrived in Carentan. While the ambulance picked its way through rubble-strewn streets, its passengers were silent. The desolation they'd already seen left no words to express further consternation.

The road to Coigny still looked naked. The plane trees which formerly lined the route had been felled on General Rommel's orders. Cut into stakes, tipped with explosives, "Rommel's asparagus" were planted by the thousand on Normandy's beaches. On D-Day, hidden by high tide, they ripped the bottoms from Allied landing craft.

The town looked the same as when she'd left, yet how strange it was to return like this. With mounting excitement, she directed Robert along the road whose every contour she knew by heart. Finally they arrived at the open gateway and began their slow progress down the drive. Broken windows were still boarded up, the trellis in the flower garden had disappeared, and the chestnut tree had been badly damaged. But the courtyard had been raked, and welcoming lights burned in all the rooms. When Robert cut the engine, the front door burst open.

In a fever of impatience, Yvette listened to the crunch of running feet, an excited babble of voices. The back doors opened and Madame Laconte alighted. The introductions between the newcomers and their hosts seemed interminable. Finally, the servicemen lifted the stretcher out of the ambulance and cries of *"Tiens!" "Voila, Yvette!" "Ma petite fille!"* greeted her. She was engulfed in a flurry of hugs and kisses. She clung to her mother. "Maman!" she kept repeating. Tears and smiles mingled as she gazed around at the circle of faces. Even Father Giard was there.

Antoine waved a hand toward the open door. "Our house is your house," he said to the guests, and with Alice beside him, he led the way across the threshold. As the Americans carried her stretcher into the hall, Yvette inhaled the potpourri of odors coming from the kitchen: soup bubbling on the *cremaillere,* polish that was used to clean the copper pots, fresh-cut herbs on a cupboard shelf, lamb roasting on a spit. Even with her eyes closed, she would have known that she had arrived at La Hougue.

When Henri had moved her from the stretcher to a reclining chair beside the fire, Alice spread an afghan across her lap. She cupped Yvette's chin in her hand and examined her face. "So thin," she murmured in a worried tone. "We must get some good hot meals inside you." She patted her daughter's cheek, then turned to Madame Laconte. "May I show you to your room?"

While Marguerite and Claire busied themselves with putting dinner on the table, Edouard went for more firewood, and Antoine and the other brothers helped the servicemen unload the ambulance.

The Abbe drew up a chair beside Yvette. "There have been many changes since you went away," he said.

She nodded. "The room looks like a kitchen again instead of a cave."

"No more need for mattresses at the windows. Splintering glass isn't a danger any more, thank God."

"The copper pots are back, there's the blue vase on the mantle and," she smiled, "Papa's rifle has returned."

Father Giard examined the chimney with a puzzled frown. "Strange about the rifles. As soon as the Nazi left, they all showed up. Magical."

Yvette didn't answer, for she hadn't heard. Her eyes were fixed on the table where, closer to death than to life, she'd lain following her injury. She felt again the rosary pressed into her hand, heard her mother's muffled sobs. She saw the Abbe sway toward her from the doorway and listened as he administered the last rites.

"Yvette."

His voice wrenched her back from the awful memories.

"Yes, Father."

"It's over. Don't let your mind dwell on those events."

"They're not easy to forget."

"No," he agreed, "but you must not linger in the past. Look ahead to the future, my child."

What future, she thought. Dutifully she nodded.

"You're surrounded by people who love you. We'll do everything we can to help."

She looked into the steadfast eyes that had seen so much sorrow and travail. They did not offer pity. Instead they issued a silent challenge: you can sink into self-indulgence, thinking only of your own misfortune, or you can develop into a strong, resourceful human being. The choice is yours.

Tears blurred the contours of his face. "Why does it have to be so hard?"

He covered her hand with his. "Because anything worth attaining always is."

Voices from the hallway ended their talk. Alice showed the guests to their places, while Henri and Michel moved Yvette's chair closer to the table. Antoine poured an *aperitif*—La Hougue's

own brand of apple brandy, called *eau de vie,* or Calvados, then
lifted his glass. *"Vive l'Amerique; vive la France.* To our guests, we
extend the hand of friendship. To our precious Yvette, welcome
home!"

When the "Bravos," and "Hear, hear's" subsided, Claire brought
Yvette's dinner to her on a tray. "Can I help you?" she asked.

"I can manage, thanks," Yvette replied. "It looks delicious."

While the soup disappeared, Yvette was plied with questions
about Colonel Kleine, Dr. Lerossi, General Eisenhower's visit, and
finally, the reason the Americans were involved in Yvette's care
was explained to Robert and Joe.

The soup was followed by lamb, potatoes, green beans and
onions done to a turn. Bread, pitchers of milk, and crocks of butter
made the rounds. Weary of the C and K rations on which they'd
lived for so long, the Americans fell upon each dish as if it were
to be their last. They showered compliments on their hosts. The
Hamels were still amused that Americans who had so much of
everything would consider milk and butter such a treat.

Over coffee, the conversation turned to how much longer the
war would last. "We've thought the Germans were done for so
many times, nobody is predicting any more," Robert grimaced.

"What keeps them going?" Joe wondered aloud.

"A dictator who's lost all touch with reality," Antoine said.

"And Allied demands for unconditional surrender," the Abbe
suggested. "If they're going to lose everything, they might as well
go down fighting."

"One thing is certain," Henri said grimly. "The Germans hope
the English and Americans reach Berlin before the Russians do."

Despite Yvette's effort to stay awake, the stress of the day's trip
overcame her excitement at being home. Her eyelids grew heavy
and her head began to nod. Noting her fatigue, Madame Laconte
rose to her feet.

"I'd better get my patient to bed."

"Shall I bring the stretcher?" Robert offered.

"Don't bother." Henri pushed back his chair. "I'll carry her up."

Good-nights were exchanged, Henri picked up Yvette and,
with Alice leading the way and Madame Laconte behind, the

procession made its way to the hall. There, her mother kissed her daughter and smoothed her hair. "May angels guard thee through the night," she murmured.

As Henri mounted the stairs, Yvette recalled the last time she had descended them. How angry she had been. Heavy-footed, she'd clumped down to the hall and confronted him. "I milked this morning. Papa said I don't have to do it twice." But Henri had argued and cajoled, and grudgingly she'd given in. She'd gone out into the field and her life would never be the same.

What would have happened if she'd refused. If Henri had milked those cows would she be walking up the stairs, and he need to be carried?

"It's over, Yvette," the Abbe had said. "You must not linger in the past. Live for the future."

Her eyes closed, and her head dropped to Henri's shoulder. A door opened, and she felt herself lowered gently to the bed. The light grew dim, the voices faded. She sank into the feather pillow, welcomed the warmth of the down comforter. Home.

37

adame Laconte said. "Well done. You know how to bathe the patient, keep her wounds clean, and now you've mastered massage. You've earned my certificate of approval!"

Standing at Yvette's bedside, Marguerite and Claire basked in the nurse's praise.

"Thank you," Claire bobbed a curtsy.

"You are too kind," Marguerite added.

"Not at all," the nurse responded. "You've both worked hard, and you're very competent."

Marguerite winked at Yvette. "Will you trust us?" she asked.

Yvette pretended to cringe.

"I'll give you a diploma," Madame Laconte said in a loud aside to Marguerite. "That'll make her feel you know more."

"What will it say?" Claire asked.

"Exactly what I've just said," the nurse answered. "The written word always carries more weight than the spoken."

As Yvette listened to the exchange, she recalled Madame Laconte's formal manner when she'd first arrived. Her bearing had been stiff, correct; everyone was Madame, Monsieur, Mademoiselle. No one heard her laugh aloud, and she'd kept to herself instead of joining the others around the fire. But gradually, the easy give and take, the quips, the jests which were so much a part of the family's behavior had enlivened her wit, relaxed her demeanor, and now she was one of them.

"I can't believe the month is over," Yvette said on a more sober note. "Where has the time gone?"

"Where indeed?" Madame Laconte took the chair beside the bed while her two students sat facing her on the floor. "I'll miss so many things. Our walks together, Marguerite, and my cup of coffee in the afternoon, Claire. All of you have spoiled me."

"I wish you didn't have to go."

Marguerite and Claire echoed Yvette's lament.

"Duty calls," Madame Laconte replied, "though I confess I'm not ready to answer." She glanced out the window at the cloudless sky. "May is the best month of the year in Paris, but I doubt that it compares with May in Normandy." She smiled. "I'm even going to miss the cock's crow waking me at dawn."

As the last session of what had become a daily routine progressed, Yvette remarked again on how her sisters had changed during her eight months absence. Ever since Yvette could remember, Marguerite had been ill-at-ease with strangers, and shy even with people she knew. She seldom initiated a conversation, or volunteered her services. Perhaps it was the responsibilities forced on her by Gilberte's death, or satisfaction in her approaching marriage that had transformed her. Whatever the reason, it was she who had sought out Madame Laconte's company and become her friend: she, also, who'd offered with Claire's help to take over Yvette's care when the time came for the nurse to leave.

And Claire—no longer a child, her former straight-as-a-stick figure was budding into womanhood. She'd developed a talent as a *coiffeuse,* and took infinite pains in arranging her own as well as her sisters' hair into elaborate *pompadours* and elegant *chignons.* Torn between waiting for a handsome knight on a white horse to sweep into her life or pursuing a career as the *Proprietesse* of her own salon, she was buffeted by conflicting hopes and dreams. To look at Claire was to look at herself at thirteen, Yvette mused. So long ago!

"—and how did you wear your hair?" Claire's question interrupted Yvette's musings.

"Wait a minute!" Marguerite objected. "Let her finish telling us about the dress."

"Since it was a tea dance, I wore a mid-calf gown. It was my husband's favorite, rose-colored silk, with long sleeves and a full skirt—"

As Madame Laconte patiently supplied the requested details, her sisters' avid interest emphasized to Yvette how circumscribed their lives had been since the war began. For a month, like someone parched with thirst gulps water, they had drunk in the nurse's tales of attending a convent school in Lyon, then the romantic meeting with the young cavalry officer. They'd listened in rapture to her descriptions of the balls, ballets, and operas she'd attended as his wife until his tragic death in 1916 at the Battle of Verdun. They dreaded the end of these morning sessions around which they centered their days. But end they must. Tomorrow, Madame Laconte departed.

She rose now from her chair. "I think we've tarried long enough. On a day like this, Yvette should be outside. Also, I'm sure that Madame Hamel could use some help with lunch."

Reluctantly, her listeners put aside visions of a magical land that they would never experience and returned to their everyday routines. Madame Laconte readied Yvette for the stay outdoors. Marguerite left to summon one of the brothers, and Claire to offer her services to her mother. As Madame Laconte finished tidying the room, Etienne appeared, lifted his sister, and carried her down the stairs. Gently, he lowered her into the chair outside the kitchen window. *"Merci, mon frere,"* she said.

He hunkered down beside her. "You look like a different girl from the one that arrived a month ago—color in your cheeks, a sparkle in your eyes. You're even putting on weight," he pretended to grumble. "You're getting heavier all the time."

"No more desserts, Etienne. I promise."

"How's your arm this morning?"

Yvette eyed the unsightly limb lying at her side, and wished as she had a thousand times that it would suddenly surge with strength and vigor. Every exercise, each massage hurt as much as the one before. She could no longer remember what it was like to be free of pain.

"I think it's getting better," she lied.

"I'm glad." He rose to his feet and patted her head. "Papa will be after me if I don't get back to work. We're trying to fix a plough—one of the beams is broken."

"There's always something," Yvette sympathized.

She watched him hurry back to the barn. After the relative inactivity of winter, they were entering the busiest of seasons. The family had been relieved of the drudgery of her care up to now, but as of tomorrow, she needed to be even more sparing of demands on their time.

She closed her eyes and tilted her head to let the sun warm her face. A murmur of voices from the kitchen, "moos" echoing in the adjoining fields, the bang of hammers in the barn combined to form a familiar chorus. Images of James drifted through her mind: raindrops glistening in his hair, his cap set at a jaunty angle, the tilt of his eyebrows when he frowned. The rhythm of his stride, his smile, inflections in his voice was as vivid to her as the day they'd met. In her mind's eye, she saw him leaning toward her from the chaise. He was showing her the picture of his younger brother. "I hope to God the war is over before Luke turns eighteen," she heard him say. "I couldn't stand it if anything happened to the guy." His image faded, and tears rolled down her cheeks. The war continued, but whether or not it ended before Luke turned eighteen, James would never know.

"Bonjour, Mademoiselle!"

Yvette opened her eyes. It was Micheline waving from the road. "Do you want company?" she called.

"Of course!" Yvette answered, and waited impatiently while Micheline walked her ancient bicycle down the drive. Her friend had come every week to see her, always bringing a token gift. Today it was a bouquet of daisies. "They're going crazy in Maman's garden," she said, handing them to Yvette. "You pick one, and two come up in its place. How is it going, *ma petite?*" She propped her bicycle on its stand, planted a kiss on Yvette's cheeks, then seated herself cross-legged on the ground.

"I'm getting stronger all the time," Yvette answered, "but I dread tomorrow. Madame Laconte is leaving."

"That will be hard," Micheline agreed. "Will Marguerite and Claire be able to manage?"

Yvette nodded. "It's just such a grind on everyone."

"Can I help?"

"Thanks, we'll do all right. As soon as my arm decides to work again, things will get easier. Enough of me—I get so sick of myself. Tell me what's going on."

Micheline's pert features brightened. "I have some news." She took a letter from her pocket. "This just arrived from *Tante* Elizabeth, my mother's only sister. You remember—she used to come and visit us before the war—from Alencon."

"I remember. You're so much like her—pretty and vivacious. Always have a dozen things going at once."

"And never finishing any of them, eh?" Micheline grinned. "Anyway, she's decided the war is almost over. When it is, she wants me to come and live with her. Alencon is getting itself back together after the mess left by the fighting, and there are going to be openings in the lace industry. She's sure that I can find a job."

"Wonderful!" Yvette exclaimed. Then her expression grew pensive. "That means you'll leave Coigny for good."

Her friend nodded.

"Oh, dear, how I'll miss you but," she glanced toward the road where a wagon pulled by a plodding horse was the only traffic, "I don't blame you. In your place, I'm sure I would do the same."

"Coigny was a marvelous place to grow up. We had fun at the J.A.C. meetings at the Chateau, boating on the river, Sunday afternoon get-togethers at the church, but—" she shrugged, "I'm eighteen."

Yvette nodded. "Time to move on."

"My aunt has friends who may be able to pull strings," Micheline's voice quickened. "If I got into a training program, I'd be eligible to—" Her face took on a stricken look. "Here I am babbling about my plans when you—"

"Please!" Yvette interrupted. "I can't stand it when people feel sorry for me. I'm really glad for you. I just hate to lose you as a friend."

"That will never happen! I'll probably be here for months. God knows when the war will end. Besides, this will always be home. I'll come back often for visits."

Yvette felt a chill as she saw the pattern beginning to form. Micheline, her best friend, was leaving. Others would follow.

How long would it take for the town to empty of anyone her own age?

"Can I set another place at the table?" Claire called from the kitchen window.

"Thanks," Micheline got to her feet, "but Maman will be home shortly. I'm supposed to have lunch ready when she gets there. A rain check?" she asked.

"Of course," Claire answered, and waved a good-bye.

Micheline bracketed her bicycle stand. "I'll be back to see you soon, Yvette. Can I bring you anything from town?"

"Your visits are my best medicine," Yvette answered.

Micheline smiled her thanks, and with the customary kisses, and an *"A bientot,"* called over her shoulder, she hurried up the drive.

Lunch as usual was a busy affair with discussion of the morning's activities. The Hamels expressed their regret at Madame Laconte's imminent departure. "It has been a true vacation. I've enjoyed every minute," she assured them. "Getting back into harness will not be easy."

After lunch while the others went about their duties, Alice and Yvette sat beside the fire. As was their custom, Alice mended clothes, while Yvette did her exercises. Over and over, until her mind lost count, she repeated each maneuver to strengthen her arm. At the end of the session, her muscles ached and her nerves protested. When disheartened at her snail-like progress, she reminded herself of Dr. Lerossi's assurance: "It may take months, but it will come. I promise."

Alice did her mending with seeming equanimity. Her glance strayed often to Yvette, however, and when she saw her daughter wince, she too felt pain. She longed to take Yvette in her arms, to sympathize and console her. But progress did not come that way. It must be earned. So she voiced support, encouraged the trying, and no one saw her blink away the tears. At the end of an hour, Yvette's face was bathed with sweat, and her mother was emotionally drained.

Alice put down her mending. "It's time for your nap. I'll call one of the boys."

It was Edouard who appeared a few minutes later. Twenty-two years old, this youngest of the brothers was also the huskiest, and lifted Yvette with ease. "Everybody else was busy," he said, heading for the stairs, "so they saddled me with the job."

"It's high time you did something nice for me," she retorted, reverting as easily as he had to the adversarial relationship they'd enjoyed as children. 'Remember the first morning I started milking. I was so sleepy I could hardly hold my head up, and you kept bullying me. You were horrible."

"That was five years ago! You have a memory like an elephant. Besides," his smile was sugary, "I was doing it for your own good."

"Zut!"

"I knew that if I made you mad enough, you'd be able to manage. It worked, but what thanks do I get!" he growled.

She grinned. "It did work, didn't it?"

"Like a clock. You won't believe this," he started down the hall, "but I still remembered how lousy I felt the first morning I had to get up that early. I really sympathized with you."

"You had a weird way of showing it!"

"You needed the challenge," he said righteously.

In her room, he lowered her to the bed. His bantering mood disappeared. "You're being tested like never before. And you know what? As stubborn as you are, you're going to make it."

"I wish I were as sure of that as you are," she sighed.

"You won the big round—staying alive. You can win the next one."

"Don't bet on it," she advised.

"Now you tell me!" he grunted. "I've already put my money down."

She smiled as he waved from the door.

38

F ace flushed, cap awry, Henri burst into the kitchen. "It's over! The war is over! Papa and I heard the news in the blacksmith's shop."

Alice stood immobilized at the table. She stared at Henri over the stack of bowls she held poised in midair. She blinked. "Praise God!" she breathed.

Sitting by the fire, Yvette closed the book that she was reading. "The war is over?" she repeated.

"Yes," Antoine hurried through the door. "It's true." He crossed the room to turn on the radio. A sudden blare of car horns and the clang of church bells filled the room. "I'm standing at an open window overlooking the Champs Elysees," the announcer said. "From the Place de la Concorde to the Arc de Triomphe, the boulevard is jammed with people, and every one of them is making noise."

A clatter of feet on the stairs brought Marguerite and Claire; the slam of the back door announced the arrival of the brothers.

"The unconditional surrender of the German armed forces on May 7 at Reims, followed by cessation of hostilities on the 8th, has culminated in the formal ratification by the German High Command in Berlin this morning, May 9. The war in Europe has come to an end. For conqueror and vanquished alike, the relief—"

As she listened, Yvette recalled the September evening five years ago when the conflict had begun. The family had gathered then as they were gathered now around the radio and, stunned, had heard mobilization orders summon five Hamel sons to war. They had answered the call, had fought and survived intact. What a strange twist of fate it was that the dead and wounded had been daughters.

"The full force of the Anglo-American assault can now be unleashed on Japan," the commentator went on, "where the fanatical clique which is in power has decreed that the homeland will be defended with the last drop of blood."

Yvette shuddered, remembering Dr. Lerossi's comment: "When the war in Europe is over, that's only half the battle. We still have to fight the Japanese." Had he already received his sailing orders, she worried. How many of the others that she knew would have to go?

"—and though fighting continues in the Pacific, the end of the war that engulfed a continent has triggered an outburst of joy in the capitals of Europe the like of which has never been seen." The microphone panned again to sounds of jubilation outside the window. "And so good-bye from the streets of Paris," the announcer concluded. "I return you now to the studio."

"Pierre, Georges and David will come home," Alice rejoiced.

Etienne shook his head as if to clear it. "The end of the war is like the beginning, isn't it? Even though you know it's coming, it's still a shock."

When the family sat down to the noon meal, bemused silences were broken by mundane comments, as if trying to bring the momentous down to a manageable level. The appalling plight of millions of refugees, the cataclysmic destruction visited on their erstwhile enemy were beyond comprehension. Reality was the availability of gravel for the driveway, the repair of house and barns now that war had ended.

The meal finished, Alice and Yvette moved to their places beside the fire. A pile of socks lay unmended in her lap as Alice gazed out the window. "I wonder how we'll hear. Will the boys send a postcard saying they're on their way, or will Monsieur Malraux bring an official announcement."

"Don't get your hopes up too soon, Maman," Yvette cautioned. "Germany is full of foreign laborers. It may take a long time to get around to David and Pierre. As for Georges—" she shrugged, "he'll probably just show up at the door."

The end of the war in Europe brought no drastic changes to Coigny. For the Cotentin, the war was over when the Germans had been driven from Normandy. Though they mourned the mounting numbers of Allied wounded and dead that the liberation of France brought in its wake, the day-to-day battles against weather, crop failure, and ailing animals were of more immediate concern than the fight that raged on the Franco-German border. Now that, too, had ended, but nothing was very different. Cities lay in ruin, French prisoners-of-war had not returned, and shortages of everything were still the norm.

As the weeks passed and no word was received from the missing sons, Alice grew increasingly worried. The men in the household, however, had little time to fret. The sowing of the grains in March and April had been followed by planting the beet crop in the month of June. The weather had been favorable, and they labored fourteen hours a day.

Since Marguerite and Claire also had their hands full, Yvette made as few demands on them as possible. In order not to interfere with their schedules, she'd moved to the guest room after Madame Laconte had left. Here, one or the other of her sisters brought her breakfast, and tended to her needs. She read, exercised her arm, wrote letters.

Later in the morning, Marguerite came to move her from the bed to the chair by the window. She could look out over the courtyard, barns, and stables, and watch the comings and goings of the household. She also had a view of the road, and friends and neighbors passing called out greetings to her. Lunch at noon, another exercise period, and a nap. Then one of the brothers carried her downstairs to the chair outside the kitchen window.

She was there one afternoon entertained by a mother goose parading her string of goslings back and forth across the courtyard when the squeak of the gate attracted her notice. A young man, lean as a birch sapling, walked slowly down the drive. Dressed in blue pants and dark jacket, he carried a bundle under his arm. A trim dark beard covered his chin, his forehead was hidden by a cap. Looking from side to side, he hadn't seen Yvette but as he drew closer, she recognized her brother. "Georges!" she called.

"Who is it?" he asked, squinting into the sun.

"Yvette! Here!" She waved an arm.

He sprinted the remaining distance, but when he reached the courtyard he saw her clearly, and stopped in his tracks. "Yvette?" Tentatively, he approached her, his eyes filled with dismay. He kneeled beside her chair. "What happened?"

Tears rolled down his cheeks while she recounted the events of a year ago. When she told him about Gilberte, he buried his face in his hands.

A door opened behind them. "Georges!" Alice cried.

She rushed to him, and he put his arms around her. Wordlessly, she clung to him, then held him at arms' length to look him over.

"Your wandering son is home." His face clouded. "Yvette just told me the awful news."

"It's been a painful year," she agreed. "As if Gilberte's death were not enough, we thought we were going to lose Yvette, too."

"And all this time I didn't know," he murmured.

Alice gestured toward the house. "The others will be coming soon. Will you bring Yvette?"

Gently he lifted her, his face still white with shock. "Are you getting better, *ma petite?*" he asked.

"It's slow," she acknowledged, "but sure—if I keep trying."

The rest of the family welcomed the first of the absent brothers to return. His tales of his unit blowing up munitions trains at St. Malo, destroying a communication network at Brest, marching with General Leclerc in the liberation of Alencon, and helping to pin down an enemy regiment during battles in the Ardennes kept the family in their seats long after the evening meal was finished.

In a two-week period, David and Pierre returned, and the kitchen echoed again to the sounds of jubilation. Theirs were different tales. Pressed into service on a dairy farm, David had plenty to eat and had been treated kindly by the German owners. "What a crazy setup," he related. "A Belgian, two Poles and myself were imported to do the work while the three sons of the owners were shipped off to fight the Russians. Two of the sons were killed; the four of us foreigners survived."

Of the five brothers who had gone to war, Pierre's lot had been the hardest. Shunted from one dangerous job to another, he'd defused unexploded bombs, labored in a coal mine, worked in an underground factory making rockets which had terrorized London. His skin was pasty white, and nothing about the rail-thin figure resembled the stalwart, laughing, blue-eyed flirt that had left La Hougue four years ago. To look at him brought an anguished expression to his mother's face. "It's a nightmare I'll never forget," he told her, "but it's over. Please don't keep reminding me of it with your tears." And so she cried in solitude for his lost youth; for the carefree lad who had gone away— forever.

As the long hot summer continued, there was much activity at La Hougue. David and his wife came once a week, as did Denise's family. School friends stopped by, the *Contesse* visited on Tuesdays and Father Giard dropped in whenever he made parish calls. Yvette received a lot of mail. She heard from 67th Evacuation Hospital personnel as well as members of the 371st Fighter Group still stationed in Germany.

The last week of July, the family was startled by radio reports of the ultimatum issued by the Allies to Japan: unconditional surrender. Though starvation threatened, and the nation verged on collapse, the military hierarchy refused. Fears arose that this small group of fanatics would commit the nation to mass suicide rather than accept defeat. Rumors circulated of a secret weapon the Americans possessed.

Newspaper reports of American aircraft dropping leaflets over Japanese cities warning civilians of impending bombing impressed on readers the contrast between these alerts and the sneak attack which devastated Pearl Harbor. As August came, the tension mounted. Three million copies of the surrender ultimatum were loosed by bombers over the countryside. No one in the islands could plead ignorance of the offer of cessation of hostilities. Still, the tender was rejected. The final warning was given on August 5, and the next day the mushroom cloud arose over Hiroshima. With the second explosion over Nagasaki on August 9, the worldwide conflict came to an end.

"To the victor belongs the spoils," Antoine mused, staring out the kitchen window, "but in this war, everybody was a loser."

The days of August wound down. The bell ringer, Monsieur Duclos, returned from captivity, and the church bells chimed as they used to do. Pierre's friendship with an American guard at a German prisoner-of-war camp in Lithaire, a town noted for its quarries, led to a gift of several wagon loads of gravel. Again, rain or shine, the entrance to La Hougue was passable.

September came, and the heat and haze of August gave way to lucid skies. As Yvette sat in the courtyard one afternoon enjoying the change in the weather, a "Hola!" from the road attracted her attention. She replied with a wave of her hand, and watched the familiar figure, leading her bicycle, hasten down the drive. From the look of suppressed excitement on Micheline's face, Yvette guessed the reason for her visit. "My aunt sent me my train ticket!" Micheline called. "I'm leaving for Alencon tomorrow!"

A feeling of desolation crept over Yvette. Since the war's end, she'd dreaded this moment. Now it was here.

"I've only got a minute." Micheline propped her bike on its stand, and sat on the grass beside the chair. "Maman has loaded me down with a thousand things to do before I get away." She sighed. "I've waited so long, I can hardly believe it's true."

"I'm so glad for you," Yvette said.

Micheline shivered. "It's the first time I've been this far from Coigny. I'll probably die of homesickness."

"I doubt it ever killed anybody," Yvette assured her.

"I suppose not." From the grass, she plucked a dandelion. Her face grew pensive watching its petals blur together as she twirled it between thumb and forefinger. "You've always been my best friend. I wonder how I'll get along without you." She handed the dandelion to Yvette.

Yvette nodded as she took the flower. "I can't remember when I didn't know you. You've just always been there and, I thought, always would. I'll miss you."

"I wish we could leave together. You to study *couture,* and me to—"

"I've spent enough time on 'might-have-been,'" Yvette interrupted. "I wish you the best."

"I may need it," Micheline grimaced. "Joining the nine to five work force will take some getting used to."

"It will build character," Yvette told her.

They laughed at this reminder of their school teacher's many admonitions. Micheline pushed herself to her feet. "I must go." She leaned over and hugged Yvette. "Good-bye."

"Write to me when you get the chance."

"Of course I will," her friend replied.

They gazed at each other, then for the last time, Micheline guided her bicycle up the drive. At the gate, she turned and waved. As the sprightly figure, hair flying in the wind, sped off to her new life, the tears that Yvette had held in check flowed unrestrained down her cheeks.

39

Sitting in her chair, Yvette watched the rain beat against the window, listened to the wind's shrill whistle across the slate roof of the house. Swallows had departed long ago, cows and horses shivered in barns and stables, rabbits huddled together in their hutch, and in the chicken coop, hens brooded, head under their wing. How much longer would winter hold the inert landscape in its icy grip?

Yvette was tired of reading, tired of being penned up in the house, tired of everything. She longed to ask Claire to come and visit, but of course she couldn't. Marguerite's October marriage and her move to her husband's farm had left a gap in the work force that Alice and Claire must fill. A task completed only led to another waiting to be done.

The brothers' circumstances had changed also. David and Michel had already set up households of their own. Henri planned to do the same. His wedding date had been set, and he'd accepted his future in-law's invitation to take over from the ailing father of his fiancee the running of the family farm. He'd agreed to help with the spring planting at La Hougue then he, too, would be gone. It was Georges, however, who had dropped a bombshell. Since early January, he'd been moody and short tempered. Even minor provocations had set his teeth on edge. At first, his father had been patient, but as his son's behavior grew more defiant, Antoine's forbearance had worn thin. One morning, he sharply reprimanded Georges over the care of an ailing cow. All day the rebuke had festered. That night at dinner, the mere mention of the cow's name was all it took to cause Georges to erupt. He thrust himself from the table. His chair crashed to the floor. The family stared open-mouthed as he shook his fist at Antoine.

"I've led men into battle," he shouted, "but ever since I've been home you've treated me like a stable boy. I'm sick to death of the farm: of the god-damned drudgery that's turning me into someone as stupid as the cows. And so I say, to hell with it! I'm leaving." With a flick of his foot, he'd spun his upended chair aside, and stalked toward to the door.

"Georges!" Alice had cried, rising from her seat. "Wait!"

"Let him go!" Antoine's voice was granite hard.

Husband and wife stared at each other. "For two years, he led a gypsy life," Antoine said. "He reveled in it—the excitement, even the danger. But most of all he loved the freedom from responsibility. That's what he wants to find again. Well, he can try. It may take awhile for him to learn there's no such thing."

The family had slept fitfully, if at all, that night. Alice's eyes were red and swollen as she served the morning coffee. Antoine paid his son the wages that he'd earned. Then Georges had bid the family a strained farewell, and trudged up the driveway, head ducked into his shoulders against a glacial wind. When he disappeared through the gate, Antoine had put a comforting arm around his wife. "He survived for two years in the *Maquis*," he reminded her. "You may still think of him as your little boy, but he's a man and it's time he acted like one."

Staring out at the dreary landscape, Yvette wondered where he was and what would become of him. She'd mourned his departure, but it wasn't as if he hadn't known the rules. Like all farmers' sons in the Cotentin, he'd learned them at an early age. There could be only one head to a household, and his word was law. Mothers might be loved, revered, but it was the fathers on whom everyone's livelihood depended. They were the absolute authority. Georges had challenged that. Now Georges was gone.

Was it the farm's isolation during this gloomiest of seasons that had sparked his discontent? Yvette thought back to the busy days of fall. The harvesting of the wheat had been a grand affair. After the rows of golden grain had fallen under the scythe, the itinerant Monsieur Dufour had arrived with his threshing machine. Farmers and their families in the region had gathered at La Hougue, the men to bundle the chaff and sack the grain, the women to prepare their meals. At intervals, Yvette had sat in her courtyard chair and enjoyed the camaraderie of the girls and young men who had come to help. When the day was done, it was time for eating and drinking, dancing and singing in thanksgiving for the food laid up against the winter that was to come.

But when the harvest season ended, what Yvette had feared would happen had indeed come to pass. Almost every week it seemed, another friend heeded the city's siren call and left for Caen, Cherbourg, Bayeux or Paris. For awhile, cards and letters had been exchanged. Then her friends had grown busy with their own pursuits, and the mail had tapered off. Communications with the American pilots had also dwindled. Eager to make up the lost years of the war, they'd hurried home to schools, to jobs, to setting up households of their own. Finally, only Dr. Lerossi's letters from the hospital in Stuttgart where he was stationed, kept her in touch at all.

"How about a cup of tea?"

Yvette blinked quickly before turning toward the door. "Maman told me not to bother with the kitchen floor today," Claire went on, crossing the room to the window. "In this kind of weather, I'd scarcely get it clean before someone tracked it up again." As she slid the tray onto the table by Yvette's chair, she noted with concern her sister's tear-clotted lashes. "Don't you think that having a cup of tea is the logical substitute for mopping a floor?"

Yvette wanted to throw her arms around Claire's neck. Instead, she frowned, pretending to give the question serious thought. "It makes sense to me."

Watching her sister pour the steaming tea into the cups, Yvette was touched that in place of the crockery *ordinaire,* Claire had used Yvette's favorite teapot—the yellow one with the green design—that was saved for special occasions. On a trip to Provence before the war, their father had bought the pot in Vallauris, a town famous for its pottery. Yvette had once remarked that its bright color always lifted her spirits.

"That smells so good!" Yvette said. "Can you stay and talk a minute?"

"You bet." Claire added milk and sugar and handed the cup

and saucer to Yvette. After fixing her own tea, she sat on the floor and leaned against the wall. "It's such a gloomy day," she sighed, "I was feeling kind of—blah. I hoped you'd help get me out of the dumps."

"I'll do my best," Yvette answered, going along with the charade of who was to be cheered, and who would do the cheering. "Let's see." She pursed her lips. "The world didn't come to an end this morning. Rain is good for the crops. And you're no longer thirteen. As I recall, thirteen was a miserable age."

"Hmmmm. That's pretty good for starters," Claire said. "I'm beginning to feel better. Keep going."

"That burgundy blouse looks good with your coloring."

She was amused to watch Claire blush at the compliment. Then inspecting her sister's porcelain-smooth complexion, Yvette's eyes narrowed. "It really is the perfect shade," she decided. "The blouse should be silk, of course, with more fullness in the sleeves. A mid-calf skirt, the same shade as your hair—"

Claire held her breath. For the first time since her accident, Yvette was noticing clothes.

"You wouldn't want a jacket," Yvette went on. "That would crush the sleeves. A cape," her eyes lit up, "that's it. Cropped just below the waist. A single strand of pearls, and *voila,* you're dressed to go to the theater."

How long it had been since Yvette's smile had not been forced! "Come to the theater with me," Claire exclaimed. "Design an outfit for yourself."

The smile faded. "The only way I can go to the theater is in my dreams. I dream a lot at night. Do you?"

"Now and again," Claire agreed.

"In my dreams, I'm whole again," Yvette mused. "I'm always on the go—running across an open field, or playing hide and seek as we used to do. Last night, I was dancing."

"Dancing! With whom? Where?" Claire asked.

"On the grass outside my salon. Davis had set up the victrola on the *chaise,* and somebody put on that record—do you remember the one the Americans used to sing about the paper doll?"

Claire nodded, smiling. "'I'm going to buy a paper doll that I can call my own,'" she sang.

"That's it. The eight pilots that Dr. Lerossi picked to visit me when I first arrived at La Londe were there. They were dressed in khaki pants and leather jackets. I wore a blue blouse and a pleated skirt made of parachute silk. The music was so lively. I'd jitterbug with one awhile, and he would pass me to another. They'd whirl me this way and that, and I knew all the steps. We laughed and sang. It was such fun. I wanted it to go on forever—"

Yvette stared out the window. "But one by one, the pilots said good-bye. When the music ended, I was dancing by myself."

Claire's eyes filled with tears.

Yvette shifted in her chair. "What a bore—blabbing about my dreams. Is there another cup of tea?"

Claire got up, and moved to the table.

"Is anything special going on downstairs?" Yvette asked in a determinedly change-of-subject tone.

"Yes," Claire answered. "I was going to tell you. A letter came just now from Michel and Juliette. They're coming for a visit. They want Father Giard to baptize their baby on Sunday."

"That's wonderful," Yvette said.

"They'll need this room, so you'll move in with me." Claire picked up the teapot. "I'll be glad to have you back. My room is too big for just one person." She reached for Yvette's cup and saucer. To help her, Yvette made a motion with her hand toward the cup. The girls stared at each other. It was her right hand that she'd moved.

"Mon Dieu!" Claire whispered.

Inch by inch, Yvette slid her hand across her lap and circled the cup with her fingers.

The teapot clattered to the table, and Claire threw her arms around Yvette. "It's happened. Just like Dr. Lerossi said it would!"

Laughing and crying, Yvette nodded. "Thank God he's always right!"

40

La Hougue
February 2, 1946
Dear Dr. Lerossi,

Thanks for your letter. As always, hearing from you brightens my day. I hope you'll be able to decipher this scribbling. It's being written with my right hand! You told me it would happen. Though discouraged at times, I never doubted that your promise would come true. It's not the prettiest hand I've ever seen, but it works!

It's hard to believe that almost a year has passed since we said good-bye in Paris. I think of you often. Your bracelet on my wrist is a constant reminder of what you have meant in my life.

The country air and Maman's cooking have made me so much stronger. It is wonderful being home, but I hope and pray that before too long a place in a rehab center will open so I'll have a chance at a more normal life. Keep your fingers crossed.

My arm tires quickly, so I must bring this to a close. My family says hello. I hope that all is well with you.

The Mule

February 9, 1946
Paris
Dear Mule,

The news about your arm is fantastic! I knew you could do it! As usual, you give me too much credit. A doctor can go only so far. It's the patient's perseverance, in cases such as yours, that brings about the cure. Congratulations on being so obstinate! I'm proud of you.

Your letter arrived as I was packing, and I didn't have time to answer it. Thus the Paris postmark. My discharge from the Army cleared sooner than I'd expected, and I'm returning to the States. After my stopover here, I fly a transport to London, then on to New York. It has been more than three years since I've been home. I hardly know what to expect.

An announcement of Frank's marriage to "the girl next door" also arrived as I was leaving Stuttgart. He sounds very happy. He plans to go back to school in the New York area, so we'll be seeing each other, I hope. Davis has given up the idea of going into medicine. It's a long, hard grind, and he doubts he has the tenacity to stick it out. He's still trying to decide what he wants to do. I've lost track of Barnes. He's a wanderer. B. J. is doing well in his aeronautical engineering studies. He has always been fascinated by aircraft design. Had a note from Colonel Kleine recently. He'll be stationed in Germany for awhile. Like many in the regular military, he's outraged that we allowed the Russians to occupy the countries of eastern Europe, and wonders if we fought that long, bloody war merely to exchange one dictator for another!

I'm enclosing an envelope containing a note for your parents. Would you deliver it to them for me? Keep on with those exercises. You must be ready in case a place becomes available. How I'd love to stop by La Hougue to see you. Alas, my discharge orders don't allow that kind of detour. By the time you get this letter, I'll already be home. I'll write you from there.

Affectionate regards,

Dr. Lerossi

Ithaca, New York
April 14, 1946
Dear Mule,

I hadn't meant to let so much time elapse before getting back in touch. Setting up my practice, however, proved to be more difficult than I'd expected. Shortages abound. In Europe, one thinks that America's resources have no limits, but such is not the case. Though rationing of most items has eased, delays in obtaining medical supplies are still common. I had to all but sell my soul to get an examining table. When it arrived, it was defective, and had to be returned. A replacement has finally showed up. I've secured the services of a nurse, my office is open, and I'm waiting for my next patient to arrive—something I never had to do overseas! So far this morning, I've had two. At this rate, I don't plan to retire any time soon.

I hope your arm continues to improve. When I was a child, I broke my right wrist, and had to be a 'lefty' until it healed. I remember trying to throw a baseball, and how clumsy it felt. You did remarkably well.

I'm glad to be home, yet it is difficult to renew ties with family and friends following a three-year absence, and especially after an experience as traumatic as the war. Those who were not there cannot understand what it was like. When you try to explain, they look embarrassed for you as if, now that it's over, it should be put aside like something you've outgrown. They don't realize that, for many of us, it will never be over.

My nurse has come to tell me that Mrs. Bancroft has arrived—she needs a mole removed—so I must leave you now. Write soon. I look forward eagerly to your letters.

Fondly,

Dr. Lerossi

La Hougue
May 7, 1946
Dear Dr. Lerossi,

If this letter doesn't make sense, it's because I'm still in shock! My parents have just told me the contents of the letter you wrote them. At the time I gave it to them, as you requested, I'd assumed you were telling them good-bye on leaving France. I did wonder about the sudden trip Papa made to Paris. On his return, he was so preoccupied, I worried that some misunderstanding had come between him and le Proprietaire, and that trouble was brewing for the farm. Maman, too, sidestepped my questions, and I just knew they were trying to protect me from bad news.

Since the mail arrives while I'm still in my room, I didn't know about the exchange of letters that went on between La Hougue and Paris. You can imagine how flabbergasted I was this morning when my parents rushed to my room with the news that, due to your efforts during your stopover there, I've been accepted at the Centre de Reeducation Eugene Napoleon. I still can't believe it's true! I was beginning to lose hope of ever walking again.

How can I thank you? You have given me so much, and I've returned so little. All I ever offer is my gratitude. To that, believe me, there are no bounds.

On May 22, Papa and I leave Carentan by train for Paris. I'm counting the hours!

Maman and Papa will write you later, but I couldn't wait to let you know how happy I am. What would I ever do without you?

Affectionately,

The Mule

Ithaca, New York
May 15, 1946
Dearest Mule,

Your letter of May 7 just received. How wonderful to know that in a matter of days, you'll be at the Centre! I'll imagine you in the various exercise rooms that I was shown, and picture your progress. Remember that it will come slowly, and that often you'll be discouraged. Press on. This time, you're working toward your final goal. I know you'll reach it!

Again, my role was a minor one. I merely convinced the administrator that you, as much as any soldier, were war-injured and deserved a chance at rehabilitation. That got the door ajar. It was your father's persistence which kept it open. Your parents are extraordinary people, and I'm proud to have known them.

My mind keeps drifting back to the summer days at La Londe. Those few weeks have taken on a dreamy quality. The anxiety, sleeplessness, and grotesqueness of the war have faded, and I remember only taking care of you. You say you have given little, yet you do not realize what you meant to me as well as to that group of men. For us you represented everything that was sweet, gentle and unspoiled. Your bravery was an inspiration, and having you among us gave a focus to our lives; symbolized in a very personal way what we were fighting for.

So many memories crowd in that often they get in the way of

daily living: the horror on your face when Barnes and I took off your cast, and then the joy when your fingers began to curl into a fist; your astonishment at the first glimpse of your birthday cake; the pleasure you took in the tea party that Davis and Barnes arranged; your fear the first morning you awoke to the roar of planes. How odd that events of the summer of '44 are more vivid in my mind than incidents that happened yesterday.

I eagerly await an account of your arrival at the Centre. I'm anxious to know the bad as well as the good, so please do not skimp on details.

Remember me kindly to your parents,

With my warmest regards,

John Lerossi

Centre de Reeducation
Paris
May 22, 1946
Dear Dr. Lerossi,

Your letter of the 15th reached the farm just as Papa and I were setting out for Paris. So much has happened since then, I feel as if I left home a week ago instead of just this morning. You asked for a description of my arrival at the Centre. Alors, I'll do my best to bring you up to date.

Naturally, I had mixed feelings on leaving home. Some of my married brothers and sisters came to say good-bye, so quite a group waved Papa and me out the gate. My brother, Henri, drove us to Carentan and put us on the train. Though uneventful, the trip was tiring and, once again, I had to accustom myself to being stared at. We were taken by ambulance from the St. Lazare station to the Centre.

I confess that my first impression of it was depressing. Everywhere I looked I saw amputees. I'd anticipated this day for so long, but now that it had arrived, I realized the Centre is another hospital, and I'll be here for a long, long time. I'm scared, I must admit. Still, I realize how very lucky I am—thanks to you—to have this chance at a normal life.

After Papa filled out the necessary papers, a male nurse carried me to the second floor where wounded officers are quartered. As I'm the only female patient, I've been given a room to myself. It's small, but well lighted by a window that overlooks a beautiful garden. Soon after the nurse left, the Commandant of the hospital arrived to welcome me, and get a detailed history of my injury and treatment to date. He's very nice, and assured us that everything possible would be done to help me. Then the Moniteur who'll be in charge of my training came to see us. Monsieur Cochet is stocky, very muscular, and has a gruff manner. He told me that he had never worked with a girl before and so we'll both be novices. He paused at the door on his way out to advise me to get a good night's sleep, because tomorrow we begin.

By that time, visiting hours were over, and Papa had to go. He'll be here tomorrow and the next day. Then I'm on my own.

Here I go again—wishing you were here. I hope that your medical practice is flourishing (how could it do otherwise for the world's greatest healer!) and that the rough places in your life will be made smooth. You are right about those weeks at La Londe. In my memory, they are so like a fairy tale, sometimes I wonder if I made them up. What a pity they had to end so soon.

Affectionately,

The Mule

Ithaca, New York
June 12, 1946
Dearest Mule,

When your letter of the 26th arrived, I kept three people waiting while I devoured it. I can hardly wait to hear what's happened since then.

I'm sorry you're in for another long haul, though I know that your own inner strength will pull you through. At this stage of your recovery, you probably hate everyone around you, every minute of your training, and most of all, me, for getting you into it.

Hang on. Things will get better.

Your hopes that my medical practice would flourish have been fulfilled. Every day I grow busier. I suppose eventually I'll reach a saturation point and must look around for a partner to share the load.

Your wish about the rough places in my life hasn't yet been realized. Settling down has proved more difficult than I ever dreamed. I'm not alone. A letter from Frank yesterday says that his wife has filed for divorce. He blames himself for the break. Though they grew up together, she says he's not the same person she knew before he went away. He isn't, of course. No one who has fought a war is unchanged. Fighter pilots, in particular, have a devil of a time returning to normal—whatever that is. Nothing in their lives can match flying a fighter in the war. The mixture of excitement and danger was a heady brew to which they got addicted. Suddenly it ended, and they were expected to take up where they'd left off. Some of them never will.

Frank has invited me to a reunion of pilots of the 371st Fighter Group who live in this part of the country. The get-together will be held in New York City on August 10th, the anniversary of Japan's surrender. It will be great to see them again; there will be lots of "remember whens." If your ears burn that evening, you will know that we are saying nice things about you.

Often when something sad or amusing happens in my practice, the words, "I must tell Yvette," flash through my mind. Then I realize how far away you are. I miss our talks—hearing your voice, watching the play of expression on your face. You and I reached an understanding of each other that two people seldom experience, and that closeness is hard to live without. I suppose that what I'm really saying is that I miss you.

Warmest regards,

John

Dear Dr. Lerossi,

It's now July 13th, and I must apologize for my delay in answering your wonderful letter of June 12. My training sessions of the past weeks have been so exhausting, I haven't had the energy or will to write. Thank God that period is behind me, and I'm able to appreciate that there's more to life than pain and frustration. My first impulse on reaching this happy state was to write you. Your interest in my progress inspired me to keep a journal, so I'll use bits and pieces of it to bring you up to date.

May 23, 9:00 o'clock. Monsieur Cochet carried me to exercise room—25 meters long—equipped with contrivances borrowed from a medieval torture chamber. He sat me in a chair, attached to each leg a rope with pulley which hung over a metal bar. A bag of sand was tied to the end of the rope. He told me to lift the bags of sand off the floor.

I tried—over and over! I was furious—cried, yelled. They didn't budge.

Next day, and the next, more of the same. I suspect le Moniteur wishes he'd never been saddled with me.

May 26: Dr. Lerossi is right. I hate everybody and everything.

May 27: 9:05. Eureka! I lifted the bags of sand!

May 28: 9:00. Moniteur keeps adding sand. I'm getting stronger.

June 16: 3:00 p.m. Monsieur C. fastened leather corset around my hips. Fixed to corset are aluminum pilons with thickly padded tops. Fitted these prostheses to my legs. Took my hands and slowly pulled me to a standing position. *Mon Dieu!* How strange to suddenly be so tall—and light-headed. I almost fainted.

Next, he positioned me between parallel bars. Told me to swing legs back and forth up to top of bar. Managed to do three in a row. How proud I was! Until he told me I must work up to fifteen minutes without stopping. I wanted to strangle him!

Added a few more each day. Getting stronger.

July 5: 9:00. Did fifteen-minute workout on parallel bars without breathing hard!

July 10: 9:15. After workout, Moniteur stationed me at one end of parallel bars, himself at other. Motioned me to come to him. I froze, my mind a blank. Couldn't remember which leg goes first. He had to come and shove my right leg forward. Some dormant reflex must have sprung to life. Without his help, I moved my left. I'VE TAKEN MY FIRST STEP! Felt like I'd climbed Mont Blanc. Even crusty old Moniteur smiled.

Voila, dear Dr. Lerossi, there's the saga of my life since I last wrote. After I leave the security of the bars, I'll use two canes, and then progress to one. Monsieur Cochet assures me that at the rate

I'm going, that won't be long at all. The moment it happens, you'll be the first to know.

I'm glad you're going to the New York reunion. It sounds like a wonderful idea. How I wish I could see all of you again. Give my love to those who remember me. I'm sorry about Frank, and hope that he's managing in spite of his troubles. I pray that you find satisfaction in your work, and gain contentment in other areas of your life. Though for millions of us the war will never be over, maybe time will ease the process of coming to terms.

During these weeks of strenuous effort, you've seemed very near. I hear your voice egging me on, and remember that you never let me get by with anything less than my best. I know you're busy, but if you can steal a few free moments, I'd love to hear from you. Your letters mean so much to me. Monsieur Cochet says he always knows when I've gotten one. I feel so good that I try extra hard.

Affectionately,

The Mule

41

Nurse Marianne helped Yvette pull the black slacks over her pilons. "Won't your father be surprised!" Yvette tucked in her shirttail, then buttoned the band around her waist.

"Yes indeed! Last month when he was here, even with you holding me by one arm and Monsieur Cochet by the other, I could barely hobble."

"Well, you certainly aren't doing *that* any more!" The nurse fixed Yvette with a mock stern eye.

Yvette smiled. On her way to the library two days ago, she'd stood at the top of the long curving staircase and decided she was ready to attempt something she'd wanted to do for some time. She'd hooked her cane over the banister, and after it had made its swift descent, she'd straddled the handrail and sailed down its entire length.

Delighted with her accomplishment, she'd dismounted at the bottom. As she'd picked up her cane, however, she was aware of someone watching her. It was the Commandant who'd come through the front door just as she'd finished her caper. With an appalled look on his face, he'd beckoned her.

"Mademoiselle," he'd said gravely, "you must never do that again!"

She'd lowered her eyes contritely. "Oui, Monsieur le Commandant." Then unable to resist, she'd smiled. "But oh it was such fun!"

"If you'd hurt yourself, that moment of pleasure would have undone months of effort on your part and ours," he'd retorted.

"I'm sorry. It was a silly thing to do," she agreed.

His expression had softened. "Your exuberance is commendable; I'm proud of your progress but," his eyes were serious, "no more. *D'accord?*"

"*D'accord,*" she'd promised.

He'd crossed the entrance hall and proceeded up the stairs, sliding his hand along the railing. Halfway to the top, he'd paused and looked at her over his shoulder, shaking his head in amazement. She'd suppressed a smile, and with a wave of her hand had hurried off to the library.

"Even with two good legs I can't slide down that banister," Nurse Marianne continued. "But then I'm not eighteen."

"Time is flying," Yvette mused. "In two months I'll be nineteen."

The middle-aged nurse inspected Yvette's face through the half-moons of her bifocals. "I don't see any wrinkles yet. I'd say you've got a couple of good years left." She patted Yvette's cheek. "What I'd give for a complexion like yours." She headed for the door. "I'll go down and tell your father you're on the way. I want to see his face when you walk into the waiting room."

Yvette crossed to the dresser and, as she ran a comb through her hair, she thought back over her improvement during the month since her father's last visit. Etched in her memory was August 10th, a week ago. The morning had followed the usual pattern: a workout on the parallel bars, a swim, and then a massage. Back in the gym, her Moniteur had fastened the leather belt around her waist as he usually did, and fitted her legs into the aluminum pilons. He'd pulled her to a standing position, then attached to each side of the belt a leather strap. Held like reins in his hands, the straps acted as a safety net. Without them, her fear of falling when she walked had proved to be an obstacle to her progress.

"Are we ready?" he'd asked.

"*Allons,*" she'd replied, taking the two canes that he handed her.

Slowly, she'd begun her circumnavigation of the room. He'd followed, holding the straps firmly in his grasp. Yvette examined herself in the full-length mirror. No longer did she swing her right leg in a semicircle as she'd done at first—"you're not scything grain," Monsieur Cochet had admonished her—but placed each pilon in its appropriate square directly in front of her. Her carriage was good: head high, shoulders squared. All in all, a satisfactory performance.

As she'd left the mirror behind and made her way along the bank of floor-to-ceiling windows, she imagined that she was promenading down one of the grand boulevards of the world. Which one would it be? The Champs Elysees, London's Mall, or New York's Fifth Avenue? Suddenly, she recalled that it was August 10th—the day that Dr. Lerossi was meeting the pilots for their reunion. At this moment, he might be on his way to the city. She pictured the boisterous greetings, the warm handclasps; imagined the toasts, the reminiscences and quiet moments in remembrance. Dr. Lerossi had written that her ears would burn when they said nice things about her. If only he could see her now—walking with two straps for support. How proud he'd be. "That's my girl!" he'd say.

"Yvette, look at me."

She paused, surprised to see that she was back at her starting point. Over her shoulder, she glanced at Monsieur Cochet. He was holding out his empty hands, the leather straps were trailing on the floor. Her heart began to pound.

"How long have they been there?" she asked.

"Quite a while," he'd answered. "You were so lost in thought you didn't notice."

Tears spilled down her cheeks.

"You've done it," he said. "You've walked alone."

"We've done it," she corrected.

He'd come to her and unhooked the straps. "You won't need these any longer."

Yvette put the comb back on the dresser. He was right. Not only had she dispensed with the straps but had progressed from needing two canes to walking with only one. She hurried out the door and down the steps. She couldn't wait to show her father how far she'd come. At the entrance to the waiting room, she saw him talking to the nurse.

"Papa," she called.

He turned expectantly and, eyes wide in astonishment, watched her walk toward him across the room. She threw her arms around his neck. He held her close. Nurse Marianne smiled with satisfaction, and left the room.

"Let me look at you," he said.

She twirled around, crossed to a chair, sat down, stood up. "I may try riding a horse next, then even climb a tree," she joked.

"I can't believe my eyes," he said.

"It's taken twelve weeks, but it's finally happened."

"What a victory," Antoine beamed. "Maman will be thrilled!"

"It's really just a way station," Yvette grimaced. "As soon as I'm completely confident with my pilons, I'll be fitted with my new prostheses. Legs and feet are heavier, and much harder to accommodate than pilons. But," she took his arm, "we won't borrow trouble. How about a stroll around the garden?"

They crossed the marble foyer, and left the gray stone building by way of the arched entrance with its tall French doors. Between the entrance and office of the Concierge ran a covered walkway. Yvette waved to the sentry of the day, then led her father on a tour of the grounds. High, vine-covered walls muted traffic noises, and it was hard to imagine that the compound was located on a busy street. The August sun had brought the gardens to their peak. Masses of larkspur, roses and hyacinth bloomed in beds which were interspersed with flowering shrubs. Magnificent oak and chestnut trees shaded wooden benches placed at random. Beside a reflecting pool, a statue of St. Joseph holding a child was a reminder of the origins of the Centre. In the Napoleonic era, the complex had been built as a haven for orphans of the city.

As usual, Yvette wanted news from home. Maman kept well, her father told her, and sent her love. Prospects were good for an abundant harvest which, God willing, would begin next week. Father Giard had been ailing lately; he pushed himself too hard. To help him, Claire was tutoring a class of girls on the catechism in preparation for their confirmation. The *Contesse* asked to be remembered.

"The big news is that Edouard is getting married."

"*Mon Dieu!*" Yvette exclaimed. "Irene?"

Antoine nodded. "As soon as the harvest season is over. He plans to leave the farm and open a butcher shop."

"What?" Yvette eyes widened.

"No one wants to farm any more," her father sighed. "The work is too hard."

"One by one," Yvette mused. "Soon, only Claire and I will be left."

"We'd like you to come home for the wedding," Antoine went on.

"Oh! I—I'd love to," she said quickly. "Seeing Edouard get married would be lovely, but—" she frowned. "On my pilons— All those people. Here, everyone's in the same boat. We encourage each other and can joke about ourselves. But there—"

"You'll have to face the real world some time, *ma cherie.* Maman will be very disappointed if you refuse."

"Let's see how things develop," Yvette hedged.

Antoine let the matter drop. "How's the good Dr. Lerossi?" he asked.

Relieved of making a commitment, Yvette told him of the pilots' reunion in New York. "I haven't heard from him since then but I'm sure they had a wonderful time."

"That reminds me," Antoine searched in the pockets of his coat. "Ah, here they are." He handed her two letters. "The one that looks like a greeting card came yesterday. The other arrived this morning."

"What a nice surprise," Yvette said.

"I remember Frank," Antoine reminisced as Yvette examined the return address. "Always joking. Good company."

"Odd," she mused. "I haven't heard from him for months. Now he's written two days in a row." Yvette glanced around. "There's a bench under the oak. Let's sit down and I'll read them aloud."

She opened the greeting card first. "Look at this! How cute!" Together, she and Antoine enjoyed the pen and ink drawing of Frisky flying a P-47. Though dressed in civilian clothes, he sported goggles and a fighter pilot's white silk scarf. As his plane wobbled across the face of the card, its contrails spelled, "Wish you were here."

All around the airplane were names and scribbled salutations.

"That's clever!" Antoine said. He tilted his head. "Turn the card over—there's something written on the back."

"Dear Yvette," she read,

"We thought you'd get a bang out of seeing your old friend, Frisky, one more time. Twenty of us from the 371st Fighter Group are in New York for a reunion at the Commodore Hotel. We've had a ball catching up on news of each other, and lying about the number of enemy planes we shot down. We've also taken time to remember the ones who never made it back.

"Dr. Lerossi had planned to be with us for cocktails and dinner. We waited awhile, but he never showed up. I guess he had some emergency. I'll call his office in the morning to tell him how much we missed him. He's kept me up-to-date on your progress. We're all proud of you, and wish you the best. Give our kind regards to your family.

"Affectionately,

"Frank."

"They were a fine group of young men," Antoine said.

Nodding absently, Yvette slipped the card back into its envelope. With pinpricks of unease, she picked up the letter. "Dr. Lerossi was so eager to be there. Why didn't he go?" she murmured.

Curiously reluctant, she opened the envelope and unfolded the sheet of onionskin paper. The penmanship of the letter was not the scrawl used on the Frisky card, but precise, as if the writer had taken pains to think through what he wanted to say.

"Dear Yvette," she began,

"I hope you've received the card that I mailed you yesterday and therefore might be somewhat prepared for what I must write to you today. It is my lot again to have to bring you bad news."

A chill settled between her shoulder blades. She looked up and met her father's troubled eyes. "Would you rather I read it?" he asked.

Dreading to go on, she nonetheless shook her head.

"As I wrote you," she continued, "Dr. Lerossi didn't come to our reunion. I phoned his office the next day, planning to tell him all about it, but when I identified myself to his receptionist, she burst into tears. 'It's terrible!' she sobbed. 'He's been killed.'"

Antoine sucked in his breath. "Good God!"

Stunned, Yvette stared at the words. They weren't true! They were too awful to be true. Frank had misunderstood. Frantic to prove herself correct, she hurried on:

"I was so shocked I only caught snatches of what his receptionist was saying. '—excited about going to the reunion—his first weekend off since he'd opened his office—happy to be with his fly boys again.' Gradually my mind focused on what had happened. He'd made hospital rounds, then stopped by his office to take care of some unfinished business. He asked her to mail a letter for him, and then was ready to go. She wished him 'Bon Voyage,' and watched him drive away.

"While catching up on paper work that afternoon, she got a call from a hospital in the town of Albany. There'd been an accident on the highway. A drunk driver had crossed the median into Dr. Lerossi's lane. The resulting collision had totaled both cars. The drunk escaped with cuts and bruises: Dr. Lerossi was killed instantly. They were trying to reach his next of kin."

Yvette felt a numbness creeping over her. Her father's "How awful!" sounded hollow, as if he were speaking in a tunnel. The writing on the paper blurred. As she stared at it trying to decipher what it meant, her father gently took the letter from her hand.

"I realize that I should try and comfort you," Frank's letter continued, "but I can't think of anything to say that makes sense. That John Lerossi survived the Normandy invasion, the Battle of the Bulge, and the conquest of Germany only to be killed riding down a road in his own home state is too ironic for soothing words. What kind of insane world do we live in?

"He and I had been friends overseas, but during the months since we've been home, he'd become the older brother that I never had. He was always there—I knew I could count on him. I can't believe he's gone.

"He spoke of you with great affection. He was so proud of your spirit, that quality in you that never gives up. When the day comes that you can walk without assistance, somehow I think he'll know.

"Sincerely,

"Frank."

Antoine reached for his daughter's hand. She gazed across the lush grass to the windows in the exercise room. On August tenth while he was driving to the reunion, she'd walked unsupported by the straps. Did he know?

"That's my girl," she'd heard him say.

42

The Commandant leaned toward her across the dinner table. "Mademoiselle, you've been preoccupied—and even silent—for the whole meal. Is something troubling you?" Yvette's eyes met the level gaze beneath the thick, graying brows. The five other officers at the table in the Commandant's private dining room paused in their eating to cast indulgent glances in her direction.

"I apologize for being so dull," she said, "but this afternoon my father brought me some very bad news."

The indulgent smiles changed to looks of concern. "Do you want to tell us about it?" the Commandant asked.

Yvette's glance circled the table, from the Captain on her left whose hands had been blown off by a grenade, to the Lieutenant on her right who, like her, had been made a double amputee by a German shell. "Yes, I do," she answered, "because all of you would understand. I've lost my best friend."

The silence was complete.

"He was the American doctor who took care of me after I was wounded." Staring at her scarcely touched plate, she was unaware of tears spilling down her cheeks. "He was so good to me. Everything that I've accomplished, I owe to him. He's the reason that I'm here."

"Dr. Lerossi!" the Commandant exclaimed.

Yvette nodded.

"Mon Dieu! What happened?"

She explained the circumstances of the accident.

The Commandant shook his head. "What a shame!"

"Please accept our sympathies, Mademoiselle," the Captain said. "Believe me, we do understand."

Yvette brushed at her eyes, then pushed back her chair. "If you'll excuse me—I'm not hungry. I think I'll go to my room."

"Of course," the Commandant agreed.

She rose from her seat and walked to the door. Gone was the brisk pace with which she usually moved. As she made her way along the hall, the effort of placing one pilon in front of the other seemed almost more than she could manage. Footsteps resounded behind her, and Nurse Marianne called her name. Yvette paused and glanced over her shoulder.

"You forgot to pick up your mail." The nurse's words echoed down the corridor. "The clerk gave me a letter for you. I put it in your room."

With a wave of her hand, Yvette acknowledged the message, then plodded on her way toward the wing where the officers were billeted. The letter aroused no interest. Sunk in despair, she'd forgotten it by the time she arrived at her quarters.

She closed the door behind her, crossed to the window and stared out into the garden. The beauty of lengthening shadows on the grass, the gentle aspect of the St. Joseph statue, the magnificence of oak and chestnut trees, the brilliance of the flowers was lost on her. She could just as well have been looking at a desert scene. The numbness that she'd felt when she'd first learned of the doctor's death had passed, and now desolation filled her soul. He, who had been the mainspring of her life, was gone. She leaned her head against the coolness of the windowpane, and gave way to her grief.

Finally, her tears were exhausted. Drying her eyes, she pondered how to pass the time until sleep released her from her melancholy. She longed for the serenity of the garden, but she would meet people there, and have to talk. To read was pointless. The words would be forgotten as soon as they were read. Perhaps knitting was the answer. She'd taken up the hobby as therapy for her hand, and had found the monotony of its repetition sometimes soothed her mind.

Looking around for her knitting bag, she noticed the letter on the table. Dr. Lerossi's handwriting leaped at her from the envelope. For a moment, she stood riveted to the spot. Then, her mind whirling, she rushed to snatch it up. Frank was wrong! Dr. Lerossi wasn't dead. Here was the proof! As if fearing it would disappear, she stared at her name, written in the familiar script, while she sank into the chair beside the table. With trembling hands, she tore open the envelope. Then she saw the date on the letter, and despair again engulfed her.

Ithaca, New York
August 10, 1946
Dearest Yvette,

I'm penning this hurried note before leaving for the city. I'd planned to write you after my return from the reunion, but I had a sudden impulse to do it now. Ordinarily, I'm not impulsive, as you well know, but when I am, I pay attention.

Your last letter was marvelous. How I wish I could have seen you take that first step. Across the three thousand miles that separate us, I offer my heartfelt congratulations. I must confess that I'm jealous of the lucky Monsieur Cochet. He sees the scowls, the angry tears, hears the muttered imprecations when obstacles block your way, then basks in the warmth of your matchless smile when the hurdles have been overcome.

Time and distance are supposed to blur one's image of a person, yet the pictures of you that I carry in my mind are sharper than any photos I could have taken. When I notice a girl who tilts her head, or shrugs, or lifts an eyebrow the way you do, my pulse races, and I can scarcely breathe. Because of you, my attention meanders when I'm listening to my patients' complaints, and they must wonder why I'm regarding them with so blank a look. You can see that being separated from you is disrupting my whole existence. And so I must put an end to that. What would you say to my coming to see you in the fall?

It has taken me all this time to realize what my feeling is for you. In the beginning, it disguised itself as pity; later, that developed into admiration. Now my eyes are open, and I recognize that you're the only one who can fill the empty place in my life. This revelation may come as a shock to you—it took me somewhat by surprise—but looking back, my sentiments seem such a natural progression. So logical. So right. I realize that you're not yet nineteen and I am thirty-two, and that you may not be ready for a romantic attachment. Do not fret, for there is time, and I can wait. Still, I hope with all my heart that you love me as I do you. I long to hear you say it. Please do not keep me too long in suspense.

My nurse, Mrs. Plucker, who mothers me, has come to urge me to get on the road. As she and I are well aware, further dawdling on my part is an open invitation for some emergency to crop up, and I'd have to cancel the trip. I'm reluctant to leave you though. At this moment, you are so close.

I'll deliver your greetings to the pilots. They'll be delighted with the progress that you've made. Have courage for what lies ahead. The coming days will bring new challenges. Some of them will seem beyond your strength to overcome and you may ask yourself if confronting them is worth the effort. I assure you that it is. I send you my love and support, confident that you will let nothing deter you now that success is within your grasp.

Au revoir, my dearest Yvette.

Yours,

John

She dropped the letter to her lap, and leaned her head against the back of the chair. Finally he'd perceived what she had been aware of for some time. And now it was too late. She pictured him writing at his desk, his fine hand racing across the page, trying to forestall his appointment with death. If Mrs. Plucker had not urged him to hurry, he might still be alive. A few moments could have made the difference. "There is time, and I can wait," he'd written. But there was no time. Bitter tears stung her eyes. What kind of God would let a drunk survive instead of Dr. Lerossi!

She sat unmoving, oblivious as twilight faded into dark. She ignored a rap on the door. Nurse Marianne came into the room, and switched on the light. The figure slumped in the chair alarmed her. She hurried to Yvette's side. "Oh, my dear!" she exclaimed.

With an effort, Yvette straightened. The letter on her lap fluttered to the floor. The older woman and the girl leaned down together to retrieve it. Holding it between them, they looked at each other.

"I recognized the handwriting when I brought it to your room," Nurse Marianne said. "The Commandant has just told me the sad news."

Yvette stared at the letter's closing line. *"Au revoir.'* That means, 'until we meet again.'"

With tears in her eyes, the nurse took the letter from Yvette's unsteady hand, and returned it to the envelope.

"It doesn't make sense, does it?" Yvette said.

"No," Nurse Marianne agreed. "Not to us. But one must keep on."

"That's what he told me," Yvette said. "He didn't say why," she added bitterly.

"Life doesn't stand still. It goes backward or forward. You have to make a choice. You know what he'd want you to do." The nurse held out her arms. "Let me help you get ready for bed."

Like a child, Yvette allowed Nurse Marianne to undress her and get her settled for the night. She was very tired, and for that she was grateful. Perhaps she would sleep. As she closed her eyes, she heard the soft hum of a lullaby.

The lights went out, the door closed, and she slept.

43

He swung his stiffened leg in a half circle before placing his foot on the floor in front of him. "Do you remember how hard it was to break that habit when you first began to walk? Pay attention, Yvette. Look at me."

"I am, Monsieur Cochet," she defended herself.

"No, you're looking through me—as you have for the past three weeks. You're doing it again—it is the lazy way," he said. "Watch."

She nodded.

He examined her pale, dejected face. "Let's take a break." He turned toward a table against the wall. "Sit down and I'll bring you something to drink."

She sank into a chair beside the parallel bars. Everything she did nowadays demanded more energy than she could muster. Exercises exhausted her, meals were something to be gotten through. A walk in the garden, climbing stairs, even engaging in conversation left her spent. She fought a daily battle with herself just to get out of bed.

"Here you are." The *Moniteur* handed her a glass, then brought another chair and sat beside her. For a few moments, he let her sip the apple juice in silence. Then leaning forward, he rested his elbows on his knees. "Up to the present, I haven't intruded into your private life. It was none of my business. But it is interfering with your training, and that concerns me." He laced his hands together. "I think we'd better talk."

She struggled to hold back the tears that lay so often now just beneath the surface. "Have you ever lost someone who was very dear to you?"

He nodded.

Her eyes searched his rugged features, so seemingly invulnerable. "How did you get over it?"

"You never do." He stared out the window. "Everybody tries something different, I guess. I stayed drunk a lot; finally realized that wrecking my health wasn't going to bring her back." He turned to look at Yvette. "Is giving up going to bring Dr. Lerossi back?"

She shook her head. "But now that he's gone, nothing seems worthwhile."

"He was proud of you. Isn't that important?"

She hadn't heard. Her eyes had that vacant look again. "He was coming to see me in the fall," she murmured.

"And if he'd come, what would he demand of you?" Monsieur Cochet persevered.

The *Moniteur's* insistence that she stay in the present irritated Yvette. "My best!" she retorted. "You *know* that."

"I do," he agreed. "You seem to have forgotten. You *owe* him that," he added.

"I owe him that," she repeated in a wondering voice. "You have given me so much, and I've returned so little," she had written him. Here was something she could give.

She handed the *Moniteur* her glass and he put it on the table. When he returned, she held out her hands and he pulled her to a standing position. "You've got to make up for lost time," he said. "It won't be easy."

It wasn't. She was back to aching muscles, and the grind of each day adding a little to what she had done the day before. Though messages from her parents encouraged her, she missed more than she ever could imagine the spur that Dr. Lerossi's love and support had provided her. For the most part now it was her own obstinacy, and Frank's "somehow I think he'll know" that kept her going.

An unexpected pleasure one afternoon was a visit from Father Giard. Though warned by her father about the priest's physical condition, Yvette was startled by how frail he looked. The robust priest striding along the road between Coigny and Baupte seemed to be a different person from the thin curate, dressed in the too-

big cassock, who sat in the waiting room. His eyes lighted when
he saw her, however, and his smile was ready.

"How wonderful to see you, Father!" she exclaimed. "What
brings you to Paris?"

"A doctor's appointment for a minor problem," he said. "I
couldn't pass up the chance to see you."

She didn't press him on the "minor problem," as he seemed
disinclined to talk about it. Instead she asked if he would like a
tour of the facility. He readily agreed, and she showed him the
chapel, workout and massage rooms, the library and pool;
introduced him to the Commandant, Monsieur Cochet, Nurse
Marianne and some of her friends. When he seemed to tire, she
suggested a bench in the garden. The afternoon heat had
dissipated before a cooling breeze, and they sat beside the
reflecting pool.

"Your agility is remarkable," the Abbe said. "I confess that
when your father bragged about what you could do, I took it with
a grain of salt."

"I'm getting there—little by little," she replied.

"What a pity that Dr. Lerossi can't see you now," the priest
went on. "He would be so pleased."

The mention of her loss put her in a reflective mood. "Why did
he have to die? What purpose did it serve?"

"I wish I had an answer," Father Giard said. "I have lived my
life and I am ill. Why not me instead of him?" He shook his head.
"It isn't given us to know the reasons."

"He loved me," she said.

"Of course he did, my child," the priest patted her shoulder,
"as we all do."

"No, Father," she answered. "Not like that. He was in love with
me." She looked up and met the Abbe's incredulous gaze. "He
told me in a letter that he wrote the day he was killed."

"Mon Dieu!" Shock mingled with concern as Father Giard
examined her despondent face: shock that the girl he'd known
since childhood was now an adult; concern that she'd been dealt
this added blow. "My dear, my dear. I am so sorry. Do your
parents know?"

She shook her head. "They have enough to worry about. I've kept it to myself. Lately, though, I've wondered if not telling anyone has made it harder for me to accept his death."

"Mourning is never easy," the priest answered. "Talking out one's grief with someone does help, I think. I feel privileged that you chose me to tell. For what small comfort it gives you," he continued, "it is a great compliment that such a fine man loved you."

She nodded, unable to speak.

"I wish I could offer you consolation, but the words I've used for so long seem empty now." He stared at the St. Joseph statue cradling the child. "The closer I draw to my own demise, the more unreconciled I become to the young dying. Life cut off in its prime is a tragedy—such a waste." He looked at Yvette. "You survived against impossible odds, and that you've come this far is a miracle. My hope is that you will get on with your life. That's what Dr. Lerossi would want for you. It won't mean that you've forgotten him. No one else can ever take his special place."

As the tears that she had held in check overwhelmed her, the curate worried that perhaps he should have used the formula words. Their very familiarity might have been a comfort to her. But as he listened to her sobs, he recognized that she had passed beyond paroxysms of grief, and that these were healing tears. And so he put his arms around her and let her weep. Finally, her crying ran its course, and with the handkerchief he gave her, she dried her eyes.

He shook his head. "There is so much sadness in the world sometimes I think we priests are fighting a losing battle."

She looked at his wan, lined face whose every contour was familiar. For as long as she could remember he'd been her family's comforter and friend. He'd rejoiced when they were glad, grieved with them in sorrow. Never had he been too tired or busy to come when he was needed. "You haven't lost this battle, Father," she told him. "I don't feel lonely any more—knowing that you know."

He smiled at her. "You have gladdened an old man's heart."

Just then, an orderly hurried toward them from the building. "Your taxi is here, Father," he called.

The Abbe waved an acknowledgment, and rose to his feet. "I was given an assignment by your mother," he said, as they made their way along the path toward the front of the Centre. "I think you know what it is."

He saw her fleeting look of dread and hurried on. "She wants you home with the rest of the family for Edouard's wedding."

"I would love nothing better than to see them, but—" she grimaced, "a hundred and ten guests! The other girls in their long, party dresses, and me in my black trousers covering my pilons. The whispered comments, the stares."

"They are people that you know! Neighbors, old friends. They wouldn't want to hurt you."

"No one realizes what it's like."

"You don't realize what this means to your mother," the curate answered firmly. "She will be very disappointed if you refuse."

He waited as she vacillated. "Your mother has thought of you so much. This time, think of her."

Filled with misgivings, Yvette reluctantly nodded. "All right."

"There, my child. That wasn't so hard, was it?"

What else could she do but nod agreement.

"I'm glad, Yvette," he said. "You will be, too."

The twentieth of September was as beautiful a day as any bridal party could hope for. The air was crisp like a sip of cold cider and fragrant with the smell of hay. Though the sun was still warm, the leaves of *la vigne vierge* had begun to turn, and overhead swallows banked and wheeled, anticipating their journey south.

Since dawn, the farmhouse had swarmed with activity. The arrival of Denise's family, Marguerite and her spouse and new baby, the married brothers, wives and children added to the hubbub. They extended good wishes to the bridegroom, and welcomed Yvette home with joy and astonishment at her progress.

Yvette's dread of the coming event mounted as she watched different groups of the family leave for the church by carriage or on foot. Finally, she would have to face the wedding guests. Though she had on her prettiest blouse, and Claire had arranged her hair in a becoming pompadour, the contrast would be painful between the other girls' colorful dresses and the black slacks she must wear over her pilons. If only she could stay at home!

"Ready, Yvette?" her mother called.

"Yes, Maman," she answered dutifully.

They met at the front door, and made their way together up the drive. In spite of her disquietude, she began to enjoy the walk. Wild flowers bloomed on both sides of the road, bird songs filled the air, and the sun warmed their backs. How sweet, too, were these moments alone with her mother. The press of people in the house made one-on-one conversations all but impossible. Here they could express their private thoughts. Alice confided her worry over Georges's continued absence.

"One never stops grieving for the wayward child," she finished.

"He'll come back, Maman," Yvette tried to comfort her. "He loves us, and his roots are here. Once a Norman, always a Norman."

Their talk turned to Gilberte. Alice had finally found the strength to go through her belongings. She'd given her clothes to a local charity and separated her jewelry and other mementos. "I'm sure that she would want you to have the cameo."

The memory of Gilberte hurled to the ground, a red stain spreading over her chest left Yvette unable to respond. She could only nod.

"We hope before too long to replace the marker on her grave with a permanent memorial," Alice went on.

"I do miss her so," Yvette lamented.

"Don't we all," Alice murmured.

Intent on thoughts of her sister, as well as the careful placement of her pilons on the rough textured road, Yvette did not notice a young man emerge from the chasse ahead of them, until her mother's exclamation, "My goodness, there's the oldest Clermont son."

Yvette recognized her former classmate. He was a likeable boy then, friendly and full of high spirits. Now, dressed in a naval uniform, he was a handsome young man. Startled by the sudden encounter, she gave him a wide-eyed smile.

"Bonjour, Alexandre. *Comment ca va?"*

Mouth agape, he stared at her pilons.

"You remember my mother, Madame Hamel, and me, Yvette?"

Still as if struck dumb, he didn't answer. His face was a study in shock, or was it repugnance, she wondered.

"We used to clean the blackboard together in Mademoiselle Leduc's school room," Yvette blundered on, hoping that by injecting humor, she might help make the chance meeting easier. It didn't help. His only response was to duck his head and hurry on his way.

Stunned, Yvette looked after him, then turned to meet her mother's unhappy gaze. "Don't let his behavior upset you," she said. "He was just—surprised, that's all."

"Surprised?" Yvette's voice was icy.

Why had she let herself be talked into coming! This encounter was a preview of what lay ahead at the church. Like Alexandre, others would turn away from her, not knowing what to say. What could they say? "My how pretty you look. Your black slacks, that don't quite hide your pilons, are so attractive!"

She took her hand from her mother's arm. "I'm going home."

"The church won't be like that," her mother objected. "Everyone is anxious to see you. Yvette, please come with me."

The more her mother entreated, the firmer became Yvette's resolve not to subject herself to further humiliation.

"Alexandre has been away. He's just arrived home and didn't know of your injury."

"That doesn't excuse his rudeness," she retorted.

The words were scarcely out of her mouth when an incident that had happened at the Centre flashed through Yvette's mind. She had chanced one afternoon to be exchanging pleasantries with the Commandant in the foyer when an army Captain had arrived to be admitted. Yvette had wondered why he was accompanied by a nurse. Hands in his pockets, he'd walked unaided, and did not seem in any way disabled. The Commandant had welcomed him, then introduced Yvette. She'd held out her hand, and the Captain had extended his. Horrified, Yvette had stared at the stump, not knowing what to do. As the Captain had murmured apologies, she'd noticed that both hands were gone. The shock unnerved her and, without a word, she'd fled upstairs to her room. After he'd been fitted with prostheses, he'd joined the group in the Commandant's private dining room, and he and Yvette had become better acquainted. She'd apologized for her rude behavior on the day they'd met. "I don't know what got into me," she said.

"It was the same with me when I met you," he'd laughed. "I was so startled to see you on pilons, I forgot I didn't have hands."

Although the Captain had excused her, she still reproached herself. Perhaps Alexandre was going through a similar remorse.

"You're right, Maman," Yvette said. "He didn't know." She slipped her hand into the crook of her mother's arm. "Shall we go?"

Yvette was unprepared for the crowd of people waiting to greet her. They pressed her hand, embraced her. The warmth of their welcome brought tears to her eyes. At the church door, Father Giard gave her a tender smile. "We are proud of you," he said.

Seated between her parents in the family pew, nostalgia overcame Yvette. How entwined her life had been with this institution. At its font she'd been baptized, knelt in its chancel for her confirmation. Her siblings had been married before its altar, and in its cemetery, Gilberte was laid to rest.

As she listened to the "Ave Maria" on the harmonium, watched light filter through the stain glass windows, she was grateful that the meeting with Alexandre had not deterred her from renewing these ties.

Irene's face glowed, and Edouard was suitably grave while Father Giard charged them with the seriousness of the step that they were taking. The ritual over, the bride and groom with eyes only for each other, hurried down the aisle to the waiting car.

The wedding feast was scheduled to begin as soon as the ceremony ended, and soon the road to the bride's family farm was filled with carriages of every sort.

Yvette rode in the car with Claire and her parents, and when they arrived, they found that the focus of activities was the largest of the barns. Scoured from top to bottom, it had been converted into a dining room. Shimmering drapes from ceiling to floor hung against the walls while lanterns and baskets of flowers were everywhere. Bouquets and streamers of ribbon decorated the center of a horseshoe-shaped table, draped in white. Around the periphery, places for a hundred and ten guests had been set. On the *table d'honneur* facing the entrance stood the multitiered wedding cake, and a large buffet against the wall held champagne, wines and the farm's own brand of apple brandy.

As the carriages arrived, guests gathered in the farmhouse courtyard where the newly married couple mingled with their guests. Any social gathering in this farm community offered isolated families a welcomed forum for catching up on news of each other, and exchanging information on market conditions. Especially enjoyed was the celebration of a wedding and this one uniting two well-known families had been anticipated for weeks. The women had ransacked closets for their most becoming outfits. Summer clothes had not yet been put away, and bright dresses supplied a pleasant contrast to dark suits worn by the men.

Many young people who had left town to seek jobs or more excitement than Coigny offered, had returned for the marriage of the popular couple. As Yvette chatted with a group of them, someone came up behind her and covered her eyes. The question, "Guess who?" was easy for Yvette to answer.

"Micheline."

Joyous exclamations were followed by embraces.

"My train was late and I missed the ceremony. I just got here," Micheline explained.

Hands clasped they separated to inspect each other. "The last time I saw you—" Micheline shook her head. "It's incredible. How did you do it?"

"Sweat, tears, frustration—and lots of help," Yvette answered.

"I'm sorry I haven't kept in touch," Micheline's face was a picture of contrition, "but life got so—busy!"

Yvette brushed aside the need for apology. "I want to hear what you've been doing." She glanced toward the barn. "The toasts are about to begin. After dinner, we must find a place to talk."

"Wonderful!" Micheline agreed.

As the guests moved toward the barn, members of the bride's family passed among the crowd with glasses of wine and champagne. In turn, Irene's father and then Antoine wished the young people a long and happy life together. After the toasts. Father Giard blessed the wedding feast. Then the guests found their places at the table.

Served by uniformed waiters hired for the occasion, an *aperitif*—Muscat, Porto or Whisky—accompanied by hors d'oeuvres started off the elaborate meal. The entree was fresh salmon bathed in Normandy cream with a touch of pureed tomato added to give it a rosy color. Mutton with garden-fresh green beans followed, then slices of roast beef au jus and small round potatoes browned to a turn. A pause while tables were cleared of dishes and cutlery signaled that it was time for the *Trou Normand*. This small glass of Calvados swallowed in a gulp was a potent restorative of sated appetites. After the green *salade* came the cheeses, the fruits and black currant tarts. The meal which had lasted five hours ended with cups of strong black coffee.

As the guests left their seats to mingle with each other, Micheline caught up with Yvette, and the two withdrew to a bench under an elm. "Now start at the beginning, from the day you left Coigny," Yvette insisted.

Micheline's eyes lit up recalling her excitement at the prospect of that voyage. "I just knew that all kinds of wonderful things would happen the minute I got on the train. The trip *was* a lot of fun. I met the cutest boy—but," the glow faded from her face, "it's been downhill ever since. Alencon hasn't much more to offer than Coigny."

"Mon Dieu! Give it a chance. You've only been there—how long?"

"A whole year," Micheline countered.

Yvette looked at her friend's petulant expression and thought of the two years of painful exercises she'd undergone just to regain the use of her hand.

"A nine-to-five job is not much fun. In fact, it's deadly dull."

"What about the training program?" Yvette asked.

"Since my aunt knew the Supervisor, I thought I'd be a shoo-in. I certainly deserved it, but the opening went to somebody else."

Her aunt was too strict, the boys were fickle, and she was trapped in a dead-end job. As Micheline's litany continued, Yvette felt she'd heard it all before. The failures had changed, but Micheline's penchant for placing the blame elsewhere than on herself had not. She was still the girl who'd abandoned the sewing class at St. Jores because the weather was too cold. Suddenly, her expression brightened. "But, guess what! I'm moving to Paris. I'm so thrilled! I just know that everything—"

Yvette stopped listening. The words were identical to those of last year when everything was going to be better in Alencon than Coigny.

"Now it's your turn," Micheline's prattle finished. "Tell me about the Centre."

Yvette blinked, not having heard her discourse end. What could she say that would be of interest to Micheline. She claimed to have endured boredom, repetition, and monotony, but in truth she barely knew the meaning of the words. Perseverance and pain were beyond her comprehension. "Let nothing deter you," would seem to her absurd, and "obstinate as a mule," a disagreeable trait. A feeling of sadness came over Yvette. How far apart their paths had diverged.

She was saved from having to answer by a trill of notes on an accordion and violins and a mandolin getting in tune. Micheline's expression brightened. 'They're going to dance! Let's join the others, shall we?"

"You go," Yvette urged. "I'll be fine right here."

With a smile and a wave, Micheline hurried toward the courtyard. For the first time since they'd known each other, Yvette was not reluctant to see her go. Was shedding outgrown friendships part of "getting on with one's life"?

Partners were chosen and the music began. Watching the couples weave in and out, Yvette relived her dream of dancing with the pilots outside her tent. What a lovely dream it was—the catchy tune, the lively tempo. How she'd hated to have it end. She sighed. Only in her dreams would she experience that carefree feeling of release.

"Would you dance with me, Yvette?"

Slowly, she turned her head. At her shoulder stood Alexandre. Too surprised to speak, she stared at him. "That song is fun to dance to, and I'm pretty good," he said.

Mesmerized, she arose and let him lead her to the courtyard. Gently but firmly he took her in his arms, and she began to sway to the music's beat. The other dancers gradually edged away, leaving the dance floor to the two of them. Smoothly and with little effort, they moved in unison. She felt outside herself, immersed in the lilting rhythm. Each patterned movement was a joy, every motion a triumph. She'd mourned that dancing was beyond her reach. Now that miracle had come within her grasp.

The music ended, and Alexandre let her go. "That's the most enjoyable dance I've ever had," he said.

Friends crowded around them. They congratulated Yvette and greeted Alexandre. Edouard clapped him on the shoulder. "It's been a long time, my friend. What are you doing here?"

"My ship made port at Cherbourg this morning," Alexandre answered. "I requested shore leave for the day, and—surprise— I got it." On reaching home he'd learned about the wedding, and had come to offer congratulations. His hosts urged him to stay for the cutting of the wedding cake, but there wasn't time, he said.

"Relatives are coming by to see me, and then I've got that Cherbourg train to catch." He wished the couple a long and happy life.

Instead of saying good-bye to Yvette, he took her by the arm. "Walk with me to the road, will you?" he asked.

She nodded, and they set out. "It's you I really came to see," he said, "to apologize for my behavior when we met this morning."

She started to protest, but he hurried on. "I was so floored when I saw you, I was speechless. I couldn't do anything but stand there like an idiot!" He clapped his hand to his head. "I still can't believe it."

"I understand," she began again, but he was not yet ready to be pardoned.

"How you must have hated me. I didn't mean to be cruel, but I didn't know you'd been wounded. I have no excuse except—shock!"

"I was hurt and angry at the time," she conceded, "but that's past. I'm O.K. now. So why don't we forget it ever happened."

"Can you?" he asked.

"Cross my heart." Her face glowed. "Besides, you made up for everything with that dance. I'd thought I never could again. It was a dream come true."

"Partners as good as you don't come along every day," he smiled.

They walked a few steps more, and he turned to face her. "There is something that's been bugging me all these years, and it's time we had it out."

His frown was so reminiscent of the boy she'd gone to school with, she made a show of bracing herself. "Well?"

"You never did your share of cleaning the blackboard."

"Says who?" she demanded. "You were so slow, it always took you longer."

"And then there were the wastebaskets," he persisted. "I had to empty them more often than you did."

"That was *my* fault? *Zut!* Your misbehaving caused all your problems. I, on the other hand, was a model student."

"Same old Yvette," he grumbled. "I still can't get the better of you."

"Growing up with seven brothers helped," she smiled.

They sifted through other memories of those bygone days, then she asked where his ship was headed. The Mediterranean, he answered. Trouble was brewing in Algeria. He wanted to know about her rehabilitation, and she briefly explained the setup at the Centre. "Learning to walk on pilons was the easy part," she said. "The real challenge comes when I return, and start training with my new prostheses—legs and feet."

He shook his head admiringly. "It's hard for me to imagine

what you've been through. Many times you must have said, 'I can't go on!'"

She nodded. "I try not to look beyond the next day."

"You can do it, Yvette. You always have accomplished what you set your mind on!"

"I'll remember that," she promised.

He heaved a reluctant sigh. "I must go."

She held out her hand, but instead of shaking it, he gave her a hug. "I hope we'll meet again some day."

"Perhaps we will," she answered. "Good-bye."

She watched him grow smaller in the distance. At the first bend in the road, he turned, raised his hands in a victory salute and called, "Bravo, Yvette!"

As he disappeared, she heard other voices encouraging her: Colonel Kleine, Dr. Glocker, Davis and Barnes, DiMarzo, James, Frank, B. J. Overriding all of them, Dr. Lerossi's challenge "Never give up," echoed in her ears. They'd started her on the road to independence; how proud they would be to see her now. Time, distance, and even death separated her from them, but when she made her way back to the wedding party, she felt them walking at her side.

Epilogue

vette returned to the Centre and underwent intensive training with her new prostheses. Although made of light-weight Duralumin, the feet and legs—especially the right leg with its articulating joint taking the place of her knee—seemed impossibly clumsy. Still, after only six weeks, she became proficient in their use. She discarded the pilons, along with the black slacks that had covered them, and dressed in the feminine styles of the day including stockings and shoes with a medium heel. Watching her cross a room, one would never suspect that she was different from any other very pretty girl. The cane she carried seemed an affectation or a whim of fashion rather than a means to steady herself.

Her dream of becoming a *couteriere* never materialized. By the time France recovered from the ravages of war and the school of design opened, Yvette was twenty-seven. The school rejected her application claiming that she was too old. She was convinced that her rebuff was due to her handicap.

She married a lawyer and bore a beautiful daughter, Martine. Her husband, a World War I hero and several years her senior, was a kind, intelligent man, and his companionship and support during Martine's childhood and school years filled her with contentment. There was a cottage on the beach in the summer, a house in Carentan in the winter and, although her parents died within a year of each other, many of her brothers and sisters lived nearby. Life was good.

In early 1980, Yvette was once again bereaved—this time by the death of her husband. In the midst of her grief, however, she was astounded to receive an invitation from the P-47 Thunderbolt Pilots Association to be their guest at their annual reunion to be

held that year in the city of Lake Charles, Louisiana. Since Martine
was taking final exams in boarding school, a niece accompanied
Yvette on the fairy-tale voyage. All aspects of the trip were taken
care of. A committee met the travelers at the New Orleans Airport
and whisked them by car to Lake Charles. At the opening session
of the reunion, Yvette stood on the stage in an auditorium filled
with a thousand people, and made a short speech in well-
practiced English, expressing her thanks and her joy at being once
again among the people she loved.

At the banquet that evening, she was reunited with Colonel
Kleine, Dr. Glocker, and a group of the pilots who on so many
occasions had stopped by her tent. Laughter and tears mingled as
the memories were recalled of events that happened so long ago.
She stayed in the home of one of the pilots in Lake Charles, and
after the festivities in that city ended, she was flown in a private
plane to Lakeland, Florida, for a visit with another pilot, and then
on to New Jersey and a sojourn with a third. Thirty-five years after
General Eisenhower extended his invitation, she had finally made
it to the United States.

In June 1994, France was again to be invaded by American
forces. Five hundred thousand of those who took part in the 1944
D-Day invasion were expected to return to wander the beaches,
rediscover villages they liberated, and, in the cemeteries, mourn
their comrades who died that this land might be free. Yvette was
again to be reunited with her friends—at the Concorde-Lafayette
Hotel in Paris. A luncheon was planned, with anticipation of
laughter, toasts and remembrances.

The sands of time are running out for all of them, however,
and this reunion may be the last hurrah. But Martine (who
translated this book into French for her mother), her husband, and
their two children will be there. Children and grandchildren of the
fliers of the P-47 will also attend, and so the story of the French girl
and the American pilots will live on in the coming generations.